ROBERT HENRYSON

Testament of Cresseid

Edited by
DENTON FOX
Victoria College
University of Toronto

NELSON

THOMAS NELSON AND SONS LTD
36 Park Street London W1
P.O. Box 336 Apapa Lagos
P.O. Box 25012 Nairobi
P.O. Box 21149 Dar es Salaam
P.O. Box 2187 Accra
77 Coffee Street San Fernando Trinidad

THOMAS NELSON (AUSTRALIA) LTD
597 Little Collins Street Melbourne

THOMAS NELSON AND SONS (SOUTH AFRICA) (PROPRIETARY) LTD
51 Commissioner Street Johannesburg

THOMAS NELSON AND SONS (CANADA) LTD
81 Curlew Drive Don Mills Ontario

THOMAS NELSON AND SONS
Copewood and Davis Streets Camden New Jersey 08103

———

First published 1968

17 173109 3

821
H52 ta

Printed in Great Britain by
Thomas Nelson (Printers) Ltd, London and Edinburgh

CONTENTS

ACKNOWLEDGMENTS

THIS edition is an offshoot of a complete edition of Henryson which will be published by Thomas Nelson and Sons: I hope in that volume to acknowledge my numerous and heavy debts more fully. But I would like to thank here, for their generous assistance in various matters connected with this small edition, Professor Geoffrey Shepherd, the general editor of this series; Mr A. J. Aitken, of the Dictionary of the Older Scottish Tongue; Dr William Beattie, the Librarian of the National Library of Scotland, and many members of his staff; Mr C. P. Finlayson, Keeper of Manuscripts in the Library of Edinburgh University; and Professor Kenneth Kee, of Victoria College.

ABBREVIATIONS

(See also list of editions)

A	Anderson's 1663 edition of the *Testament*
Barth. Angl.	Bartholomaeus Anglicus, *De Proprietatibus Rerum*, tr. Trevisa (London, 1535)
C	Charteris's 1593 edition of the *Testament*
DOST	*A Dictionary of the Older Scottish Tongue*, ed. Sir William A. Craigie and A. J. Aitken (Chicago, 1931——). Letters A–L have been published
EDD	*The English Dialect Dictionary*, ed. Joseph Wright (London, 1898–1905)
EETS (OS; ES)	Early English Text Society (Original Series; Extra Series)
Fables	Henryson's *Morall Fabillis of Esope*
JEGP	*Journal of English and Germanic Philology*
K	Kinaston's text, translation, and annotations of the *Testament* (cited with references both to the pagination of the MS and to the transcription printed in G. G. Smith)
L	Book of the Dean of Lismore
ME	Middle English
MED	*Middle English Dictionary*, ed. Hans Kurath and S. M. Kuhn (Ann Arbor, Michigan, 1952——)
MLN	*Modern Language Notes*
MLR	*Modern Language Review*
MSc	Middle Scots
OE	Old English
OED	*Oxford English Dictionary*
OF	Old French
ON	Old Norse
Orpheus	Henryson's *Orpheus and Eurydice*
PL	*Patrologia Latina*, ed. Migne
PMLA	*Publications of the Modern Language Association of America*
PQ	*Philological Quarterly*
R	Ruthven MS
SATF	Société des Anciens Textes Français
SND	*The Scottish National Dictionary*, ed. William Grant and David D. Murison (Edinburgh, 1931——)
STS (I; II; III)	Scottish Text Society (First Series; Second [*or* New] Series; Third Series)
T	Thynne's 1532 edition of Chaucer
Tilley	Morris P. Tilley, *A Dictionary of the Proverbs in England in the Sixteenth and Seventeenth Centuries* (Ann Arbor, Michigan, 1950)
TLS	*Times Literary Supplement*
Whiting	B. J. Whiting, 'Proverbs and Proverbial Sayings From Scottish Writings Before 1600', *Mediaeval Studies*, **11** (1949), 123–205; **13** (1951), 87–164

INTRODUCTION

HENRYSON'S *Testament of Cresseid* is one of the most immediately attractive of all late-medieval poems. It has the advantage of an exceptionally lurid and pathetic plot: Cresseid, the most beautiful and most adored of women, becomes a prostitute, is smitten with leprosy, forced to join a band of leprous beggars, and, after she has seen Troilus once again, dies repentant. It has also the interest for modern readers which comes from its connection with Chaucer and from Henryson's remarkable audacity in attempting to write a continuation of *Troilus and Criseyde*—an attempt which, ironically, was so successful that Henryson himself was forgotten, while the *Testament* was for centuries thought to be by Chaucer himself. But the most important quality of the poem is simply its obvious merit: most people would agree, I suppose, that it is the best poem, English or Scottish, of the fifteenth century—perhaps even the best poem ever written in Scotland.

Yet the *Testament*, if immediately attractive, is also a more intricate poem than it may seem at first sight, since Henryson's characteristic method is to work by indirection and to conceal a considerable amount of complexity underneath an apparently simple surface. An intelligent fifteenth-century reader would have had no trouble in penetrating beneath the surface, but a modern reader may lack the necessary information or the proper expectations. For example, though the poem does not appear to be technical or learned, it is filled with references, often important ones, to late-medieval ideas about medical and natural science, astrology, and the pagan gods. Or again, the poem is, apparently, an account of the savage revenge taken by some pagan gods, so that it is sometimes thought to be frivolous, sadistic, or an attack on the cruelty of divine justice. But this is only because Henryson took for granted an audience who would see, because they were looking for it, the evidence that his poem was serious, moral, and Christian. The most pervasive surface disguises of the poem, however, are its apparently rambling style and its imbecilic narrator. A fifteenth-century reader, trained to recognise conventions and to value poetry for its rhetoric and, in the best sense, its contrivance, would not be likely to confuse the narrator with the poet, or to think that Henryson's concealed art was clumsiness or an amiable *naïveté*. But a modern reader may find helpful some information about the conventions which Henryson is manipulating, and some analysis of his rhetorical manoeuvres. The poem is certainly solid and intricate enough to withstand and repay any amount of analysis, just as it is valuable enough to justify any labour spent in attempting to arrive at a correct text.

The most important source for the text of the *Testament*, and the basis for this edition, is the Edinburgh print of Henry Charteris, dated 1593 (C). The next most important is the text printed in Thynne's 1532 edition of Chaucer (T). There are three more texts which have some authority, though their value is much less: the edition of 1663, published probably in Edinburgh by Anderson (A), the stanza in the Book of the Dean of Lismore (L), and the three stanzas included in the Ruthven MS (R). The other surviving MSS and prints are completely without authority, to the best of my knowledge.

It is possible to trace two textual traditions of the *Testament*, one in Scotland, which includes all of the witnesses mentioned above except T, and one in England, which is based solely on T. The earliest information we have about the Scottish tradition is in the table of contents of the Asloan MS, usually dated *c.* 1515, where there is an entry, 'Itm̄ þe testament of Cresseid'.[1] Unfortunately, most of the poems originally in the Asloan MS, including this one, are in the part of the MS

[1] *The Asloan Manuscript*, ed. W. A. Craigie, STS II 14, 16 (Edinburgh, 1923–5), I, xiii.

which has disappeared. But the existence of the entry lends some slight support to Laing's suggestion that the *Testament* was printed by Chepman and Myllar, who were printing in Edinburgh around 1508. The text of Henryson's *Orpheus and Eurydice* which is in the surviving part of the Asloan MS seems to be copied from the Chepman and Myllar print of the poem, and there is a close relationship between other Chepman and Myllar prints and the corresponding items in Asloan.[1]

In any case, it is certain that the *Testament* was printed in Scotland before 1593. Robert Gourlaw or Gourlay, an Edinburgh bookbinder, had in his possession, at the time of his death in 1585, three copies of the 'Testament of Cresside', valued at 4d. each.[2] It is not unlikely that there were still other editions printed before 1593 which have disappeared.

The first extant Scottish edition is the black-letter quarto of ten leaves published in 1593 by Henry Charteris, one of the most important Scottish printers of the sixteenth century, and one who seems to have been particularly interested in vernacular literature.[3] The title-page reads: 'The Testament of / CRESSEID. / Compylit be M. Robert / Henrysone, Sculemai- / ster in Dunfer- / meling. / [Ornament] / Imprentit at Edin= / burgh be Henrie Charteris. / M.D.XCIII.'[4] The collation is A—B⁴, C².

It is reasonably certain that this edition was set up from an earlier print; it is possible that it is a paginary reprint of

[1] See Laing, p. 257, and *Asloan MS*, ed. Craigie, I, vi; II, vii, ix. A collation of the Chepman and Myllar and the Asloan texts of *Orpheus* makes a very close relationship between them certain, though there are a few puzzling discrepancies. The extant Chepman and Myllar prints have been reproduced in a facsimile edited by William Beattie (Edinburgh Bibliographical Society, 1950).

[2] *The Bannatyne Miscellany*, Bannatyne Club, II (Edinburgh, 1836), p. 214.

[3] A black-letter quarto of Henryson's *Fables* was printed by Lekpreuik for Charteris in 1570. For Charteris's other work, see R. Dickson and J. P. Edmond, *Annals of Scottish Printing* (Cambridge, 1890), pp. 348–76.

[4] A facsimile of the title-page is given in G. G. Smith, III, facing p. 2. My transcriptions are simplified.

an earlier edition published for or by Charteris. The other
literary works published by Charteris in the years 1592–4
seem to be reprints of this sort: his 1592 edition of Lindsay's
works is a reprint of his 1582 edition (itself a reissue of the
1580 edition printed for him by John Ross); his 1594 edition
of Lindsay's *Historie and Testament of Squyer Meldrum* is,
according to Hamer, a reprint of a 1580 edition printed for
him by Ross, of which no copy has survived; his 1594 edition
of Blind Harry's *Wallace* is a reprint of the 1570 edition
printed for him by Robert Lekpreuik.[1] This hypothetical
early Charteris edition of the *Testament* may be the one of
which Gourlaw held three copies, since at the time of his
death Gourlaw had a stock of other works printed for Charteris,
and was in his debt.[2]

The inventory of Charteris's stock, made after his death in
1599, states that he possessed 545 'Testamentis of Cresseid,
at iiij d. the pece'.[3] But only one copy of the 1593 edition
survives; now British Museum C. 21. c. 14.

There were other editions after 1593 of which no copy
survives. The inventory of the stock of the Edinburgh printer
Robert Smyth, made after his death in 1602, lists the large
number of 1638 'Cressedis'.[4] The catalogue of the Harleian
library lists copies of two other octavo editions: 'Henrison's
Testament of Cresseid, *black Letter*—1605' and 'Testament
of Cresseid, *black letter*,—Edinb. 1611'.[5]

---

[1] See Harry G. Aldis, *A List of Books Printed in Scotland before
1700* (Edinburgh Bibliographical Society, 1904); Sir David Lindsay,
Works, ed. Douglas Hamer, STS III 1, 2, 6, 8 (Edinburgh, 1931–6),
IV, 54–7, 63–4; Dickson and Edmond, *Annals of Scottish Printing*,
pp. 367–70. Some indication of the number of reprints of vernacular
texts which were published in Scotland in the sixteenth century,
and of the number of editions of which no copy now survives, is
given in Douglas Hamer, 'The Bibliography of Sir David Lindsay
(1490–1555)', *The Library*, Fourth Series, **10** (1929), 1–42.
[2] *Bannatyne Miscellany*, II, 209–216.
[3] Ibid., II, 224.   [4] Ibid., II, 234.
[5] *Catalogus Bibliothecae Harleianae*, ed. Samuel Johnson *et al.*
(London, 1743–5), IV, p. 644, No. 13734; V, p. 378, No. 12728.
As far as I know, all the references which have been made to these
editions are ultimately based only on these catalogue entries,

The second surviving Scottish edition is preserved in a unique copy in the library of Trinity College, Cambridge (II.12.217). The title-page reads: '/ THE / TESTAMENT / OF / CRESSEID. / [rule] / Compyled by Master / *Robert Henrison*, Schoole- / master of *Dumfermeling*. / [rule] / [square of ornaments] / [rule] / Printed in the Year, 1663.' 8vo, A⁸, B⁴, black-letter. Laing, probably because he identified the ornaments, said it was printed 'apparently at Glasgow by Andrew Anderson' (p. 259). The authorities of the National Library of Scotland were kind enough to compare a photograph of the title-page of this edition with other books known to have been printed by Anderson at this time, and they confirm Laing's guess. But they point out that it must have been printed, not in Glasgow, but in Edinburgh, where Anderson was working in 1663.[1]

This late and anglicised print has not been thought to have any authority. But for all its corruptions it is of some value, since it is plainly not a descendant of C: it sometimes agrees with T, against C, on a correct reading, and in a few other places it has readings superior to those in either C or T.[2] It is probably a direct or indirect descendant of a Scottish print which antedates C. One can hypothesise that the immediate ancestor of A was another small print which had about four stanzas, or twenty-eight lines, to a page (the full pages in C have usually 33 lines; in A, usually 29 lines). The evidence

---

unless Chalmers had some authority for his statements, which he makes without any reference to the Harleian catalogue, that there is a 1605 edition printed by Robert Charteris and a 1611 edition printed by Thomas Finlason (*Robene and Makyne, and the Testament of Cresseid*, ed. George Chalmers, Bannatyne Club [Edinburgh, 1824], p. vii). It is not unlikely that Finlason was the printer of one of these editions, since in 1602 he purchased from the heirs of Robert Smyth the privileges of printing various books, among them 'the feabillis of Esope' (presumably Henryson's) and 'the testament of Cressed and the winter night' (H. G. Aldis, 'Thomas Finlason and his Press', *Publications of the Edinburgh Bibliographical Society*, Vol. I, No. 20: the 4th paper of the 1893–4 session).

[1] See Aldis, *Books Printed in Scotland*, p. 107.
[2] See pp. 14–15, below.

for this is that in A four stanzas, 302–29, follow 357, and so are four stanzas away from their correct position. This misplacement is undoubtedly connected with the fact that both 302 and 330 begin with *Than* (*Then* in A). Since 302 and 330 both fall in the middle of a page in A, the most probable explanation of the error would seem to be that the copy-text for A contained the comparatively rare error of incorrect imposition.[1] If 301 had fallen at the bottom of a page, the catch-word would have been *Than* or *Then*, and this could easily have led to the next two pages being reversed in the forme.

There are fragments of the *Testament* in two Scottish manuscripts. A single stanza (lines 561–7) is contained in the Book of the Dean of Lismore, in the National Library of Scotland.[2] This MS, which was compiled in Scotland between 1512 and 1529, is an important collection of Gaelic poetry, written in an attempt at phonetic spelling. It also contains a few scraps in Middle Scots and Latin: verses, accounts, and various chronological, historical, legal, and religious notes. Between pages 92 and 93 there are two unnumbered leaves which measure about 4×6 inches, and which were apparently made by folding horizontally one of the normal 6×8 inch leaves of the MS. These two unnumbered leaves do not differ noticeably in hand or in matter from the rest of the MS, and are probably contemporary with it. Since the MS has now been inlaid, it is impossible to tell whether or not these leaves were originally bound in their present position.

The stanza from the *Testament* is on the recto of the first of the two unnumbered leaves, and is headed 'In bocas þat

---

[1] See R. B. McKerrow, *An Introduction to Bibliography* (Oxford, 1927), pp. 259–60.

[2] Gaelic MS XXXVII (deposited by the Highland Society of London). A bibliography and short description of this MS is given in *Treasures from Scottish Libraries* (Edinburgh: National Library of Scotland, 1964), p. 29. The existence of this stanza was pointed out to me by A. J. Aitken, who possesses a transcription of the Middle Scots parts of this MS made for the *Dictionary of the Older Scottish Tongue* by Professor M. L. Anderson.

wes full gwd'. The reference is perhaps a mistaken one to Lydgate's *Fall of Princes*, an adaptation of Boccaccio's *De casibus virorum illustrium*. Two stanzas from the *Fall of Princes* occur on p. 184 of this MS, where they are headed 'quod bochas anent dalyda & sampsone', and other extracts from the *Fall*, particularly of anti-feminist passages, are common in other MSS.[1] But the stanza may have been assigned to Boccaccio simply because of his double role as authority on Troy and on anti-feminism. The compilers of this MS seem in any case to be careless about attributions: two stanzas from an anonymous Scots attack on women are written on p. 77, where they are attributed to 'chawschir'.[2] The stanza from the *Testament* was presumably included in this MS only because the compilers had a taste for anti-feminist verse.

A transcription of the text of this stanza is given below, in the Appendix. It contains three variants, one trivial (564 Quhome CTA; *þat* L) and two of some interest: 562 for quhome CA; for whan T; q*uhair*for L.   563 thairout CA; throughout T; about L. These are the only two places in the stanza where C and T differ, and the fact that L, the earliest of the witnesses, differs from both C and T in both these places, suggests the possibility that some of the differences between C and T elsewhere are due to corruption at a fairly early stage in the transmission of the text.

The other surviving Scottish MS is the fragment in the Ruthven MS, in the University of Edinburgh Library. This MS is a copy of Douglas's translation of the *Aeneid* and is

---

[1] The two stanzas in this MS are I, 6371–7, 6441–7 (*Fall of Princes*, ed. H. Bergen, EETS ES 121–4 [London, 1924–7]). The second stanza was used again by Lydgate in his *Examples Against Women* (*Minor Poems*, ed. H. N. MacCracken, EETS ES 107, OS 192 [London, 1911–34], II, 444). For similar extracts in other MSS, see F. L. Utley, *The Crooked Rib* (Columbus, Ohio, 1944), pp. 168, 270, and Lydgate, *Minor Poems*, I, xvi.

[2] They are from the poem 'The beistly lust the furius appetyt' (Bannatyne MS f. 262[a], Maitland Folio MS pp. 325–6) which has sometimes been attributed to Dunbar, though there is no evidence for this.

described in D. F. C. Coldwell's edition of that work;[1] Professor Coldwell has suggested to me that it must be dated about 1520–30. The text of the *Aeneid* ends on f. 300[b]; f. 301, the last leaf of a gathering of twelve, is blank on the recto, but has on the verso the first three stanzas of the *Testament*.[2] Above these stanzas is written, apparently in the same hand (a hand different from the text of the *Aeneid*), 'Patrik Drummond'. Below the stanzas is written, in another hand, 'Partenet Wilhelmo / Dno de Ruthven'. Below this there is a sketch of the Ruthven arms, and then 'Deid Schaw', their motto.[3] The owner of the MS who is referred to here is presumably William, fourth Lord Ruthven and first Earl of Gowrie, who was born about 1543, became Master of Ruthven between 1556 and 1561 (because of an elder brother's death); Lord Ruthven in 1566, was created Earl of Gowrie in 1581, and was executed in 1584.[4] This name, then, was probably written after 1556 or 1566 and before 1581.[5] The stanzas appear, from the spacing of the page, to have been written earlier than the name.

'Patrik Drummond' is so common a name that it cannot be traced with certainty, but it is tempting to speculate that it refers to Patrick, third Lord Drummond, who was born about 1550, came into the title in 1571, and died in 1602 or soon after. His father, David, died in 1571, but was survived by his second wife, Lilian, who was the daughter of William, second Lord Ruthven, and so provides a connection between

---

[1] Gavin Douglas, *Virgil's Aeneid*, STS III 25, 27, 28, 30 (Edinburgh, 1957–64), I, 98.

[2] There is also a poem on f. 1[a] of this MS. See Edith Bennett, 'A New Version of a Scottish Poem', *MLR*, 33 (1938), 403.

[3] Sir Bernard Burke, *The General Armory . . .*, 2nd ed. (London, 1884), p. 882.

[4] *The Complete Peerage*, ed. G. E. C[okayne], new ed. (London, 1910–59), VI, 40–1; XI, 249.

[5] It is probably not the signature of the fourth Lord Ruthven himself. It is at least unlike his usual Italianate signature, which is on f. 1[b] of the MS and can be found in other places: e.g. J. G. Nichols, *Autographs of . . . Remarkable Personages* (London, 1829), Plate 33, No. 17, and in Laing Charter No. 125, Box 4 (University of Edinburgh Library).

the two families.[1] If these speculations—and they are no more than that—are correct, the stanzas were presumably written in the 1560s.

The text of the stanzas contains a number of errors, and was probably copied from memory. A transcription of it is given in the Appendix. This MS does provide one almost certainly correct reading at a place where all the other witnesses are in error (see note to line 6).

To turn now to the English tradition, the earliest surviving text of the *Testament*, and the ancestor of all the extant six-teenth-, seventeenth-, and eighteenth-century editions of the poem (except for C and A) is in Thynne's 1532 edition of Chaucer.[2] Chaucer's *Troilus and Criseyde* ends on Qq3ᵃ of this edition and is followed by a colophon: 'Thus endeth the fyfth and laste booke of Troylus: and here foloweth the pyteful and dolorous testament of fayre Creseyde.' The title is below, 'The testament of Creseyde', and then the poem itself, which is concluded on Qq6ᵇ with the colophon: 'Thus endeth the pyteful and dolorous testament of fayre Creseyde: and here foloweth the legende of good women.' Editors since Chalmers have pointed out that the *Testament* must have been added after the rest of the volume had been printed, since there is a gap in the foliation—Qq3 is numbered 219, and the next number, 220, is on Qq7; and since Qq is a gathering of nine, although the volume is regularly printed in sixes. It is fairly easy to reconstruct what must have happened. Thynne first printed, or at least set up, Qq as a gathering of six. Qq1–2 contained the text of the close of *Troilus and Criseyde*; the original Qq4–6, now Qq7–9, con-

---

[1] *The Complete Peerage*, ed. G. E. C[okayne], IV, 471.
[2] A brief description of the print and references to the literature on it are given in E. P. Hammond, *Chaucer: A Bibliographical Manual* (New York, 1908), pp. 116–18. A facsimile has been edited by Skeat (Oxford, 1905). In the few copies of this edition which I have collated, there are no important variations in the text of the *Testament*. But at least one copy (B.M. 75. h. 14) reads *bore* in 166 and *uat* (inverted *n*?) in 283, where other copies (B.M. G. 11623, Bodleian Douce C. subt. 19, and Bodleian Ash. 1095) read *bor* and *nat*.

tained the text of the beginning of the *Legend of Good Women*;
the original Qq3 must have contained, on the recto, the last
two stanzas of *Troilus* and the colophon, and on the verso
the title of the *Legend of Good Women*, perhaps in the form
of a full title-page. Thynne then decided to insert the *Testament*
after *Troilus*, and for this purpose he cancelled Qq3 and in its
place inserted four leaves which contained the *Testament*
sandwiched between the matter on the cancelled leaf. But it
is impossible to know why Thynne made this change: he
may belatedly have acquired a print or MS of the *Testament*,
or simply have had a happy afterthought.[1]

A characteristic of this edition, and of all the later English
texts, is that the stanzaic form of Cresseid's Complaint is
garbled. For the seven nine-line stanzas in C, Thynne prints
seven stanzas which have, respectively, nine, nine, eight,
five, six, eight, and eight lines.

Each of the editions of Chaucer's works for the next century
contains a *Testament*, always placed after *Troilus*, and always
with a text which is based on the immediately preceding
edition. Each edition makes fresh mistakes, which are per-
petuated by its successors. To give a single example for each
edition: Thynne's edition of 1542 reads in 442 *is al now ago*,
where his edition of 1532 reads *nowe is al ago*; his undated
third edition (1545–50?) reads in 181 *And in* for *In* of the
earlier editions; Stow's edition of 1561 reads in 399 *bitter* for
better of the earlier editions; Speght's edition of 1598 reads
in 98 *that* for *than* in the earlier editions; his edition of 1602
reads in 558 *and* for *on* in the earlier editions.[2] So these

---

[1] There is some evidence that Sir John Thynne, William Thynne's
nephew, was interested in Scottish literature: see Coldwell's edition
of Douglas's *Aeneid*, I, 100. Sir John was himself a book collector,
and was one of the two overseers named in William Thynne's will of
1540 (Francis Thynne's *Animadversions*, ed. G. Kingsley and F. J.
Furnival, EETS OS 9 [London, 1865], pp. xl, xliii). So it is con-
ceivable that he brought the *Testament* to William Thynne's attention.

[2] These editions are described in Hammond, *Chaucer*, pp. 118–27.
There are exceptions to this rule: in 401, for instance, Thynne's
1st edition reads *ouerheled*; his 2nd edition reads (nonsensically)
on euery syde; in his 3rd edition he returns to *ouerwheled*. But it is

editions have no authority, and their only use is to show us where T was thought to be in need of emendation in the sixteenth century or, especially with the glossary of Speght's 1602 edition, to indicate what some of Henryson's words were then thought to mean.

There are also two English MSS of the *Testament*. One of them is St John's College, Cambridge, MS. L. 1, a vellum MS which contains an important text of Chaucer's *Troilus*, in a hand of the early (?) fifteenth century, and, in a different hand, a text of the *Testament*.[1] This MS has sometimes been thought to be of importance for Henryson: Wood, for instance, gives a collation of it. But unfortunately both the vellum it is written on and the association with the Chaucer MS are misleading. It is in fact only an inaccurate copy of Speght's 1602 edition.[2] This can be proved by noting that, for instance, it agrees with Speght's 1602 edition in reading *shrill* in 20 (earlier English editions, *shill*); *The* in 76 (earlier, *Than*); *Phlegone* in 216 (earlier, *Philologee*); *in* in 309 (earlier, *on*); *way* in 427 (earlier, *pane*); *and* in 558 (earlier, *on*); *Toun* in 607 (earlier, *the toun*). No attempt at deception is involved here: the owner of the Chaucer MS doubtless made, or had made for him, a copy of the *Testament* to be bound up with it.[3] MS copies of printed books are common up to a surpris-

still certain that each printer used the immediately preceding edition as a copy-text. It should be noted that the 1598 edition exists in two states, one of which includes a list of corrections.

[1] Described in M. R. James, *A Descriptive Catalogue of the Manuscripts in the Library of St. John's College Cambridge* (Cambridge, 1913), No. 235. See also R. K. Root, ed., *The Book of Troilus and Criseyde* (Princeton, 1926), p. lviii.

[2] It was guessed as early as Laing that it was 'evidently transcribed from one of the printed editions of Chaucer's Works in a hand of the seventeenth century' (p. 257). But since then the MS has been incorrectly described as being in a sixteenth-century hand.

[3] It is written on vellum of the same size as that of the Chaucer MS, but of a much greater thickness, perhaps the sort of vellum that was still being used for legal purposes. The watermark on the paper fly-leaves of the volume suggests that the volume was bound not long after the *Testament* was written (E. Heawood, *Watermarks Mainly of the Seventeenth and Eighteenth Centuries* [Hilversum, Holland, 1950], Nos. 249–317).

ingly late date: in this case antiquarianism, or the greater permanence and prestige attributed to vellum MSS, may be responsible.[1] Except as a bibliographical curiosity, and perhaps as an indication that the English prints had led people to think of the *Testament* as a necessary appendix to *Troilus*, this MS is of no value for Henryson.

The other English MS is the Kinaston MS, Bodleian MS. Add. C. 287, which is dated 1639 on the title-page. This very interesting MS contains a text of Chaucer's *Troilus* and Henryson's *Testament* in which each stanza is followed by Kinaston's translation of it into an accentual Latin verse which imitates the metre and rhyme scheme of rhyme royal. There are occasional notes, in English, interspersed in the text, and the *Testament* is followed by sixteen closely written pages of Latin annotations. A very full account of the MS and its history, together with a transcription of the Latin and English texts of the *Testament* and a selection of the annotations is given in G. G. Smith, I, xcvii–clxii.

Kinaston's English text of the *Testament* is taken from Speght's 1598 edition. This is proved on the one hand by its agreement with the earlier editions, against the 1602 edition and the St John's MS, in the readings listed above for lines 76, 309, and 607; and on the other hand by its agreement with the 1598 edition, against the 1561 edition, in reading in 28 *paas* (against *pas*), in 98 *that* (against *than*), in 154 *austern* (against *austrine*), and in 380 *ben* (against *be*). Kinaston's text has been thought to be of more value than it is, and its dependence on the 1598 edition has been obscured, because Kinaston was a man of considerable learning and poetic ability who was forced to produce an English text which made sense before he could translate it into Latin. Accordingly, he emended the 1598 text wherever necessary— sometimes correctly, but more often not. In line 20, for instance, *shill*, the reading of the 1598 edition, is crossed out and *shrill* added; in 48 *Esperus* (=1598) was written but then

[1] See Curt F. Bühler, *The Fifteenth-Century Book* (Philadelphia, 1960), pp. 32–9, 117–22.

altered to *Esperance*; in 195 *horne blew* (=1598) has a *he* interlineated before *blew*; in 220 *His* (=1598) has been altered to *Her*; in 272 *vacation* (=1598) has been crossed out and the clever but erroneous emendation *conuention* added, and so on.[1] The only correct emendation in Kinaston which is not fairly obvious is in 194, where he correctly reads *tulliure*, and points out, in a note, that almost all editions wrongly read *tulsure*.[2] This emendation argues more familiarity with Scots than Kinaston was likely to have had: G. G. Smith suggests that he may have been helped here by some of his Scottish friends (I, cliv); the 'almost all editions' may imply that one of these friends had access to a Scottish print where the correct reading was preserved (as it is in C). But there is no other indication that Kinaston had access to a Scottish text. It is noteworthy that although Kinaston (p. 500) expresses dissatisfaction with the irregular stanzaic form of Cresseid's Complaint, as it appears in the English texts, he has no other solution than to omit one of the truncated stanzas, and to reduce to seven lines all the stanzas of eight or nine lines. A glance at a Scottish print would have enabled Kinaston to solve his problem more easily.

THE CONSTRUCTION OF A TEXT

Except for four stanzas of the poem, there are only three witnesses which have authority. C is probably a fairly accurate copy of another late print: the 1570 and 1571 prints of Henryson's *Fables* (for which there are, in part, earlier witnesses), as well as the appearance of C itself, suggests that these late prints are modernised, smoothed-out, but tolerably reliable.[3] T is earlier, and was probably printed from a copy-

---

[1] The MS is probably not a holograph (G. G. Smith, I, xcix). The English text may have been copied directly from Speght by a scribe, and Kinaston's emendations added later. Most of the alterations are not noted by G. G. Smith.

[2] 'Propter ignorantiam veræ significationis Scotici vocabuli *Tullieur* erratum est fere in omnibus impressionibus in quibus perpaeram describitur *Tulsur*.' Page 519; G. G. Smith, I, cliv.

[3] Protestant expurgation is fairly common in the prints of the *Fables*, but I have noticed only one example (line 363) in the *Testament*.

text more accurate than the immediate ancestor of C, but it is heavily anglicised and emended. A shares T's faults to an even greater degree, but still has some authority: A and C apparently have an ancestor, or ancestors, in common, but A is not descended from C. T, C, and A all descend ultimately from a text which contained major errors, and so was not likely to be one of Henryson's own copies.

The variants can be sorted roughly into three classes. (1) Cases where C and A agree against T. In the majority of such cases T is in error, often because the printer did not understand or did not like a Scottish word or idiom (e.g. 10, 32, 45, 52, 70). But in some cases T preserves words which are replaced by more modern words in C and A (see the notes to 94, 164, 286, 401), and in a fair number of cases there are other grounds for preferring the reading in T (see notes to 205, 328, 408, 432, 614). In the cases where there are no grounds for choosing between the reading of T and that of CA, the only recourse is to follow, though without confidence, CA. It should be remembered that the agreement of C and A indicates no more than that they had a common ancestor which they do not share with T.

(2) Cases where T and A agree against C. When T and A agree on a reading there is a strong presumption that this reading existed in the archetype from which all three witnesses are derived, and that C has made an independent error. In some cases the error in C is obvious (e.g. 178, 218, 275, 290, 479); in other cases both C and TA offer possible readings, but the agreement of T with A makes their reading preferable (see the notes to 109, 382, 420). Majority rule is not a safe method of textual criticism, however, and sometimes it is necessary to follow C even against the agreement of T and A. In some places T and A agree only because they both find the same English equivalent for a Scots word or idiom (e.g. 142, 287, 577, 583, 593); in other places they agree apparently because of coincident error (see the notes to 357, 445, 481, 568–74). Coincident variation is more common than might be supposed: A, for instance, is certainly not related to the St

John's MS, but they agree in reading, against C and T, *frosts* in 19, *couth* (*could* A) *on her* in 371, and *before her face* in 500.[1]

(3) Cases where C and T agree against A, or where all three witnesses disagree. The majority of these instances are trivial. There are so many modernisations or simple errors in A that it has not seemed worth while to include them all in the apparatus, e.g. 1 *doolie* CT; *Dolefull* A. 34 *be* CT; *the* A. 35 *baith I haue* CT; *I have both* A. 45 *abraid* CT; *abade* A. 47 *wanhope* CT; *vain hope* A. And often when the three witnesses all differ, this means only that T and A have tried, in different ways, to emend a difficult word which is preserved in C (e.g. 156, 167, 194). But there are some interesting and important instances where the correct reading seems to be preserved only in A. In one or two of these cases, the better reading in A may simply be the result of emendation: such, I suspect, is *esperance* in 48. In two other cases, A has confirmed simple emendations which I had made before I had noticed the readings in A: *With* in 222, and *fane* in 544. Both of these, but particularly the second, are emendations unlikely to be made by a seventeenth-century printer. A alone contains the certainly correct *efflated* in 549 and the probably correct *sound* in 411: neither of these readings can be emendations. There are still other cases where A may contain the best reading, though I have not ventured to follow it: see notes to 73, 140, 267, and 605.

ORTHOGRAPHY AND ANGLICISATION

The text of the *Testament* is of little value for linguistic purposes: C was published probably over a hundred years after the poem was written, and follows the fairly standardised orthography of the late sixteenth-century Scottish printers,

---

[1] A good account of coincident variation is given in the introduction of *Piers Plowman: The A Version*, ed. George Kane (London, 1960). I have leaned heavily on Kane's description of the various types of scribal error: one additional type which is important for Henryson is the scribal tendency to make each line a complete unit of sense. See notes to lines 6, 568–74.

not Henryson's own spelling. Although T is, of course, anglicised, in a few places it contains forms, or the hints of forms, which are probably closer to the original than the corresponding forms in C. But C is so far from Henryson's own usage that it seems futile to emend it in these few places. The usual MSc distinction between the present participal in -*and* and the gerund in -*ing* is, for instance, hopelessly obscured in C.

In the *Testament* as in his other poems, Henryson occasionally uses southern forms. One finds, for instance, normal Scots rhymes (with unrounded OE /ā/) such as *cair*: *mair*: *bair*: *sair* (407–11) besides rhymes with southern forms, such as *soir*: *moir*: *thairfoir* (100–3). In some cases Henryson's -*ai*- spellings may be represented by -*oi*- in C: see note to line 163. On the other hand, the concluding couplet, 'as I haue said befoir. / Sen scho is deid I speik of hir no moir', where one might have expected 'as I haue said ʒow air / . . . mair' (see *Fables*, 1784), suggests that Henryson may deliberately have used anglicisms, whether because of a desire to write in a high style or because of the Chaucerian influence.

AUTHORSHIP AND DATE

We know very little about Henryson's life. His title of Master suggests that he may be the 'Magister Robertus Henrisone' who, already a licentiate in arts and a bachelor in decrees (canon law), was incorporated at the newly founded University of Glasgow in 1462.[1] If so, he must have been born before 1440, but there is no other evidence for the date of his birth.[2] He was almost certainly a schoolmaster at Dunfermline, and

---

[1] Laing, p. xii; the identification is questioned by G. G. Smith (I, xx). Laing's investigations into Henryson's life have still not been superseded, except in trifles. As he points out, the great difficulty is that Robert Henryson was an extremely common name.

[2] An earlier date of birth is generally given for him, on the strength of Kinaston's scatological anecdote in which it is stated that Henryson was 'very old' (p. 475; G. G. Smith, I, ciii). But this anecdote (which dates the *Testament* about 1532) is plainly apocryphal: the report of his old age probably comes from the frequent appearance of old men in his poems.

was probably also a notary public.[1] The only evidence for the date of his death is given by a reference to him in Dunbar's *Lament for the Makers*, which proves that he was dead by 1505.[2]

Most of Henryson's poems cannot be dated. It has been argued that several of his *Fables* contain borrowings from Caxton's translation, *Reynard*, and therefore must be later than 1481, when it was printed,[3] but the existence of these borrowings is far from certain. There is, however, some evidence which suggests that the *Testament* was in circulation by 1492. In *The Spektakle of Luf*, a prose treatise in the Asloan MS, there is a list of notorious women who are briefly described in order to show why men 'suld eschew þe delectatioun of luf'. Among them is Cresseid: it is said that she abandoned Troilus for Diomeid, 'And þare efter went common amang þe grekis And syn deid in gret mysere & pane' (*Asloan MS*, ed. Craigie, 1, 279). G. Myll, the author, dates his work 10 July 1492 in his conclusion, and says that he translated it from Latin, though an original has not been found. B. J. Whiting, who first noted this passage, examined the possible explanations and came to the tentative conclusion that 'the safest, and most satisfactory, solution would seem to be to agree that Master

[1] For the references to a Magister Robertus Henrison as a notary public, see Laing, pp. xiii–xiv. He is called 'Sculemaister in Dunfermeling' on the title-pages of C and of the early prints of the *Fables*; the geographical location is born out by Dunbar's 'In Dumfermelyne he [Death] hes done roune / With Maister Robert Henrisoun' (*Lament for the Makers*). For the position of a schoolmaster in Henryson's time, see John Durkan, 'Education in the Century of the Reformation', in *Essays on the Scottish Reformation 1513–1625*, ed. David McRoberts (Glasgow, 1962), pp. 145–68. Other schoolmasters at this time were notaries: see Durkan, p. 167.

[2] Henryson is the fourth from the end in Dunbar's list of dead poets. Of the last two, Dunbar says 'he [Death] hes now tane, last of aw, / Gud gentill Stobo and Quintyne Schaw'. Stobo died in 1505 (J. W. Baxter, *William Dunbar* [Edinburgh, 1952], pp. 133–4). The fact that Henryson's name is late in the list, but that his death is not referred to as a recent event, suggests that a death-date of *c.* 1500 would not be far wrong.

[3] See G. G. Smith, I, xl–xliii. A more precise dating has been attempted by David K. Crowne, 'A Date for the Composition of Henryson's *Fables*', *JEGP*, **61** (1962), 583–90.

G. Myll had read Henryson's *Testament* sometime before 10 July 1492, and that he could not resist introducing [Cresseid]'.[1] Myll's echo of lines 76-7 ('scho walkit . . . commoun') and 82 ('go amang the Greikis') makes this solution almost certain, I think.[2]

There is no doubt that Henryson is the author of the *Testament*: the external and the internal evidence are equally unambiguous. But Henryson's authorship was only belatedly recognised in England, and was forgotten for a time even in Scotland. It is difficult to be sure whether Thynne knew that the poem was by Henryson, not Chaucer: it seems likely, though not certain, that he at least wished his readers to think that it was by Chaucer. (He may, of course, simply not have cared who wrote it.) Skeat states that 'Those who, through ignorance or negligence, regard Thynne's edition of Chaucer as containing "Works attributed to Chaucer" make a great mistake'. His argument is that Thynne's title, 'The Workes of Geffray Chaucer newly printed, with dyuers workes whiche were neuer in print before', must be construed as 'dyuers workes [*of various authors*]'.[3] This title is certainly ambiguous, but the phrasing is repeated in the preface in such a way that the 'dyuers workes' must be works of Chaucer: 'I attayned . . . nat onely vnto such as seme to be very trewe copies of those workes of Geffray Chaucer / whiche before had ben put in printe / but also to dyuers other neuer tyll nowe imprinted'.[4] Skeat points out further, with special regard to the *Testament*, that line 64, 'Quha wait gif all that Chauceir wrait was trew?',

---

[1] 'A Probable Allusion to Henryson's "Testament of Cresseid" ', *MLR*, 40 (1945), 46-7.

[2] James Kinsley, who independently noted Myll's reference, conjectured that Henryson found his germinal idea in the *Spektakle* (*TLS*, 14 November 1952, p. 743). But this seems improbable: apart from other considerations, it is not likely that Henryson had access to the *Spektakle* (see James Gray, *TLS*, 13 March 1953, p. 176).

[3] Skeat, p. ix.

[4] This preface was written by Sir Brian Tuke, but it gives an accurate account of Thynne's work. See Francis Thynne, *Animadversions*, p. xxvi, and T. R. Lounsbury, *Studies in Chaucer* (New York, 1892), I, 266-8.

must have made it plain that the poem is not Chaucer's (p. lv). This argument has some force, but the references to Chaucer may have been missed, or taken as ironic self-allusions.

In any case, Thynne's inclusion of an anglicised text of the *Testament* in his edition ensured that it would be accepted as Chaucer's in the sixteenth century.[1] The first Englishman to state that the poem was not Chaucer's was Francis Thynne, in his *Animadversions* (1599, but not printed until the nineteenth century): 'yt wolde be good that Chaucers proper woorkes were distinguyshed from the adulterat, and suche as were not his, as the Testamente of Cresseyde, The Letter of Cupide, . . . &c. whiche Chaucer never composed, as may suffycientlye be proued by the thing*es* them selues' (p. 69). The first Englishman to recognise Henryson's authorship was Kinaston, who prefaced his translation with a note: '. . . I haue very sufficiently bin informed by Sr Tho: [altered from *James*] Eriskin late earle of Kelly & diuers aged schollers of the Scottish nation, that it was made & written by one Mr Robert Henderson . . .'[2] But the first English statement in print of Henryson's authorship was made by Urry, who had access to the Kinaston MS, and who in his 1721 edition of Chaucer copied, without acknowledgement, Kinaston's note.[3] It was not until the nineteenth century, however, that the poem was universally recognised as Henryson's, not Chaucer's.

In Scotland, Henryson's authorship was presumably recognised as long as the small Scottish editions, which assigned the poem to him, were in circulation: A, in 1663, may have been the last of these. But Thomas Ruddiman, who was probably more learned in such matters than any other Scot of his time, assigned the *Testament* to Chaucer in his 1710 edition of Douglas's *Aeneid*, and Alexander Chalmers, in his 1810 *Works*

---

[1] All of the English references to the poem which give an author name Chaucer. So, for instance, Puttenham (see note to line 408), and see further G. G. Smith, I, xlvi.

[2] Page 475; G. G. Smith, I, ciii, see also pp. xx–xxi.

[3] Hammond, *Chaucer*, pp. 396, 458.

of the English Poets, prints it among the genuine works of Chaucer, not among the 'Poems Imputed to Chaucer or by Other Authors'.[1]

The attribution of the *Testament* to Chaucer cheated Henryson of his rightful fame, but it also won for him a greatly expanded audience: there was certainly no other MSc poem which was known to nearly as many English readers in the sixteenth and seventeenth centuries. The plot of the *Testament* was constantly alluded to, and the poem itself often quoted or echoed.[2] One can usually assume that any mention of *Troilus and Criseyde* made between 1532 and 1721—and often later—is a reference to both Chaucer's and Henryson's poems. Ironically, Henryson's Cresseid tended even to supersede Chaucer's: Hyder Rollins points out that 'For authors and for readers up to 1600 Henryson's Cressid was *the* Cressid; but lacking his sympathy, they regarded her as a light-of-love who finally paid for her faithlessness and unchastity by leprosy'.[3]

THE POEM

The most obvious fact about the *Testament* is that it is a continuation of Chaucer's *Troilus and Criseyde*, and a companion-piece to the fifth book of that poem. In lines 40–60 Henryson's narrator takes up a *quair*, a small book, and, telling us what he finds in it, gives an accurate summary of the contents of Chaucer's fifth book, the final sorrows of Troilus. Then the narrator takes another *quair*, presumably an imaginary one, and describes its contents: in short, 'the fatall destenie / Of fair Cresseid, that endit wretchitlie'; in

---

[1] See Douglas Duncan, *Thomas Ruddiman* (Edinburgh, 1965), p. 58*n*; Hammond, *Chaucer*, p. 135; William Geddie, *A Bibliography of Middle Scots Poets*, STS I 61 (Edinburgh, 1912), p. 171.

[2] Many of these references are gathered together in Hyder E. Rollins, 'The Troilus-Cressida Story from Chaucer to Shakespeare', *PMLA*, 32 (1917), 383–429. See also Caroline F. E. Spurgeon, *Five Hundred Years of Chaucer Criticism and Allusion 1357–1900*, 2nd ed., 3 vols (Cambridge, 1925), especially III, 1–62.

[3] 'The Troilus-Cressida Story', p. 400.

full, the rest of the *Testament*. The parallel between the two
quairs is stressed by the parallelism of the wording: 'I tuik
ane quair . . . And thair I fand . . .' (40, 43); 'ane vther quair
I tuik, / In quhilk I fand . . .' (61–2).

There is nothing very unusual about a fifteenth-century
poet writing a continuation of another man's poem—there
were three different continuations of the *Aeneid* written during
the century, for instance.[1] But there is no reason to assume
that Henryson was making any simple-minded attempt to
provide the next instalment of an interesting story, or that
he was being compulsively tidy about the loose ends which
he thought Chaucer had left. The *Testament* stands, I think,
in a complex relationship to Chaucer's poem. To begin with,
it is a *tour de force*, an imitation of 'worthie Chaucer glorious',
and one not without irony—'Quha wait gif all that Chauceir
wrait was trew?'. The poem is filled with Chaucerian echoes,
many of them coming from the fifth book of *Troilus*, and has
an extremely Chaucerian narrator. It is literary, witty, and
sophisticated, like Henryson's other major poems: the *Fables*,
which are in part rhetorical exercises, clever reworkings of
common school texts; and *Orpheus and Eurydice*, an ingenious
and humorous retelling of one of the most familiar of all
myths. But the *Testament* is also *about* Chaucer's poem, in
the sense that a critical essay is about a piece of literature,
or in the sense that the *moralitas* of one of Henryson's *Fables*
is about the fable. It offers, by implication, a remarkably
accurate and penetrating analysis of *Troilus*. Here again it
resembles Henryson's other poems: both the *Fables* and
Orpheus and Eurydice are attempts to bring out the most
profound meaning of the pre-existing narratives. But as well
as being both an occasionally ironic tribute to Chaucer and a
commentary on his poem, it is also a serious moral poem
parallel to *Troilus*. Henryson takes Chaucer's characters and
situation, and uses them to explore the same problems that
Chaucer deals with—the meaning of earthly 'wele and wo',

[1] See Anna Cox Brinton, *Maphaeus Vegius and his Thirteenth Book
of the Aeneid* (Stanford, 1930), pp. 1–2.

for instance—though he does not always arrive at the same answers. The resemblance with Henryson's other poems still holds, for both the *Fables* and *Orpheus* are, in the end, serious poems about morality.

In considering Henryson's sources, there seems no reason to believe that he used any of the non-Chaucerian literary treatments of the Troilus story.[1] Henryson differs from Chaucer in a few details, most notably in the characterisation of Calchas. Henryson shows him as a sympathetic and loving father, and as a priest of Venus; Chaucer more orthodoxly has him a priest of Apollo, and implies that he is avaricious, sly, and selfish. But Henryson clearly introduces these changes for good reasons: Calchas must be sympathetic so that the whole blame for Cresseid's sins can be placed on her own wilfulness; it increases both the irony and the cohesiveness of the poem to make him a priest of the goddess whom Cresseid blasphemes. Henryson's other characters are, if not precisely the same as Chaucer's characters, at least extrapolations from them. Chaucer's Diomede, bestial, slippery, and sudden, is unchanged in his selfish lust. Like Chaucer, Henryson damns him without abusing him: his character is shown by his action of dismissing Cresseid with a letter, and especially by the powerfully unpleasant *And mair* in the famous lines, 'Quhen Diomeid had all his appetyte, / And mair, fulfillit of this fair ladie' (71–2). Henryson's Troilus is as noble, generous, and sensitive as Chaucer's: if he seems a bit more mature, this may be only because he, like Criseyde in the fifth book of *Troilus*, is seen mostly at a distance. Cresseid's character, of

[1] The most thorough treatment of Henryson's possible debt to other versions of the Troilus story is in Sydney J. Harth, 'Convention and Creation in the Poetry of Robert Henryson: A Study of *The Testament of Cresseid* and *Orpheus and Eurydice*', Diss. University of Chicago, 1960, pp. 9–24. Mrs Harth makes a case for his debt to some of these versions, but concludes that 'It has so far been impossible to determine on any specific source, beyond Chaucer, which Henryson definitely used for his poem' (p. 22). There is also a discussion of Henryson's characters, and their sources, in Marshall W. Stearns, *Robert Henryson* (New York, 1949), pp. 48–54.

course, changes during the course of the *Testament*. At the beginning, she seems to be a very good guess at what Chaucer's Criseyde might have become after she had passed through the hands of Diomede and others, and grown older, harder, and more unhappy. In the fifth book of *Troilus*, Chaucer depends for the effect of his portrayal of Criseyde upon the contrast between the immensely attractive character who is created in his first four books and the base actions which she performs in the last book. Henryson works in the opposite direction: he takes a weak, selfish, and unfaithful, even lascivious, woman and manages to make her into such a pathetic and much-abused beauty that we are tempted to comfort her and, with Calchas, say 'Douchter, weip thow not thairfoir'. But he uses the same method as Chaucer for simultaneously revealing the sin and making the sinner sympathetic: a stupid and passionately involved narrator who is able to say, in consecutive lines, '. . . Sa giglotlike takand thy foull plesance! / I haue pietie thow suld fall sic mischance' (83-4).

Henryson's great innovation is, of course, Cresseid's leprosy, the central fact of the poem. It is impossible, by the very nature of the case, to prove that Henryson did not borrow this idea from an earlier lost poem, the 'vther quair' which he cites as his authority. But I think it is reasonably safe to accept Henryson's originality here: it is unlikely that a poem with so striking a conception would have survived only through him, and, a more subjective but perhaps more telling argument, Henryson gives very much the impression of working out a detailed and precise idea, not of struggling with a pre-existent plot. Henryson's notion of Cresseid's later promiscuity, however, may have been suggested by her despairing remark in *Troilus*, 'To Diomede algate I wol be trewe' (V, 1071), with its strong implication that just the opposite will happen. And in view of the references in the *Testament* to Cresseid as a flower who becomes changed 'in filth' and 'maculait' (78-81), Henryson may have had in mind Criseyde's speech:

And also thynketh on myn honeste,
That floureth yet, how foule I sholde it shende,
And with what filthe it spotted sholde be,
If in this forme I sholde with yow wende.

(IV, 1576–9)

But this can hardly be counted as a source.

Leprosy, however, was not an especially far-fetched choice, if Henryson were looking for a disease to give Cresseid. The history of leprosy is difficult, if not impossible, to trace, because there has always been a widespread confusion between leprosy, which is a disease with a large range of symptoms, and various other skin diseases, while leprosy itself may have changed over the centuries. Rather less is known about medieval leprosy than has been written, but it seems clear, at least, that true leprosy, which had been an exotic disease to the Greeks and Romans, became endemic in Europe during the Middle Ages.[1] Its frequency has probably been over-estimated, because people have wrongly thought that the very common medieval spitals were always leper-houses and were always full.[2] But it is likely that most people would have seen lepers. The disease generally died out towards the end of the Middle Ages, but it lingered on in the north, in Scotland and in Scandinavia. There are plenty of references to lepers in

---

[1] A recent selective bibliography of the voluminous literature is in Patrick Feeny, *The Fight Against Leprosy* (London, 1964). Among the most useful works for leprosy in England are Charles Creighton, *A History of Epidemics in Britain*, Vol. I (Cambridge, 1891); R. M. Clay, *The Mediæval Hospitals of England* (London, 1909); and George Newman, 'On the History of the Decline and Final Extinction of Leprosy as an Endemic Disease in the British Islands', in *Prize Essays on Leprosy* (New Sydenham Society Publications, CLVII), pp. 1–149 (London, 1895). The standard work on leprosy in Scotland is Sir James Y. Simpson, 'On Leprosy and Leper Hospitals in Scotland and England', in his *Archæological Essays,* ed. John Stuart (Edinburgh, 1872), II, 1–184.

[2] This is pointed out by W. P. MacArthur, 'Some Notes on Old-Time Leprosy in England and Ireland', *Journal of the Royal Army Medical Corps*, 45 (1925), 410–22. For the Scottish spitals, see John Durkan, 'Care of the Poor: Pre-Reformation Hospitals', in *Essays on the Scottish Reformation*, ed. McRoberts, pp. 116–28.

the Scottish public records of the fifteenth and sixteenth centuries.

Cresseid's particular case of leprosy seems ordinary enough, too. Of the symptoms which she is stated or implied to have, the discoloration of the skin (339, 396), the dark facial lumps (340, 395), the deformed face (349, 448), the hoarse voice (338, 443-5), and the loss of hair (314-5) are all standard symptoms of leprosy, according to both medieval and modern thought. Most of the medieval medical writers, inveterate plagiarists, give much the same account of the disease: a short quotation from Bernard de Gordon can serve as a specimen:

> The secret signs which mark leprosy when it is beginning are these: the colour of the face is red, tending towards black; the breath begins to be altered; the voice becomes rather hoarse; and the hair begins to become thin and scanty . . .[1]

These descriptions are picked up by the encyclopedists: Bartholomaeus Anglicus, for instance, writes:

> In theym [lepers] the flesshe is notably corrupte, the shappe is chaunged / the eyen be come rounde: The eye lyddes ben reuelyd, the syght sparcleth, and namely in leonina: the nosethrylles ben streyted and reueled, and shronke: The voyce is horse namely in Elephancia: Swellynge groweth in the bodye / and manye smalle botches and whelkes harde and rounde . . . also in the bodye bene dyuerse speckes / nowe redde, nowe blacke, nowe wanne, nowe pale.[2]

Another symptom Henryson mentions, 'ene mingit with blude' (337), is probably a reference to the lesions of the eye which often accompany leprosy:[3] red eyes are listed in

[1] *Lilium Medicinae* (Lyons, 1559), p. 90 (I, xxii). An almost identical description appears in John of Gaddesden, *Rosa Anglica* (Pavia, 1492), f. 56[b]. The resemblance between Henryson's description and the details in the medical texts was first noted by Johnstone Parr, 'Cresseid's Leprosy Again', *MLN*, 60 (1945), 487-91, who gives further quotations. See also W. C. Curry, *Chaucer and the Mediaeval Sciences*, rev. ed. (New York, 1960), 37-45.

[2] *De Proprietatibus Rerum*, tr. Trevisa (London, 1535), Bk VII, Ch. lxv.

[3] See Sir Leonard Rogers and Ernest Muir, *Leprosy*, 2nd ed. (Bristol, 1940), pp. 189-91.

3

medieval accounts as one of the characteristic symptoms of the disease.[1] Some medieval writers classify leprosy into four types, corresponding to the four humours, but these distinctions do not seem helpful here.[2] All we can say, I think, is that Henryson, probably relying on the medical works of his time,[3] has given Cresseid a textbook case of ordinary leprosy.

A more important and more complicated matter is the multiple causation which Henryson suggests for Cresseid's leprosy. Here again he follows medieval medical theory, according to which the cause of a disease could be looked for on three levels. First, a disease could be caused by physical factors, such as an improper diet, a sudden unseasonable change of weather, or an infection coming from another person already diseased. Secondly, a disease could be caused by astrological factors, from the influence of planets in malevolent conjunctions. Thirdly, a disease could be caused by God, as a punishment for sin. Henryson's contemporary, Leoniceno of Lombardy, summed up these three levels when he stated, in 1497, that syphilis is caused

by divine wrath, as the theologians believe; by the influence of the

[1] See Parr, 'Cresseid's Leprosy Again', pp. 490–1.
[2] For the origins of this classification, see Klibansky, Saxl and Panofsky, *Saturn and Melancholy* (London, 1964), pp. 86–90. Stearns (pp. 45–7) suggests that Cresseid has *elephancia* or *elephantina*, the variety which comes from melancholy alone, but though this is possible there is no real evidence for it. A modern physician might consider Cresseid's symptoms to indicate nodal or lepromatous leprosy, not the anaesthetic or neural type (which is the type that causes partial anaesthesia and a consequent injury to and loss of members).
[3] In some places Henryson seems even to have followed their phraseology. See the notes to lines 81, 448. Stearns argues (p. 46*n*) that Henryson relied on 'firsthand observation', but the question is not a real one, since Henryson doubtless would have had the traditional symptoms in mind when he looked at actual lepers. It has been suggested that Cresseid's spital is St Leonard's hospital in Dunfermline (Stearns, pp. 12, 43). But there is no evidence that Henryson thought of Cresseid as a Scot, or that he was referring to any of the three hospitals which existed in Dunfermline (John Durkan, 'Care of the Poor . . .', p. 118).

stars, as the astrologists declare; or by certain unseasonableness of the air, as physicians think.[1]

It should be noted, however, that these three levels are not mutually exclusive, since God rules the planets, who in turn govern earthly affairs. Physicians were notoriously apt to concentrate only on the physical and astrological causes, but orthodox thought recognised the importance of all three levels, and the linkage between them.

The physical causes of leprosy are explained in the medieval medical texts. According to them, leprosy can be caused by a tainted heredity or by an unwholesome diet, two causes which can be adduced for almost any disease, but also, and this is more unusual, it can be acquired by infection from another leper, as a venereal disease. Most of the authorities mention this cause of leprosy,[2] and often they dwell upon it at length. Bernard de Gordon, for instance, gives more than half of his account of the causes of leprosy to a discussion of it as a venereal disease, and he includes an anecdote about how one of his assistants had acquired leprosy through lying with a leprous countess who was his patient.[3] Henryson could have expected his audience to be acquainted with some of the medical texts: all educated men, in the Middle Ages, were expected to know something about medicine.[4] And in any case, the idea that leprosy was a venereal disease was un-

[1] Quoted in B. L. Gordon, *Medieval and Renaissance Medicine* (London, 1960), p. 538.
[2] e.g., John of Gaddesden, *Rosa Anglica*, f. 56[a], f. 61[a]; Gilbertus Anglicus, *Compendium Medicinae*, ed. Michael de Capella (Lyons, 1510), f. 344[a b]; Bartholomaeus Anglicus, VII, lxv.
[3] Bernard's discussion of the causes of leprosy is given in facsimile (of a fourteenth-century MS) and in translation by R. C. Holcomb, 'The Antiquity of Congenital Syphilis', *Bulletin of the History of Medicine*, 10 (1941), 148–77. This article is also valuable for its numerous references to medieval authorities who believed that leprosy was transmitted venereally, though Holcomb's conclusions about the antiquity of syphilis in Europe should not be accepted uncritically.
[4] See L. C. MacKinney, 'Medical Education in the Middle Ages', *Journal of World History*, 2 (1954–5), 835–61.

doubtedly current in popular thought.[1] This notion appears to be almost universal, except for the modern Western world. It was believed in ancient China, and is commonly believed now by the natives of the various tropical and sub-tropical regions where the disease still remains: oddly enough, some modern medical authorities think that it has some slight basis in fact.[2]

This unattractive fact has seemed worth dwelling upon, because it is, I think, a fact important to the poem, though it has never been brought into consideration.[3] It helps, for instance, to explain some details that Henryson gives about Cresseid's earlier life. Towards the beginning of the poem it is suggested obliquely (lines 77 and 82–3, perhaps also 285) that Cresseid, after she was abandoned by Diomede, took other lovers, and perhaps became a prostitute. Henryson makes this suggestion partly in order to emphasise that when Cresseid accepts Diomede as a lover she is, in effect, prostituting herself, trading her body for attention and security. But more important is the connection which is made between her misuse of her flesh and the resulting corruption of her flesh, a connection which is moral as well as medical. This connection is made explicit early in the poem, long before Cresseid contracts leprosy, when the narrator remarks:

> O fair Creisseid, the flour and A per se
> Of Troy and Grece, how was thow fortunait
> To change in filth all thy feminitie,
> And be with fleschelie lust sa maculait . . .
> (78–81)

---

[1] Creighton, *History of Epidemics*, I, 103–4, quotes Edward III's ordinance of 1346 which remarks that lepers, 'by carnal intercourse with women in stews . . . taint persons who are sound, both male and female'.

[2] Rogers and Muir, *Leprosy*, pp. 83–4.

[3] Mrs Beryl Rowland, in a note which I saw after this was written, 'The "seiknes incurabill" in Henryson's *Testament of Cresseid*', *English Language Notes*, I (1964), 175–7, suggests that Henryson afflicted Cresseid with syphilis. See, however, below, p. 35, fn. 2.

The narrator here is using metaphors to describe a moral corruption, but later in the poem the metaphors become literally true. Cresseid trades her beautiful *feminitie* for the genderless filth of a leprous body living in a spital, and, because she has been *maculait*, 'spotted', with lust, becomes physically 'ouirspred with spottis blak'. *Maculait*, a Latinate past participle, is in fact frequently used in Latin texts to describe the spotted skin of a leper.[1]

Parenthetically, since it is important for Cresseid's later history, it might be added that Shakespeare and the Elizabethans had especially strong reasons for thinking that leprosy was a venereal disease. On the one hand, there was sometimes a confusion between syphilis, then a comparatively new disease, and leprosy; on the other hand, syphilitics were commonly housed in the old leper-houses, which by this time were little used.[2] This explains such references as Pistol's:

> O hound of Crete, think'st thou my spouse to get?
> No; to the spital go,
> And from the powdering-tub of infamy
> Fetch forth the lazar kite of Cressid's kind,
> Doll Tearsheet she by name, and her espouse . . .[3]

And, in *Timon*:

> this is it [gold]
> That makes the wappen'd widow wed again;
> She, whom the spital-house and ulcerous sores
> Would cast the gorge at . . .[4]

[1] See note to line 81.

[2] See Simpson, 'Leprosy . . . in Scotland', p. 94; J. Johnston Abraham, 'The Early History of Syphilis', *British Journal of Surgery*, **32** (1944), 234–5; and Creighton, *History of Epidemics*, I, 98. Various entries in the *Accounts of the Lord High Treasurer of Scotland* indicate that syphilitics were put in spitals: e.g., 'Item, that samyn day, at the toune end of Striuelin, to the seke folk in the grantgore' (I, p. 378, A.D. 1497).

[3] *Henry V*, II, i, 77–81. A *powdering-tub* is a sweating-tub used for the cure of venereal diseases.

[4] IV, iii, 37–40. The meaning of *wappen'd* is uncertain: it has been suggested that it is a cant word meaning 'sexually exhausted'.

Or, in Donne:

> By thee the seely Amorous sucks his death
> By drawing in a leprous harlots breath . . .[1]

The connection between leprosy and syphilis in Scotland is established by such imprecations as 'missaell lipper hwyr' ('leprous leper whore', 1565) and 'grandgorie lipper' ('syphilitic leper', 1619).[2] So Cresseid's extreme degradation in England and Scotland in the sixteenth century can be partly explained by this historical accident.

The next problem to consider is the astrological causation of Cresseid's leprosy. After Cresseid blasphemes against Venus and Cupid, she falls into a swoon and sees Cupid ringing a silver bell. The seven planets then appear, and in turn, going from the highest to the lowest, they are each described, partly as planets and partly as gods. The charge of blasphemy is laid against Cresseid; Saturn and the moon are delegated to punish her; and they afflict her with leprosy.

In part, this episode is traditional. There are innumerable English, French, Italian, and German poems in which a sin against love or an insult to Venus and Cupid is punished by a quasi-legal court made up of the pagan gods.[3] But, though astrology and mythology were fused together often enough elsewhere in the Middle Ages,[4] poems of this type did not

---

[1] Elegy IV, lines 59–60.

[2] See *DOST*, s.v. *lipper*, a., and *grandgorie*. Dunbar, in his *Flyting*, suggests that Kennedy is both syphilitic and leprous, and that he lives in 'Ane laithly luge that wes the lippir menis' (lines 83, 154, 161).

[3] See W. A. Neilson, *The Origins and Sources of the Court of Love* (Boston, 1899). In view of Cresseid's initial complaint, the *Testament* also has an ironic relationship to the group of poems in which 'l'amoureux désespéré vint porter ses griefs devant le dieu d'Amour lui-même, d'où toute la série des jugements, procès, revisions de procès, qui aboutira aux *Arrêts d'Amours* de Martial d'Auvergne' (Alain Chartier, *La Belle Dame sans Mercy*, ed. Arthur Piaget [Lille, 1949], p. xiii). Despite Stearns (pp. 70–72), there is no evidence that Henryson was much indebted to the *Assembly of Gods*: the resemblances between the two poems come mostly from their common reliance on standard legal procedure.

[4] See Jean Seznec, *The Survival of the Pagan Gods*, tr. Barbara F. Sessions (New York, 1953), and cf. Chaucer's *Knight's Tale* and *Complaint of Mars*.

ordinarily describe the gods in astrological terms. And
Henryson to an unusual degree makes the descriptions of the
gods important for the meaning of the poem.

Cupid, the convener of the court, is not the blind boy, but
'Cupide the king', the ruler of gods and men, and he perhaps
represents the love which holds the universe together. Of the
seven planetary gods, Jupiter and Phoebus are represented as
benevolent: Jupiter is 'God of the starnis in the firmament /
And nureis to all thing generabill'; Phoebus causes 'lyfe in all
eirdlie thing, / Without comfort of quhome, of force to nocht /
Must all ga die that in this warld is wrocht'.[1] Saturn and Mars
are shown, in accordance with traditional astrological theory,
as highly malevolent. Venus is described as a goddess of
variation, dissimulation, and mutability, 'In taikning that all
fleschelie paramour . . . Is sum tyme sweit, sum tyme bitter
and sour'. Mercury appears in two guises: first as a rhetorician
and poet; then as a physician—there are ironic implications
that he, like Chaucer's physician, is avaricious and dishonest.
The moon is described more neutrally—her chief characteristic
is that she is black.

This pantheon, then, is a balanced one, with two benevolent
gods or planets, Jupiter and Phoebus, two malevolent ones,
Mars and Saturn, and two who, though described inauspici-
ously, are neutral, Mercury and the moon, while Cupid and
Venus are paired but contrasted, for there is no suggestion
that Cupid has anything to do with fleshly love. But Cresseid,
by her blasphemy, has tilted the balance against her: Jupiter
and Phoebus become neutral, while the neutral figures,
Mercury and the moon, become malevolent. Mercury, who
is appointed the speaker of the parliament, is the one who
selects Saturn and the moon to punish Cresseid, and so is
indirectly responsible for her leprosy. Since he is both a
doctor and a poet, there is a double ironic appropriateness in

---

[1] Henryson does not follow the usual tradition which classifies
Jupiter and Venus as beneficent planets. For the details of Henryson's
reliance on, and divergence from, the astrologers, see the notes to
lines 151–263.

this. The moon, a fickle planet apt to take on the colour of the planet with which she is joined, is paired with Saturn, the most ominous planet, and so becomes malevolent.

But Saturn and the moon need to be considered further. Henryson probably knew that, according to some astrologers, Saturn and the moon are the two planets which jointly cause leprosy, though I am not sure whether he would have expected his audience to know this.[1] Again, it is possible that he knew the theory stated by John of Rupescissa in the fourteenth century, that 'The sun and Jupiter prefigure heaven, while Saturn and the moon represent eternal Gehenna',[2] but he could not have taken this to be common knowledge. What Henryson would have expected from his audience, however, was a thorough knowledge of the four elements and the four humours. Henryson and his contemporaries would have known almost instinctively what we are acquainted with only as an exploded theory: that there are four basic qualities in the world, cold, heat, dryness, and moisture, and that they, in combination, cause the four elements—cold and dryness causing earth, for instance, or heat and moisture, air—and also the four parts of the human body—cold and dryness causing black bile or melancholy, for instance, and heat and moisture causing blood. This view of the world is important throughout the poem, but especially in connection with its astrological elements. Leprosy was always considered to be a disease caused by an excess of melancholy, that is, of cold and dryness. Saturn is a planet notoriously cold and dry, and Henryson's description emphasises these qualities. He shows Saturn as being an old man with a wrinkled face, a lead-coloured skin, lean cheeks, and ugly hair, who walks 'crabitlie'. Bartholomaeus Anglicus provides a gloss for this passage:

> drynesse . . . draweth the skynne togyders, and maketh it ryueled /
> and hasteth age, and maketh the body euyl coloured & deformed,

---

[1] See the note to lines 253–63. For the origins of the connection between Saturn and leprosy, see Klibansky, Saxl and Panofsky, *Saturn and Melancholy*, pp. 127–33.

[2] Quoted in Lynn Thorndike, *A History of Magic and Experimental Science*, Vol. III (New York, 1934), p. 365.

. . . & spoilleth the heed of the heare, . . . and draweth togyders &
maketh croked the toes and fyngres of the fete and hondes: as it
is sene in leprous men . . . [and causes] slowe mouyng.

(IV, iii)

Saturn's coldness is plain without a gloss: he is shown with
shivering teeth, a dripping nose, and with a quiver of arrows
'Fedderit with ice and heidit with hailstanis'. Dryness and
cold are the worst qualities, because they negate the vital
heat and moisture: to quôte Bartholomaeus again, 'by
moysture and heate all thinges ben bred, . . . and thynges
gendred bothe nourysheth and fedeth' (IV, iiii).

Saturn's junior partner, the moon, is astrologically con-
sidered to be cold and moist. But Henryson does not describe
her as moist, but only as being nocturnal and without any
light of her own—and therefore cold. Like Saturn, she has
the appearance of being herself leprous: 'Haw as the leid, of
colour nathing cleir', while her gown is 'full of spottis blak'
(260), the same 'spottis blak' (339) which later appear on
Cresseid's face.

After Saturn and the moon have determined Cresseid's
punishment, they pass down to her and inflict it. Saturn
lays on Cresseid's head a frosty wand, and says 'I change thy
mirth into melancholy . . . Thy moisture and thy heit in cald
and dry'. These terms echo almost exactly the medical
descriptions of the disease: 'the immediate cause of leprosy
is melancholy [*materia melancholica*], and a bad constitution,
cold and dry,'[1] leprosy comes 'by extraction of the natural
warmth and moisture'[2] or from 'dryness drying the moisture
of the blood, and cold congealing the blood'.[3] The moon, in
strict accordance with her astrological nature, concerns herself
only with cold, and says 'Fra heit of bodie here I the depryue'.

Henryson, however, is not simply concerned with providing
an adequate astrological causation. More important is the
contrast made between Cresseid, pitiful and helpless, and

---

[1] Bernard de Gordon, *Lilium Medicinae*, p. 90 (I, xxii).
[2] Gilbertus Anglicus, *Compendium Medicinae*, f. 336[b].
[3] John of Gaddesden, *Rosa Anglica*, f. 56[a].

the planet-gods, terrible and all-powerful. One thinks of the similar situation in Chaucer's *Knight's Tale*, where Palamon and Arcite, in the arena, are dwarfed and made into puppets by the overtowering figures of the gods. Henryson's planet-gods seem to be symbols of the inexorable natural order: when Cresseid becomes promiscuous she throws the pantheon out of balance, and a mercilessly just retribution is inevitable. On this level, at least, the poem is as bleak and cruel as it has sometimes been called.

But Cresseid's leprosy can also be considered on the religious level, as a punishment sent by God. Henryson's planet figures have, of course, two aspects: they are pagan gods as well as astrological powers. The use of pagan gods either as symbols for some aspects of divine power or as surrogates for God himself is common enough in all Christian poetry: the advantage for an author of being able to represent both man and God by fictional characters is obvious. An interesting parallel to the *Testament*, and to Henryson's use of planetary gods as both astrological and divine figures, is the medical poem *Syphilis*, written in Latin by the Italian Fracastor, and published in 1530.[1] In this poem, which is certainly not derived from the *Testament*, the shepherd Syphilus (from whose name Fracastor coined the term *syphilis*, which was later adopted as a replacement for the invidious national names of the disease) blasphemes against the sun-god, because of the excessive heat, and is punished with syphilis. Fracastor refers to divine, astrological, and natural causes for syphilis, and includes a council of the gods.[2]

There are various indications in the *Testament* suggesting that the pagan gods are to be taken as being in some sense surrogates for God. Calchas is a 'preist', albeit a priest of Venus; when Cresseid commits her blasphemy she is in an oratory, and the rest of the people are in the 'kirk'. Jupiter,

---

[1] Edited by Heneage Wynne-Finch, with an introduction by J. J. Abraham (London, 1935).

[2] He also says that the disease is driven through the world by 'Saturnus . . . atrox' (I, 413–4).

the god of the stars, is said to have in his hand a spear, 'Of his father the wraith fra vs to weir' (182). Although this is a traditional detail, the reference to Christ the intercessor is inescapable.[1]

Henryson's contemporaries often thought that diseases were sent by God to punish blasphemy. The Mandate of Maximilian, for instance, which was issued in 1495 and which contains the first definite mention of syphilis, states that the disease was due to the anger of God against the prevailing sin of blasphemy.[2] And leprosy, above all other diseases, was thought of as a punishment sent by God. This is perhaps due partly to the intrinsic strangeness and horror of the disease, and partly to the Old Testament. Gehazi, Miriam, and Uzziah were all punished with leprosy, and the sins of Miriam and Uzziah, at least, could be construed as blasphemy. These biblical stories produced other similar stories. Constantine the Great, for instance, was punished by God with leprosy, and then miraculously healed when he became baptised.[3] Clay records the case of one Gilbert de Saunervill who committed sacrilege and 'was smitten with leprosy, whereupon he confessed with tears that he merited the scourge of God'.[4]

Since leprosy was considered a result of sin, it therefore naturally became a symbol for sin. Sometimes it is a general

[1] See also the note to line 182.
[2] See Abraham's introduction to Fracastor, p. 9, and B. L. Gordon, *Medieval and Renaissance Medicine*, p. 538. Some scholars believe that syphilis was indigenous in Europe before Columbus; they argue that medieval writers, when they discuss a leprosy that could be transmitted venereally, are really talking about syphilis. But whatever the merits of this view (and there seems to be very little evidence to support it), it is at least clear that a sudden and terrifying epidemic of syphilis swept through Europe in the last years of the fifteenth century, after the *Testament* was written. For its effect on Scotland, see R. S. Morton, 'Some Aspects of the Early History of Syphilis in Scotland', *British Journal of Venereal Diseases*, 38 (1962), 175–80.
[3] See Caxton's *Golden Legend*, ed. F. S. Ellis (Hammersmith, 1892), I, 314–15. In some versions of the Titus and Vespasian legend, Vespasian is stricken with leprosy by God. See *Titus and Vespasian*, ed. J. A. Herbert, Roxburghe Club (London, 1905), introduction and lines 1165–1226.
[4] R. M. Clay, *Mediaeval Hospitals*, p. 66.

symbol, as in the *Cursor Mundi*: 'þe fowl syn of meselri, / Es likend to fowle sin and dedly'.[1] Most often, however, leprosy is taken as a type of heresy: Hrabanus Maurus, for instance, says that 'Leprosy is sin, or false doctrine . . . Lepers are heretics'.[2] Henryson may possibly have this meaning of leprosy in mind, since the speech Cresseid makes to Venus and Cupid is clearly heretical. There is an interesting passage by John of Salisbury in which he remarks (apropos of Gehazi) that 'Certainly concupiscence is a miserable and wretched leprosy . . . Whoever does not moderate this love, let him fear leprosy and dread greatly the blindness of the eyes which it threatens'.[3] But though this idea is obviously relevant to the

[1] Ed. Richard Morris, EETS OS 57, 59, 62, 66, 68, 99, 101 (London, 1874–93), lines 29194–5 (Cotton Galba). Some other instances are given in Morton W. Bloomfield, *The Seven Deadly Sins* (Michigan State College Press, 1952), pp. 111, 119, 408, a work which is generally useful for the relationship between sin and disease. See also Angus Fletcher, *Allegory: The Theory of a Symbolic Mode* (Ithaca, New York, 1965), pp. 199–209.

[2] *PL* 112, col. 985. For further references see *A Dictionary of the Bible*, ed. James Hastings (New York, 1898–1904), III, 98. The author of a Northern ME sermon (*c.* 1400) uses leprosy as a figure both for sin in general and for heresy in particular: 'Be þis leprus men ich vndirstonde . . . al maner o volk þat liggen her e þis world e þe siknes & te sorw of dedli synne', and 'lepir is coruptif of clernes, & ter-bi it bitokenid wikkid doctrin & falsnis of techyng . . . þis fowl lepir of herisie' (the second sermon in *Three Middle English Sermons from the Worcester Chapter Manuscript F. 10.*, ed. D. M. Grisdale, Leeds School of English Language Texts and Monographs, V [Kendal, 1939], lines 235–6, 613–14, 660). The connection between leprosy and heresy may be derived either from Leviticus 13–14, where it is stated that the priest shall both condemn and cleanse lepers, or, as Gregory the Great says, from the fact that 'In leprosy part of the skin becomes bright, while part remains a healthy colour. Thus lepers signify heretics, because when they mix the perverse with the correct, they sprinkle the healthy colour with spots' (*PL* 75, col. 694).

[3] *Policraticus*, ed. C. C. I. Webb (Oxford, 1909), I, 176 (Bk III, Ch. iii). I owe this reference to Harth, 'Convention and Creation', p. 36n. Alain de Lille also speaks of the 'leprosy of licentiousness' (*The Complaint of Nature*, tr. D. M. Moffat [New York, 1908], p. 57 [Prose V]). Bloomfield points out that in the *Pricke of Conscience* leprosy is the purgatorial pain allotted to lechers, and that Gower, who in the *Mirour de l'omme* likens each of the sins to a disease, couples lechery with leprosy (*Seven Deadly Sins*, pp. 177, 196). The author

Testament, we cannot be sure that Henryson was acquainted with it.

The connection which Henryson established between Cresseid's blasphemy and her disease has, of course, further implications. Her verbal blasphemy is itself a symbol: Henryson makes her swear at Venus and Cupid in order to show that her life has been a blasphemous sin against the laws of love, of nature, and of God. And her leprosy is the inevitable and proper punishment for a corrupt, unnatural, and sinful life.

We need now to turn from the causes and implications of Cresseid's leprosy, and to consider Cresseid herself, as a fictional character. In the first part of the *Testament*, Cresseid is pre-eminently beautiful and pre-eminently pathetic. Her desire is all for security and love: she wants to be the admired centre of attention. But instead, she becomes more and more 'excluded': this word and similar expressions are repeated. It is said that Diomede 'hir excludit fra his companie' (75), and that 'destitute / Of all comfort . . . Richt priuelie, but fellowschip' (92-4) she passes to her father's house. Because she does not want people to know 'Of hir expuls fra Diomeid the king' (119) she goes into a 'secreit orature' (120), where she complains to Venus and Cupid that she is made an 'vnworthie outwaill ['outcast']', 'fra Diomeid and nobill Troylus . . . clene excludit, as abiect ['outcast'] odious', and 'fra luifferis left, and all forlane' (129-40).

Cresseid's leprosy, then, can be seen as the final step in her exclusion and alienation.[1] Lepers, in theory if not always in practice, were kept strictly apart from other people; when Cresseid goes begging, she, like other lepers, must carry a

---

of the ME sermon quoted in the preceding note says that leprosy 'be-tokeneþ excesse *in* etyng & dryngkynge', and that this makes a man fall into lechery (lines 265, 316). The symbolic connection between lechery and leprosy perhaps arose from the notion that leprosy was a venereal disease.

[1] Henryson underlines the connection by a verbal parallel. When Saturn passes sentence on Cresseid he says, 'Thy greit fairnes and all thy bewtie gay . . . Heir I exclude fra the for euermair' (313-15).

clapper with which to announce her coming, so that people can flee from her. There is a savage irony in this: where before men begged for Cresseid's favour, now she herself must beg for the bare means of sustenance. The metaphorical complaint of the abandoned lover, which Troilus might have used, 'They fle from me that sometyme did me seke',[1] is now something that Cresseid could say in grim earnest.

Henryson repeatedly stresses the irony of the situation. Cresseid is often referred to, for instance, as a flower: 'of eirdlye wichtis flour' (435), 'the flour . . . Of Troy and Grece' (78–9), and when she curses Cupid she says to him,

> ʒe causit me alwayis vnderstand and trow
> The seid of lufe was sawin in my face,
> And ay grew grene throw ʒour supplie and grace.
> Bot now, allace, that seid with froist is slane . . .
> (136–9)

This metaphor is borrowed from the *Roman de la Rose*: Cresseid is suggesting that her face was like the magic well of Narcissus, in which Cupid sowed the seed of love, so that anyone who looked into it must fall in love. But she does not know that the fresh and springlike beauty of her face will in fact be slain by the cold of leprosy, which will congeal her blood. And 'seid of lufe' is, though she does not realise it, ambiguous: she intends it to mean 'origin and cause of love', but it can equally well refer to the black lumps or grains of leprosy, which are also the seeds of love, being caused by her promiscuity.

A similar irony occurs when Cresseid calls out against Venus and Cupid and asks 'Quha sall me gyde? Quha sall me now conuoy . . .?' (131). Henryson has her repeat this question, I think, because he wishes to remind readers of the symbolic scene in *Troilus* where Criseyde leaves Troy, after her friends say 'almyghty God hire gide!' (IV, 693), is escorted by Troilus, who later says, 'And to the yonder hille I gan hire gyde' (V, 610), and is then turned over to Diomede, 'that ledde hire by the bridel' (V, 92). But Cresseid's question is

---

[1] Wyatt, *Collected Poems*, ed. Kenneth Muir (London, 1949), p. 28.

answered a little later, when her father 'Conuoyit hir' (389) to the leper-house.

If the poem ended with Cresseid's admission to the leper-house, Henryson would indeed be the harsh and dour moralist which he has been called.[1] But at this point there is still more than a third of the work remaining, and it is in the end of the poem that Henryson's meaning emerges most clearly. Before considering this part, however, it is useful to return briefly to the medieval opinions about leprosy.

In the Middle Ages, lepers were segregated, mostly because they were loathsome and incurable themselves and the carriers of infection for others, partly because of the detailed instructions for the seclusion of lepers in the Book of Leviticus, and partly because lepers were thought to have been struck by the hand of God, and so set aside from ordinary human beings.[2] This segregation was carried to such a point that, at times, when a person was declared a leper, the last rites were read over him, a mock-burial was held, and he was pronounced

[1] T. F. Henderson, for example, says that in the *Testament* 'a strenuous morality has extruded not merely adequate emotional pathos, but even true poetic art' (*Scottish Vernacular Literature*, 3rd ed. [Edinburgh, 1910], p. 124). Tatyana Moran says that 'unlike Chaucer, he [Henryson] felt no sympathy, not even the slightest compassion for his heroine, but only contempt and a kind of sadistic pleasure in describing her degradation', '*The Testament of Cresseid* and *The Book of Troylus*', *Litera*, 6 (1959), p. 23.

[2] Extremely strict laws for the seclusion of lepers were promulgated repeatedly, though not always enforced. The question is discussed by most writers on medieval leprosy: see particularly Newman, 'Extinction of Leprosy', and, for Scotland, Simpson, 'Leprosy . . . in Scotland'. The actions of Calchas and Cresseid in the *Testament* conform perfectly to the Burgh Laws of Scotland: 'Gif ony that duellis in the kyngis burgh or was borne in it be fallyn in lepyr, that is callit mysal, gif that he hafe gudis of his awne thruch the whilk he may be sustenyt and cled he sal be put in the spytaile of the burgh. . . . And it is to wyt that mysal men sal nocht entre in the toune gangand fra dur to dur, bot anerly to pas the he way thruch the toune, and thai sal sit at the toune end and thar ask almous at furth passand men and ingangand. And mar attour na man sal tak on hand ony mysal man in his house to herbery na reste wythin the burgh on payn of a full forfalt' (*Ancient Laws and Customs of the Burghs of Scotland*, Vol. I, A.D. 1124–1424, Scottish Burgh Records Society, I [Edinburgh, 1868], p. 28).

to be henceforth dead, in the eyes of the law and the church, though he was permitted to continue to exist, as a living corpse.[1]

This procedure is sufficiently terrible, surely, but on the other hand, it is not altogether terrible. Seclusion from mundane society need not be bad, if it is considered in religious terms; while if leprosy is a divine punishment, this indicates, at the least, that there is a special relationship between the leper and God, and, at the best, that the suffering of the leper may be a holy and purifying suffering.

The relationship between leprosy and Christianity is particularly important here. Medieval scholars found even more lepers in the Bible than are in fact there.[2] Job, for instance, was thought to have had leprosy, and, as St Job, was a patron saint of lepers.[3] The beggar Lazarus, who lay, full of sores, at the rich man's gate, and was carried by the angels into Abraham's bosom, was also thought to be a leper. This Lazarus was confused, in the Middle Ages, with the Lazarus whom Christ raised from the dead,[4] and since this composite figure was firmly attached to leprosy, as the words *lazaretto* and *lazar-house* suggest, there was a strong implication that leprosy was a disease which preceded a raising to eternal life.

---

[1] It is not certain in what areas, or during what times, this ritual was actually performed. See Feeny, *Fight Against Leprosy*, pp. 29–34, and Clay, *Mediaeval Hospitals*, who quotes the office at the seclusion of a leper (Appendix A). But the complete legal disability of lepers suggests that the fiction of their death was widespread. See Newman, 'Extinction of Leprosy', pp. 18–19.

[2] The leprosy referred to in the Bible is usually considered now not to be true leprosy, but this was, of course, not known in the Middle Ages.

[3] Louis Réau, *Iconographie de l'art chrétien*, II, 1 (Paris, 1956), 312. Some authorities think that Job was, in fact, a victim of leprosy; see George Thin, *Leprosy* (London, 1891), p. 11, and F. Delitzsch, *Biblical Commentary on the Book of Job*, tr. F. Bolton, I (Edinburgh, 1866), 69–70, 120–1.

[4] The confusion is important, partly because it reinforces the idea that lepers will be raised from death to life, and partly because of the special love and solicitude which Christ showed for the brother of Martha and Mary. Guy de Chauliac recommends that lepers be reminded that 'God loved the leper Lazarus more than others' (quoted in Simpson, 'Leprosy . . . in Scotland', p. 98).

Christ was connected with the disease, partly because of the
lepers which he healed, but most notably because of one of
the servant songs in Isaiah, where it is said (in the Vulgate) of
the man of sorrows, in a passage which was always taken as a
prophecy of Christ's passion, 'We thought him as it were a
leper, and as one struck by God and afflicted'.[1] Job, in his
sufferings with 'leprosy', was thought, too, to be a type of
Christ, suffering on the cross.[2]

When lepers were cast out from human society, then, they
entered into a specially close relation with God, as the term
sometimes used of them, *pauperes Christi*, would suggest.[3]
Guy de Chauliac brings this out neatly, when he says that
lepers should be told 'that the sayd dysease is penau*n*ce
salutary for the saluacion of theyr soules, and . . . shuld be
theyr purgatory in this worlde. For albeit that they were
refused of the worlde / yet they were and be chosen of God'.[4]

It seems likely that a medieval reader would have been
ready to regard Cresseid's leprosy ambivalently, as an affliction,
yet one which set her above other human beings. Literature
is of course so full of characters with similarly ambivalent
afflictions that one could fill a large hospital with them.
Through suffering comes knowledge, and the last part of the
Testament is devoted, I think, to showing how Cresseid is
brought, by means of her leprosy, into an understanding of
herself and of the world. For this purpose Henryson uses a

[1] 'et nos putavimus eum quasi leprosum . . .' (Isa. 53:4). Clay,
Mediaeval Hospitals, pp. 66–8, 274, cites several instances where this
verse was used to comfort lepers and to equate them with Christ.
This verse is probably also behind John Audelay's statement that, when
Christ was crucified 'vayns *and* seneus h*i*t brast, *and* bone, / þat euere
ioynt me*n* my3t e-se; / He was most lyke a leperus mon' (*Poems of
John Audelay*, ed. E. K. Whiting, EETS OS 184 [London, 1931],
p. 98, lines 45–7.
[2] This is explained in detail in Gregory the Great's influential
Moralia in Job.
[3] See Creighton, *History of Epidemics*, I, 79–86.
[4] Tr. Robert Copland, *The Questyonary of Cyrurgyens* . . . (London,
[1542]), Q2ᵃ. One of the redactors of the *Amis and Amiloun* story
says that Amiloun's leprosy is a proof of God's love for him. See
Amis and Amiloun, ed. MacEdward Leach, EETS OS 203 (London,
1937), pp. xxvi–xxvii, lxiii.

4

series of recognition scenes in which Cresseid is made to
realise what she is, and what her life has been.

The first of these scenes is simple enough. After Cresseid
has awakened from her vision, she looks in a mirror, examines
herself superficially, and sees that her face is deformed with
leprosy. But she sees without understanding; though she
realises she has paid 'full deir' for her blasphemy, she again
speaks profanely of 'Our craibit goddis' (353).

Then her father takes her secretly to the spital, where,
weeping alone in a dark corner, she delivers a formal complaint
in seven nine-line stanzas. A lyrical complaint with an elevated
style is a common enough feature of narrative poems: Chaucer
himself gives Criseyde a 'heigh compleynte'.[1] But Henryson's
is derived rather from Chaucer's *Compleynt of Anelida*, as his
change from the rhyme royal of *Troilus* to the intricately
rhymed stanza, *aabaabbab*, used in part of *Anelida* would
indicate.[2] Henryson may have imitated Chaucer's poem in
order to underline the ironic use he is making of the usual
complaint. Anelida is a deserted lover who says, exquisitely,
the old commonplaces: 'ye sleen me with the peyne; / That
may ye se unfeyned on myn hewe', 'I voyde companye',
'ferther wol I never founde / Non other helpe, my sores for
to sounde . . . I wil non other medecyne', 'For in this world
nis creature / Wakynge, in more discomfiture / Then I . . .'[3]
Cresseid, too, is a deserted lover, if also an unfaithful one,
and she has, in a completely non-metaphorical sense, a pain
caused by love which slays her and which can be seen in her

---

[1] *Troilus*, IV, 742–805. See Charles Muscatine, *Chaucer and the
French Tradition* (Berkeley, 1957), p. 26.

[2] The Anelida stanza is also used by Dunbar in the *Golden Targe*,
and by Douglas in the first two parts of the *Palice of Honour* and the
prologue to Book III of his *Aeneid*.

[3] Lines 288–9, 295, 241–4, 325–7. Henryson may also have in mind
the complaint of Chaucer's Criseyde:

> . . . I am as out of this world agon, . . .
> And of myn ordre, ay til deth me mete,
> The observance evere, in youre absence,
> Shal sorwe ben, compleynt, and abstinence.
>
> (IV, 780–4)

hue; a seclusion from society; and sores that cannot be healed
by any medicine.

Cresseid's complaint is also an ironic transversion of a very
different genre. She laments, quite naturally, that her beauty
is changed to loathliness, and that her luxurious chamber,
beautiful clothes, and elegant diet are all replaced by the
squalor and poverty of the spital. But in doing this she
produces an excellent specimen of a common medieval
genre: the poem on death which stresses the transitoriness of
all the joys of the flesh and dwells on the repulsiveness and
corruption of the dead body. In the Middle English *Dispute
between the Body and Soul*, for instance, the soul speaks to
the dead body in much the same way that Cresseid speaks to
herself.

> Ne nis no levedi, briȝt on ble,
> Þat wel weren iwoned of þe to lete,
> Þat wolde lye a niȝth bi þe,
> For nouȝth þat men miȝte hem bihete.
> Þouȝ art unsemly for to se,
> Uncomli for to cussen suwete;
> Þouȝ ne havest frend þat ne wolde fle,
> Come þouȝ stertlinde *in* þe strete.[1]

The *ubi sunt* formula which Cresseid follows is traditionally
used in these poems on death, and even the details which
Cresseid laments, the 'burely bed', the spices and delicate
meats, can be paralleled.[2]

Both of these genres, the lover's lament and the poem on
mutability, are potentially ambivalent. The lament can be
used to stress the nobility of the lamenter—the power of her
emotions and the fineness of her susceptibilities—or, alterna-
tively, it can be used to stress the suffering which love brings.
The transitoriness of earthly pleasure is an obviously ambigu-

[1] Laud MS 108, lines 257–64, from 'Þe Desputisoun Bitwen Þe
Bodi and Þe Soule', ed. W. Linow, *Erlanger Beiträge zur Englischen
Philologie*, I (1889) (I. Heft), 1–209.
[2] See notes to lines 416–33, 417, 418–21. For a summary of the
scholarship on the *ubi sunt* formula, see Edelgard Dubruck, *The Theme
of Death in French Poetry of the Middle Ages and the Renaissance*
(The Hague, 1964), pp. 45–9.

ous theme: the poet can use it to lament that the joys of life are so fleeting, and to suggest that we gather rosebuds while we may; or he can use it with a religious and didactic purpose, to show that the pleasures of the flesh are so short-lived that they should be rejected in favour of eternal life.

All of these potentialities are used in Cresseid's lament. She begins as another Anelida, a tragic heroine of 'greit royall renoun' (424) lamenting her cruel fate: 'Fell is thy fortoun, wickit is thy weird' (412). Henryson ironically remarks on the nobility of her mourning when he says that the other lepers 'presumit, for hir hie regrait / And still murning, scho was of nobill kin; / With better will thairfoir they tuik hir in'. (397–9). And she grieves for the comforts of her luxurious life which have suddenly been snatched from her. But at the end of her lament, she no longer sees herself as a noble heroine, nor does she think that 'hie honour' or 'welth in eird' is any better than wind. She no longer speaks in egocentric terms, but instead says,

> O ladyis fair of Troy and Grece, attend . . .
> Be war in tyme, approchis neir the end,
> And in ʒour mynd ane mirrour mak of me:
> As I am now, peradventure that ʒe
> For all ʒour micht may cum to that same end . . .
> Nocht is ʒour fairnes bot ane faiding flour . . .
>
> (452, 456–9, 461)

It is usually a corpse who is made to speak in this way: in Henryson's own *Thre Deid Pollis*, for instance, the three skulls say,

> O sinfull man . . .
> . . . Behold oure heidis thre,
> Oure holkit ene, oure peilit pollis bair:
> As ye ar now, Into this warld we wair . . .[1]

In his debate, *The Ressoning betuix Aige and Yowth*, Henryson employs a variation, and has an old man speak as the mirror of mortality:

[1] Lines 1, 3–5. Henryson makes Death, in *The Ressoning betuix Deth and Man*, speak in the same way: 'O mortall man, behold, tak tent to me, / Quhilk sowld thy mirrour be baith day & nicht' (lines 1–2).

I was . . .
als glaid, als gay, als ying, als yaip as yie;
Bot now tha dayis ourdrevin ar & done;
Luke thow my laikly luking gif I lie:
O yowth, thy flowris fadis fellone sone.[1]

In the *Testament*, Henryson has skilfully introduced a walking corpse onto the stage, in the form of a character who has undergone the quasi-death of leprosy. But paradoxically, Cresseid is both the warner and the warned: both the *memento mori* and the young person who is taught mortality by being made to consider the *memento mori*. As Guy de Chauliac suggests, the quasi-death of leprosy gives its victim a chance to pass through purgatory before death.[2] And the change in Cresseid's lament from grieving for the loss of her past sensual pleasures to holding herself up as a lesson for all women shows that her purgatory is educating her. Cresseid's first reaction to her leprosy was to exclaim repeatedly that her happiness was gone:

All eirdlie ioy and mirth I set areir.	(355)
. . . my mirth is gone!	(368)
. . . all mirth in this eird	
Is fra me gane . . .	(384–5)
Gane is thy ioy and all thy mirth in eird . . .	(409)

But never again does she mention *ioy* or *mirth*; towards the end of the poem she realises the illusory nature of earthly happiness. The change in her is neatly indicated by the two mirrors in the poem. The mirror into which Cresseid looks when she awakens from her swoon is symbolic of vanity and sensuality: Luxuria and Venus are frequently represented

---

[1] Lines 27, 29–32. This poem is interesting because in it Henryson plays with the ambiguity of the transitoriness theme. The opposed refrains of the old man and the youth are paradoxically coupled at the end: 'O yowth, be glaid in to thy flowris grene! / O yowth thy flowris faidis fellone sone!'.

[2] This idea occurs elsewhere, for instance in Jean Bodel, who asks God to count his leprosy as penance, 'for two hells would be too much' (lines 70–2: see below, pp. 48-9, fn, 1). In *Piers Plowman* lepers are among those who are said to have 'Here penaunce & here purcatorie vpon þis pur erþe' (*The A Version*, VIII, 88).

holding a mirror in their hands.[1] But when Cresseid says 'ane
mirrour mak of me', *mirrour* has the sense of 'warning'.[2] She
does not yet realise that it is she, not the gods, who is to blame
for her leprosy, but she does realise that beauty is but a
fading flower, and that the outward corruption of her flesh is
an outward sign of the essential and permanent corruption of
all flesh.

After Cresseid finishes her complaint, she is advised by
another leper to stop her futile weeping and, in an interesting
phrase, to 'mak vertew of ane neid'. Cresseid follows this
advice: she goes out with the company of lepers and so, for
the first time in the poem, makes a gesture towards submitting
to her fate and accepting her penance. While no one would
want to exaggerate the joys of comradeship in a leper band,
it is still true that this is also the first scene in the poem where
Cresseid is not shown as an isolated and lonely figure.

There follows immediately the most famous recognition
scene in the poem, though it might be more precisely described
as a non-recognition scene. Troilus, riding back to Troy after
a successful battle, hears the begging cries of the leper band,
and, 'Hauing pietie', rides towards them. Cresseid looks up
at him, but does not recognise him; Troilus looks at her, does
not know her, but thinks that he had seen her face somewhere
before, and then thinks of the 'sweit visage and amorous
blenking / Of fair Cresseid, sumtyme his awin darling'.
Henryson, following the orthodox Aristotelian psychology of

---

[1] See Seznec, *Survival of the Pagan Gods*, pp. 107–8, 197, and
Guy de Tervarent, *Attributs et symboles dans l'art profane 1450–1600*
(Geneva, 1958–9), II, cols. 273–4.

[2] Henryson is probably following two traditions here. On the one
hand, *mirrour* is a *memento mori*, as in the quotation above, p. 44n,
or in Lydgate's *Dance Macabre*: 'haue þis mirrour euere in remem-
braunce / Howe (I) lie here . . . wormes food' (E. P. Hammond, ed.,
English Verse between Chaucer and Surrey [Durham, North Carolina,
1927], p. 141, lines 637–40). On the other hand, *mirrour* is 'that
which reflects something to be avoided', as in the *Mirror for Magistrates*
tradition: 'my fall . . . be hold / Lett it a myrror be / that ye not
enfecte . . .' (Cavendish, *Metrical Visions*, in Hammond, *English
Verse*, p. 377, lines 1176–7). See further Peter Ure's edition of
Richard II (London, 1956) in the Arden Shakespeare, p. lxxxii, fn.

his time, explains in some detail how this happens. An image, he says, may be so deeply imprinted in a man's memory that his physical senses are deluded, and he may think that he sees the image in external reality, though it is actually only in his mind. So Troilus, seeing the image of his love, trembles and changes colour, and then, 'For knichtlie pietie and memoriall / Of fair Cresseid', throws rich gifts in Cresseid's lap, and rides off sadly.[1]

It is plain why Troilus does not consciously recognise Cresseid: her face is so deformed that it is far different from the image in his mind. But in his delusion, or what we might now call his subconscious recognition, he sees Cresseid for what she is and was: frail and corruptible flesh. And, seeing more truly than he has in the past, he acts more truly, and gives her presents, not out of physical love, but out of pure charity.

Henryson does not offer any explanation for the strange fact that Cresseid looks at Troilus but does not recognise him —his motive for this omission, I suspect, is that he wants us to consider the reason for her lack of recognition.[2] And the reason, presumably, is that Cresseid does not know Troilus. This has been suggested throughout the poem: Cresseid has coupled Troilus with the despicable Diomede,[3] and has

---

[1] Henryson probably intends there to be an ironic contrast between this scene and the scenes in Chaucer's poem where Troilus, in company with other men, comes riding by Criseyde's house. In these scenes, too, Troilus changes colour (II, 645, 1258). Though this is more doubtful, Henryson may also be remembering Criseyde's letter to Troilus:

I herteles, I sik, I in distresse! . . .
Come I wole; but yet in swich disjoynte
I stonde as now, that what yer or what day
That this shal be, that kan I naught apoynte.
(V, 1594, 1618–20)

[2] Elliott suggests that 'Troilus fully armed and helmeted would not be immediately recognizable, and leprosy would have impaired Cresseid's sight' (p. 155). But there is no suggestion that Troilus's face is concealed by a helmet, or that Cresseid's sight is impaired: she can at least see well enough to cast her eyes on Troilus (line 498) and to write her will (575).

[3] A writer for the *TLS* notes aptly, with reference to line 132, that 'the distortion of her standards is emphasized by her failure to dis-

thought of them both merely as men who can protect her and
make love to her. But her recognition of Troilus's true nature
is not delayed long: Troilus has indeed demonstrated it by
his act of charity. Cresseid asks another leper, 'Quhat lord is
ȝone . . . Hes done to vs so greit humanitie?', and she is
answered, 'Schir Troylus it is, gentill and fre'. Cresseid
swoons, and from this swoon, as from her earlier one, she
awakens to a knowledge of her own corruption:

> Sa efflated I was in wantones . . .
> My mynd in fleschelie foull affectioun
> Was inclynit to lustis lecherous:
> Fy, fals Cresseid; O trew knicht Troylus! . . .
> Nane but my self as now I will accuse.
>
> (549, 558–60, 574)

In the earlier part of the poem Cresseid was obsessed by a
false shame which was rooted in pride. Because she did not
wish to give 'the pepill ony deming / Of hir expuls fra Diomeid
the king' she went to her father 'Richt priuelie' and would
not enter the temple; because she did not wish to be recognised
as a leper she went to the spital 'in secreit wyse . . . that na
man suld espy'. Her final public and humble confession shows
that she has come through her purgatory to purification and
wisdom; she sees what she is and what she has been, and she
is now free to die. But first she makes her testament: a spon-
taneous act of giving, as opposed to the taking which has
characterized her life.[1] She cheerfully bequeaths her 'corps

tinguish between the loves of Troilus and Diomede' (9 April 1964,
p. 290).

[1] Cresseid's list of bequests occupies only lines 577–88. But her
preceding confession can also be considered part of her testament,
because the will proper and the final confession were often combined.
See W. H. Rice, *The European Ancestry of Villon's Satirical Testaments*
(New York, 1941), p. 15. In a broader sense, the whole poem can be
considered Cresseid's testament, just as the whole New Testament
was regarded 'as the Last Will and Testament of Our Lord' (E. C.
Perrow, 'The Last Will and Testament as a Form of Literature',
Transactions of the Wisconsin Academy of Sciences, Arts, and Letters,
17, Part I [1913], 707). Literary testaments of various types were
of course very common in the Middle Ages, but Henryson does not
seem to be indebted to any of them. It is unlikely that he was
acquainted with the early thirteenth-century testamentary *congés* of

and carioun / With wormis and with taidis to be rent': the physical corruption which, as leprosy, distressed her so, does not worry her now. She gives to Troilus the ring, a symbol of love and of unity, which he had formerly given her. She gives all her gold and ornaments to the lepers, and so transforms her worldly wealth into charity. And, as a final bequest, she leaves her spirit to 'Diane, quhair scho dwellis, / To walk with hir in waist woddis and wellis'. These lines parallel the usual clause of a medieval will in which the testator conveys his soul to God.[1] Diana here, as frequently, is differentiated from Cynthia: she is 'Of chastitè the goddes and the quene; ... Her lawe is for religiositee'.[2] Cresseid's choice of so pure a goddess proves that she, at least, thinks that she has emerged from her purgatory, and that she will be accepted as one of Diana's maidens.

But before we consider the final meaning of the *Testament*, we ought to look briefly at the poem's beginning and at the narrator. Cresseid's career is symbolically summed up, in a curious meteorological way, by the first stanzas of the poem. Henryson follows the convention of beginning with the description of a season appropriate to the poem's theme, and

---

Jean Bodel and Baude Fastoul in which the writers, as lepers retiring from the world, bid farewell to their friends. See G. Raynaud, ed., 'Les Congés de Jean Bodel', *Romania*, 9 (1880), pp. 216–47, and 'Che sont li Congié Baude Fastoul d'Aras', in *Fabliaux et Contes des poètes françois*, ed. E. Barbazan, rev. M. Méon, I (Paris, 1808), 111–34 (also contains Bodel's *congé*, pp. 135–52). If Henryson had needed a hint, he could have found one in the lament of Chaucer's Criseyde: 'Myn herte and ek the woful goost therinne / Byquethe I, with youre spirit to compleyne ...' (IV, 785–6).

Cresseid's will need not be taken as a bit of poetic license: though lepers were regarded as already legally dead and so forbidden, at least at times, to make wills (see Simpson, 'Leprosy ... in Scotland', p. 154, and Clay, *Mediaeval Hospitals*, pp. 56–8), wills made by English lepers do exist (see MacArthur, 'Notes on Old-time Leprosy', pp. 412–4).

[1] This is noted by Rice, *The European Ancestry of Villon's Satirical Testaments*, p. 103.

[2] *The Court of Love*, lines 1129, 686, in *Chaucerian and Other Pieces*, ed. W. W. Skeat (Oxford, 1897). See further the note to line 587 below.

he underlines the relevance of the season by the *sententia* of
the opening lines: 'Ane doolie sessoun to ane cairfull dyte /
Suld correspond and be equiualent'. But the season Henryson
describes is an unorthodox combination of spring, con-
ventionally used as the beginning of a poem about love, and
a cold stormy season, which according to a less widespread
convention was used to open sombre or satirical poems.[1] The
narrator says that it was spring when he began to write, the
sun was in Aries, and the weather was very hot, but then
came a hailstorm and great cold. By the sixth stanza it has,
surprisingly, become a 'winter nicht'. There is an obvious
parallel between Cresseid's blighted life and this 'winterlie
springe', as Gabriel Harvey called it.[2] The analogy between
the seasons of the year and the seasons of man's life was so
common in the Middle Ages that a spring storm became
almost a standard symbol for a premature death. So Lydgate,
for instance, writes:

> When Ver is fresshest of blosmes and of floures,
> An vnware storme his fresshnessse may appayre,
> Who may withstonde the sterne sharpe schoures
> Of dethes powere, where hym list repayre?
> Though fetures fresshe, angelyke, and fayre
> Shewe out in chyldhode as ony crystall clere,
> Deth can difface hem withynne .xv. yeer.[3]

But it is not so obvious that Henryson is making a precise
use of the standard tradition that 'Spring, the air, childhood,
sanguineness are warm and wet . . . Autumn, the earth, man-

---

[1] For autumn and winter openings see D. A. Pearsall's note to
lines 1–3 of *The Assembly of Ladies* (in his edition of *The Floure and
the Leafe* [London, 1962]), and Rosemond Tuve, *Seasons and
Months: Studies in a Tradition of Middle English Poetry* (Paris, 1933),
pp. 109–10, 205. Some further examples are Chaucer's *House of Fame*,
the Middle English *Dispute between the Body and Soul*, Lydgate's
Look in Thy Merour, and *Deeme Noon Othir Wight* (*Minor Poems*,
II, p. 765) and *The World is Variable* (*Minor Poems*, II, p. 844), and
Dunbar's *Meditatioun in Wyntir*.
[2] *Gabriel Harvey's Marginalia*, ed. G. C. Moore Smith (Stratford-
upon-Avon, 1913), p. 159. Harvey's comment on Book V of *Troilus*,
'A cold spring' (p. 230), underlines the parallel between the two
works.
[3] *Minor Poems*, I, p. 343, lines 374–380.

hood, melancholy are cold and dry'.[1] At the beginning of the
poem, the spring is warm, as it should be, but then comes the
north wind, which is traditionally cold and dry,[2] and so
produces the appearance of autumn:

> In herust . . . the eeyre wixeth colde *and* dry, the wynde of the
> Northe oftymes turnyth, Wellis wythdrawen ham, grene thynges
> fadyth, Frutes fallyth, the Eeyre lesyth his beute . . . Than semyth
> the worlde as a woman of grete age, than nowe wox a colde and
> hade nede to be hote clothyde, for that the yowuthe is Passyde,
> and age neghyth, Wherfor hit is no mervaile yf beute she hath
> loste. This tyme is dry and colde by kynde, and than rengnyth blake
> coler, that is callid malencoly . . .[3]

Cresseid, too, is suddenly transformed by cold and dryness,
loses her beauty, and becomes 'as a woman of grete age'.

The hailstorm is a natural result of the sudden access of
cold and dry;[4] Cresseid's flesh undergoes the same change,
and from the same causes. Aretaeus says that leprosy

> is a refrigeration of the innate heat not in a small degree, or rather
> a congelation as when the water by the severity of winter is con-
> verted into snow or hail, or after concreting chrystalizes . . . the
> flesh is full of small bumps, which in size somewhat resemble hail
> stones . . .[5]

Henryson underlines the parallel between the hailstorm and
Cresseid's leprosy when he mentions that Saturn's arrows
are 'heidit with hailstanis' (168).

The heat and cold of the first stanza also suggest the
burning passion and cold pangs of love: in the description of
love which Resoun gives in the *Romaunt of the Rose* the same
mixed season appears:

[1] Bede, as summarised by H. Henel, in his edition of Aelfric's
De Temporibus Anni, EETS OS 213 (London, 1942), p. 103. See
Tuve, *Seasons and Months*, pp. 46–70, and Klibansky, Saxl and
Panofsky, *Saturn and Melancholy*, pp. 9–11.

[2] See notes to lines 4–6 and 17–19 below.

[3] *Secreta Secretorum*, ed. R. Steele, EETS ES 74 (London, 1898),
p. 245.

[4] See note to lines 4–6 below.

[5] Aretaeus, *Consisting of Eight Books, on the Causes, Symptoms and
Cure of Acute and Chronic Diseases*, tr. John Moffat (London [1785?]),
pp. 279, 282–3.

[Love is] full of froste, somer sesoun;
Pryme temps full of frostes whit,
And May devoide of al delit,
With seer braunches, blossoms ungrene,
And newe fruyt, fillid with wynter tene.[1]

A precise parallel to the *Testament* occurs in *The Floure and the Leafe*, where extreme heat ('the sonne so fervently / Waxe whote', lines 355-6) is followed by 'a storme of haile' (368). And in both poems the allegorical meaning is the same: the heat is the heat of sensuality, and the hail the ensuing torments.[2] Henryson may also have known—it is appropriate enough to Cresseid's life—that hail is a figure for 'the hardness of faithlessness, frozen by the torpor of vice'.[3]

In the second stanza the narrator says that 'Titan had his bemis bricht / Withdrawin doun'. This sunset, which follows the hail, is analogous to Cresseid's death, which follows her leprosy: the sun, as we are told later, causes 'lyfe in all eirdlie thing, / Without comfort of quhome, of force to nocht / Must all ga die that in this warld is wrocht' (201-3). But then the weather clears: 'The northin wind had purifyit the air / And sched the mistie cloudis fra the sky'. There is an unmistakable parallel here to Cresseid's own final purification. Henryson has neatly emphasised the meaning of this clear weather by introducing, later in the poem, a sunset of a different sort: 'The day passit and Phebus went to rest, / The cloudis blak ouerheled all the sky'.[4] This comes after Cresseid has entered the spital, but before she has started her complaint and begun to clear her murky and tempestuous soul.

---

[1] Lines 4746-50. Jean de Meun is here following the series of oxymorons which Alain de Lille uses to define love: '. . . vernal winter, wintry spring . . .' (*Complaint*, tr. Moffat, p. 47).

[2] See Pearsall's note to line 368 of *The Floure and the Leafe*. Hail 'is mentioned in Scripture 31 times, and always as an instrument of divine judgment' (Hastings, *Dictionary of the Bible*, s.v. *hail*, II, p. 282).

[3] Isidore of Seville, *De natura rerum*, XXXV, 2 (*Traité de la nature*, ed. J. Fontaine [Bordeaux, 1960]). See also Gregory the Great, *PL* 76, col. 497.

[4] Lines 400-1. The metaphors of a storm, clear skies, and black clouds are all used together in Lydgate's *Temple of Glas*, 610-14:

If the weather at the beginning of the poem gives an exact parallel to Cresseid's life, a more ironic and partly inverted parallel is provided by the figure of the narrator. He is an aged servant of love, an unintelligent, low-minded and agreeable old man who is the exact contrary of Henryson's other old men: the venerable and moralising Aesop of the *Fables* (lines 1349–97); Age in *The Ressoning betuix Aige and Yowth*; and the old man in *The Prais of Aige*, with his refrain, 'The more of age the nerar hevynnis blis'. Unlike these models, he refuses to accept his age and to contemplate moral or religious matters; instead, he thinks longingly about love.

Physically, he resembles Cresseid as she is towards the end of the poem; mentally, he resembles her as she is at the beginning. He has a preponderance of the cold and dry qualities, as is natural for an old man, but he hopes that Venus will make his 'faidit hart . . . grene'. He complains repeatedly of the cold, and then goes in to warm himself by the fire, remarking wistfully, 'Thocht lufe be hait, ȝit in ane man of age / It kendillis nocht sa sone as in ȝoutheid'. His real trouble, it appears, is that he is so cold and dry that he has lost his sexual powers.[1] And therefore he tries to use artificial methods to restore heat and moisture, so that he may prolong his virility: 'To help be phisike quhair that nature faillit'. He toasts himself by the fire, and then 'tuik ane drink, my spreitis to comfort', presumably both because of his dryness and because 'A lecherous thyng is wyn'.[2] Like the

> Alas! when shal þis tempest ouerdrawe,
> To clere þe skies of myn aduersite,
> The lode ster when I [ne] may not se,
> It is so hid with cloudes þat ben blake.
> Alas when wil þis turment ouershake?

[1] 'Whatever is cold and dry stops sexual love', Constantinus Africanus, quoted in M. Bassan, 'Chaucer's "Cursed Monk", Constantinus Africanus', *Mediaeval Studies*, 24 (1962), 137. Cf. *Fables*, 518–19, 'Off chalmerglew, Pertok, full weill ye knaw, / Waistit he wes, off Nature cauld and dry', and Lindsay's *Satyre*, 2162–3, 'Howbeit that swingeour can not swyfe, / He is baith cauld and dry'.

[2] Chaucer, *Pardoner's Tale*, VI, 549. January also takes spiced wine 't'encreesen his corage' (*Merchant's Tale*, IV, 1808).

young and healthy Cresseid, he equates love with the sexual act; unlike Cresseid, he does not come to wisdom when he is no longer apt for love.

We have seen that Henryson established a cause for Cresseid's leprosy on the natural, astrological, and divine levels; in this opening section of the poem he hints, half-humorously, at other ominous portents on each of these three levels. On the natural level, the sudden change in weather is likely to cause disease:

> Galene saythe, that Ipocras meanethe, that tymes of the yere brede not syckenesse, but chaungynges of complexion of the selfe time. Whan the complexion of the ayre, which ought to be according to the time, is torned into the contrary: as whan the complexion of springyng tyme, that shuld be hote and moyst torneth / & is made colde and drye, as it were in Herueste tyme / and so of other. For if the ayre of springynge tyme be generally colde and dry, and in the winter afore the ayre was as it were in springynge tyme hote and moyst, than it must nedes folowe, that many menne shall be sicke in sprynge tyme.
>
> (Barth. Angl., IV, iiii)

On the astrological level, Venus is said to be in opposition to the sun. This is extremely ominous: 'aspectus oppositus . . . is worste: for it is the sygne of perfyghte enmyte / and sygnyfyeth and bytokeneth worste happes' (Barth. Angl., VIII, ix). Astronomically, this situation is impossible, since Venus is never that far from the sun; Henryson is apparently suggesting an unnaturally great malevolence to match the unnatural weather.[1] On the religious level, there is a mis-guided and aborted prayer: the narrator intends to pray to Venus, but is stopped by the cold. This is, of course, irrever-ence at most, not blasphemy, but it still is a plain anticipation of Cresseid's more seriously misguided and aborted prayer.

The opening section has the function of providing a properly portentous beginning and of setting up the narrator and Cresseid as parallel characters, but it also indicates some of the peculiar things that Henryson is doing with a traditional genre. The *Testament* could be described as a poem which begins in spring, with a narrator who is worried about problems

[1] See note to lines 11–14.

of love, and who, instead of sleeping, takes up a book which turns out to deal with his problems: later in the poem other problems of love are discussed by a court of mythological figures. This description shows how traditional the framework of the poem is: Henryson, the innocent reader might suppose, is writing yet another of the innumerable poems explaining and praising courtly love.[1] But the spring, as we have seen, is unorthodox, and the narrator is equally strange. His age is not in itself unusual: *The Cuckoo and the Nightingale*, for instance, is also told by an 'old and unlusty' lover,[2] and Chaucer's narrators are not in their first youth. There are various advantages in an old narrator: he can be shown as an impartial and detached figure who has outgrown passion, or as an experienced and hence wise figure. But Henryson, instead, uses his old man as an example of foolish and sinful attachment to sensuality.[3] He is, to be sure, a perfectly orthodox follower of the code of *fine amour*: according to the seventeenth statute of this code, as explained in the *Court of Love*,

> Whan age approchith on,
> And lust is leid, and all the fire is queint,
> As freshly than thou shalt begin to fon,
> And dote in love . . .
>
> (456–9)

But he is also, like January, a figure illustrating the folly, self-delusion, and sterility of lust. For all his amiability, it would not be going too far to see him as St Paul's *vetus homo*, the 'Old Man' which represents unredeemed man, corrupt and concupiscent. Henryson makes him, like Cresseid herself, a figure who is both sympathetic and sinful, so that we must condemn him at the same time that we see him to be like us.

---

[1] See Neilson, *Court of Love*. Some of the poems which conform more or less to this pattern, such as the *Parliament of Fowls*, are, of course, not uncritical of courtly love.

[2] Skeat, *Chaucerian and Other Pieces*, p. 348, line 37.

[3] The aged lover who is the narrator of Gower's *Confessio Amantis* is a character of the same type, but he, unlike Henryson's narrator, acquires wisdom during the course of the poem.

The narrator, again like Cresseid, is a votary both of 'courtly love' and of concupiscence: the two turn out to be identical. And so, where the more serious-minded narrators of the *Parliament of Fowls* and the *Kingis Quair* read philosophical works, Macrobius and Boethius, our narrator naturally reads Chaucer's *Troilus*, the great handbook of love. The fifth book of *Troilus* and the 'vther quair' about Cresseid's death should teach the narrator about the illusory nature and the bitter end of earthly love. But he learns nothing, and his reaction to Cresseid's plight is morally imbecilic, if 'normal' enough: 'Poor girl, she's so pretty she shouldn't have been faithless, but anyway it's all the fault of Fortune'. It is interesting that the narrator remains on the scene only so long as he and Cresseid are of the same mind. His last obtrusive comment is in lines 323–9, where he anticipates Cresseid's remark about 'Our craibit goddis' (353), and asks 'cruell Saturne . . . On fair Cresseid quhy hes thow na mercie . . .?' When Cresseid begins to repent and to spurn earthly love she passes beyond the narrator's sympathy or comprehension.

Henryson, then, uses the framework traditionally devoted to 'courtly love' poems in order to reveal the vanity of sexual love. He does this by repeating the pattern of the fifth book of *Troilus*. Chaucer, in this book, tells how Troilus is abandoned and how his consequent suffering leads him both to death and to wisdom: he recognises, at the end, that 'This wrecched world [is] . . . al vanite' (V, 1817). Henryson's Cresseid goes through precisely the same cycle: abandonment, suffering, death, wisdom, and salvation. The different varieties of suffering which Troilus and Cresseid undergo are appropriate to their different characters as well as to the different themes of the two poems: Troilus's sufferings are intellectual, connected with his intellectual error in making an earthly creature into an object of religious devotion; Cresseid's sufferings are physical, connected with her excessive desire for earthly safety and comfort, and with her sexual indulgences. The difference between the ends of the two poems, a smaller difference than at first appears, comes partly because Henryson is a more decorous writer than Chaucer, a poet so brilliant that he is sometimes a bit flashy. Chaucer breaks the framework of his poem at the end by rejecting 'payens corsed olde rites' in favour of the Christian God, and by explicitly condemning earthly love, 'al oure werk that foloweth so / The blynde lust'. Henryson stays within the conventions he has set himself: he makes no explicit condemnation of earthly love, though he does make Troilus as 'Honest and chaist' (555) a lover as possible, and the closest he comes to introducing Christianity explicitly is to let Cresseid use a Christian formula when she bequeaths her spirit to Diana.[1] But Christianity and the condemnation of earthly love are clearly enough implicit in the end of the *Testament*.

The interpretation which I have suggested, that Cresseid is redeemed at the end of the poem, is by no means new. Sir Herbert Grierson expressed it finely by quoting Plato's *Gorgias*:

> '. . . those who are punished by gods and men, and improved, are those whose sins are curable; still the way of improving them is by pain and suffering; for there is no other way in which they can be delivered from their evil.' . . . we see her [Cresseid] healed and repentant by the way of suffering, and we are left in mind at peace with her as with Troilus.[2]

But this view has recently been attacked by Spearing, who says that 'it is difficult to agree with what seems to be the usual view of the *Testament* as a humane work . . . She [Cresseid] is repentant, certainly, but there is no suggestion of healing',[3] and by Douglas Duncan, who suggests that the

---

[1] It is tempting to suppose that Henryson knew the tradition which equated Diana with the Trinity or with the divine essence. See *Ovide moralisé en prose*, ed. de Boer (Amsterdam, 1954), pp. 91, 116. But in any case Diana is a fairly obvious surrogate for God—or possibly for the Virgin Mary, with whom she was sometimes compared. See Seznec, *Survival of the Pagan Gods*, p. 266.

[2] 'Robert Henryson', *The Modern Scot*, 4 (1933–4), 302. The whole passage from the *Gorgias* (525) is relevant to the *Testament*. See also E. M. W. Tillyard's admirable essay on the *Testament* in *Poetry and its Background* (London, 1955) (originally published under the title *Five Poems 1470–1870* [London, 1948]).

[3] A. C. Spearing, *Criticism and Medieval Poetry* (London, 1964), p. 144.

Testament 'questions the divine order quite peremptorily'.[1] Duncan's more extreme position is the logically sounder one: if Henryson wrote a poem in which repentance brought no healing he was presumably questioning the divine order. But these interpretations seem both impossible historically and unjustified by the poem—even Cresseid cannot continue to regard herself as a wronged heroine—and they doubtless arose because modern readers do not have what Henryson took for granted in his audience: an unquestioned belief in the culpability of sexual love, in the efficacy of penance, and in the existence of an afterlife. Yet these sombre interpretations, if ultimately false, have the value of emphasising Henryson's honesty and clearsightedness. Unlike his narrator, he is not a sentimentalist, and the earth he shows consists of an inescapable concatenation of causes and effects. He maintains a precise and coldminded balance: there is justice in the world, but not a justice always comprehensible to man; there is also a very real suffering and horror, but they are not gratuitous or meaningless.[2] Men cannot evade the consequences of their actions, but they do have free will, and are able to make atonement for their sins.

[1] 'Henryson's *Testament of Cresseid*', *Essays in Criticism*, **11** (1961), 129.

[2] There is an interesting parallel and contrast between Cresseid and Emma Bovary. Both turn to infidelity and finally to prostitution out of a combination of romantic illusion and sexual desire, and the bodies of both become corrupt as a result of their moral corruption. But where Cresseid dies peacefully, Emma dies vomiting blood, and laughing 'd'un rire atroce, frénétique, désespéré'. Henryson is careful never to let Cresseid's suffering become overwhelmingly vivid: her leprosy is never described objectively, for instance, but is shown only, by anticipation, in the formal sentences of Saturn and the moon, and in the stylised phrases of her own lament.

NOTE TO THE TEXT

The text followed is that of the Charteris print (C). All letters or words added to C, or substituted for its readings, are enclosed in brackets. My omissions of letters or words in C, or alterations in its word-order, are not marked in the text, though they are shown in the apparatus. (Such omissions or alterations are made in lines 109, 238, 290, 334, 337, 374, 382, 408, 432, 442, 477, 489, 491, 493, 554.) Abbreviations in C have been expanded silently: they consist only of four ampersands, four macrons over vowels to show nasals, and single cases of contractions of *that*, *the*, and *with*. C follows the usual practice of using *z* for ȝ (yogh) and also for *z* itself, in its rare appearances (here only in *lazarous*); I have transcribed this symbol as ȝ, except in *lazarous*. C very occasionally uses *y* (as a thorn) for *th*; I have transcribed it as *th*. Punctuation and capitalisation are modernised, but the word-division of C has been preserved wherever the printer's intentions are clear.

The apparatus is intended to include all of the substantive variants in T; variants in A, in cases where C and T are in agreement, are not recorded except when they seem interesting or possibly authentic. Some variants are given from R for lines 1–21, and from L for lines 561–7. Variants of dialect, form, or spelling are given only for special purposes. Such variants as the following, for example, are ignored: 33 (*and passim*) quhilk] C; which TA.   117 kirk] C; churche TA. 132 (*and passim*) sen] C; sithe T; since A.   252 (*and passim*) culd] C; couth T; could A.   341 (*and passim*) ilk] C; eche TA. When a variant is followed by several sigla, the spelling of the variant is that of the print denoted by the first sigil. For the sigla used (C, T, A, R, L), see Introduction, p. 2.

THE TESTAMENT OF CRESSEID

Ane doolie sessoun to ane cairfull dyte
Suld correspond and be equiualent:
Richt sa it wes quhen I began to wryte
This tragedie; the wedder richt feruent,
Quhen Aries, in middis of the Lent,   5
Schouris of haill [gart] fra the north discend,
That scantlie fra the cauld I micht defend.

3it neuertheles within myne oratur
I stude, quhen Titan had his bemis bricht
Withdrawin doun and sylit vnder cure,   10
And fair Venus, the bewtie of the nicht,
Vprais and set vnto the west full richt
Hir goldin face, in oppositioun
Of God Phebus, direct discending doun.

Throw out the glas hir bemis brast sa fair   15
That I micht se on euerie syde me by;
The northin wind had purifyit the air
And sched the mistie cloudis fra the sky;
The froist freisit, the blastis bitterly
Fra Pole Artick come quhisling loud and schill,   20
And causit me remufe aganis my will.

1 to] CA; onto R; tyl T
4 the wedder] CTA; *with* wedd*eris* R
6 gart] R; can CTA
7 defend] CRA; me defende T
8 within myne] CTA; In tyll ane R
10 sylit] CA; sellit R; scyled T
15 Throw out] CTA; Out throw R
17 northin] CR; northern TA
18 the (1)] CRA; his T
20 quhisling] C; wystland (?) R; whisling A; whiskyng T

For I traistit that Venus, luifis quene,
To quhome sum tyme I hecht obedience,
My faidit hart of lufe scho wald mak grene,
And therupon with humbill reuerence
I thocht to pray hir hie magnificence;
Bot for greit cald as than I lattit was
And in my chalmer to the fyre can pas.

Thocht lufe be hait, ȝit in ane man of age
It kendillis nocht sa sone as in ȝoutheid,
Of quhome the blude is flowing in ane rage;
And in the auld the curage doif and deid
Of quhilk the fyre outward is best remeid:
To help be phisike quhair that nature faillit
I am expert, for baith I haue assaillit.

I mend the fyre and beikit me about,
Than tuik ane drink, my spreitis to comfort,
And armit me weill fra the cauld thairout.
To cut the winter nicht and mak it schort
I tuik ane quair—and left all vther sport—
Writtin be worthie Chaucer glorious
Of fair Creisseid and worthie Troylus.

And thair I fand, efter that Diomeid
Ressauit had that lady bricht of hew,
How Troilus neir out of wit abraid
And weipit soir with visage paill of hew;
For quhilk wanhope his teiris can renew,
Quhill esper[ance] reioisit him agane:
Thus quhyle in ioy he leuit, quhyle in pane.

25

30

35

40

45

32 doif] C; doufe A; dul T
36 mend] CA; made T
37 ane] CA; I T
42 worthie] CA; lusty T
45 of] CA; of his T
48 esperance] A; Esperus C; esperous T
49 leuit] CA; lyued *and* T

Of hir behest he had greit comforting,   50
Traisting to Troy that scho suld mak retour,
Quhilk he desyrit maist of eirdly thing,
For quhy scho was his only paramour.
Bot quhen he saw passit baith day and hour
Of hir ganecome, than sorrow can oppres   55
His wofull hart in cair and heuines.

Of his distres me neidis nocht reheirs,
For worthie Chauceir in the samin buik,
In gudelie termis and in ioly veirs,
Compylit hes his cairis, quha will luik.   60
To brek my sleip ane vther quair I tuik,
In quhilk I fand the fatall destenie
Of fair Cresseid, that endit wretchitlie.

Quha wait gif all that Chauceir wrait was trew?
Nor I wait nocht gif this narratioun   65
Be authoreist, or fenȝeit of the new
Be sum poeit, throw his inuentioun
Maid to report the lamentatioun
And wofull end of this lustie Creisseid,
And quhat distres scho thoillit, and quhat deid.   70

Quhen Diomeid had all his appetyte,
And mair, fulfillit of this fair ladie,
Vpon ane vther he set his haill delyte,
And send to hir ane lybell of repudie
And hir excludit fra his companie.   75
Than desolait scho walkit vp and doun,
And sum men sayis, into the court, commoun.

51 suld] CA; wolde T   52 of] CA; of al T
55 than] CA; in T   58 the] CA; that T
63 fair] CT; false A   that] C; whiche T; who A
66 fenȝeit] CA; forged T   67 Be] CA; Of T   throw] CA; by T
70 thoillit, and quhat deid] CA; was in or she deyde T
73 he set his haill] C; sette was al his T; set his whole A
74 lybell of] C; lybel T; Letter of A
77 And] CA; As T   into] CA; in T   commoun] CA; as
    commune T

O fair Creisseid, the flour and A per se
Of Troy and Grece, how was thow fortunait
80   To change in filth all thy feminitie,
And be with fleschelie lust sa maculait,
And go amang the Greikis air and lait,
Sa giglotlike takand thy foull plesance!
I haue pietie thow suld fall sic mischance!

85   Ʒit neuertheles, quhat euer men deme or say
In scornefull langage of thy brukkilnes,
I sall excuse als far furth as I may
Thy womanheid, thy wisdome and fairnes,
The quhi[l]k Fortoun hes put to sic distres
90   As hir pleisit, and nathing throw the gilt
Of the—throw wickit langage to be spilt!

This fair lady, in this wyse destitute
Of all comfort and consolatioun,
Richt priuelie, but fellowschip o[r re]fute,
95   Disagysit passit far out of the toun
Ane myle or twa, vnto ane mansioun
Beildit full gay, quhair hir father Calchas
Quhilk than amang the Greikis dwelland was.

Quhen he hir saw, the caus he can inquyre
100 Of hir cumming: scho said, siching full soir,
'Fra Diomeid had gottin his desyre
He wox werie and wald of me no moir.'
Quod Calchas, 'Douchter, weip thow not thairfoir;
Perauenture all cummis for the best.
105 Welcum to me; thow art full deir ane gest!'

79 was] C; wast A; were T   82 air] CA; early T
84 thow] CA; the T   86 brukkilnes] CA; brutelnesse T
89 quhilk] quhik C; whiche TA   92 in] CA; on T
94 but] CA; without T   or refute] T; on fute CA
95 Disagysit] C; Disaguised A; Dissheuelde T   far] CA; om T
97 Beildit] C; Bylded T; Builded A
102 of] CT; have A

This auld Calchas, efter the law was tho,
Wes keiper of the tempill as ane preist
In quhilk Venus and hir sone Cupido
War honourit, and his chalmer was neist;
To quhilk Cresseid, with baill aneuch in breist,   110
Vsit to pas, hir prayeris for to say,
Quhill at the last, vpon ane solempne day,

As custome was, the pepill far and neir
Befoir the none vnto the tempill went
With sacrifice, deuoit in thair maneir;   115
Bot still Cresseid, heuie in hir intent,
Into the kirk wald not hir self present,
For giuing of the pepill ony deming
Of hir expuls fra Diomeid the king;

Bot past into ane secreit orature,   120
Quhair scho micht weip hir wofull desteny.
Behind hir bak scho cloisit fast the dure
And on hir kneis bair fell doun in hy;
Vpon Venus and Cupide angerly
Scho cryit out, and said on this same wyse,   125
'Allace, that euer I maid ȝow sacrifice!

'Ȝe gaue me anis ane deuine responsaill
That I suld be the flour of luif in Troy;
Now am I maid ane vnworthie outwaill,
And all in cair translatit is my ioy.   130
Quha sall me gyde? Quha sall me now conuoy,
Sen I fra Diomeid and nobill Troylus
Am clene excludit, as abiect odious?

'O fals Cupide, is nane to wyte bot thow
And thy mother, of lufe the blind goddes!   135

109 was] TA; was thame C   110 aneuch] CA; enewed T
125 on this same] CA; in this T
134 is nane to] CA; none is to T   135 the] CA; that T

ʒe causit me alwayis vnderstand and trow
The seid of lufe was sawin in my face,
And ay grew grene throw ʒour supplie and grace.
Bot now, allace, that seid with froist is slane,
140   And I fra luifferis left, and all forlane.'

Quhen this was said, doun in ane extasie,
Rauischit in spreit, intill ane dreame scho fell,
And be apperance hard, quhair scho did ly,
Cupide the king ringand ane siluer bell,
145   Quhilk men micht heir fra heuin vnto hell;
At quhais sound befoir Cupide appeiris
The seuin planetis, discending fra thair spheiris;

Quhilk hes power of all thing generabill,
To reull and steir be thair greit influence
150   Wedder and wind, and coursis variabill:
And first of all Saturne gaue his sentence,
Quhilk gaue to Cupide litill reuerence,
Bot as ane busteous churle on his maneir
Come crabitlie with auster luik and cheir.

155   His face fro[ns]it, his lyre was lyke the leid,
His teith chatterit and cheuerit with the chin,
His ene drowpit, how sonkin in his heid,
Out of his nois the meldrop fast can rin,
With lippis bla and cheikis leine and thin;
160   The ice schoklis that fra his hair doun hang
Was wonder greit, and as ane speir als lang:

136 alwayis vnderstand] CA; vnderstande alway T
137 in] CA; on T   138 supplie and] CA; souple T
139 slane] CT; shorn A   140 forlane] CT; forlorn A
142 spreit, intill] C; spirte in T; spirit in A
144 ringand] CA; tynkyng T   145 vnto] CA; in to T
150 coursis] CA; course T   152 Quhilk] C; Whiche T; Who A
153 on] CA; in T   154 auster] C; austryne T; austern A
155 fronsit] frosnit C; frounsed T; frozned A
156 cheuerit] C; sheuered T; checkered A.
157 how] CA; hole T
158 of] CA; at T

Atouir his belt his lyart lokkis lay
Felterit vnfair, ouirfret with froistis hoir,
His garmound and his gy[te] full gay of gray,
His widderit weid fra him the wind out woir,   165
Ane busteous bow within his hand he boir,
Vnder his girdill ane flasche of felloun flanis
Fedderit with ice and heidit with hailstanis.

Than Iuppiter, richt fair and amiabill,
God of the starnis in the firmament   170
And nureis to all thing generabill;
Fra his father Saturne far different,
With burelie face and browis bricht and brent,
Vpon his heid ane garland wonder gay
Of flouris fair, as it had bene in May.   175

His voice was cleir, as cristall wer his ene,
As goldin wyre sa glitterand was his hair,
His garmound and his gy[te] full [gay] of grene
With goldin listis gilt on euerie gair;
Ane burelie brand about his middill bair,   180
In his richt hand he had ane groundin speir,
Of his father the wraith fra vs to weir.

Nixt efter him come Mars the god of ire,
Of strife, debait, and all dissensioun,
To chide and fecht, als feirs as ony fyre,   185
In hard harnes, hewmound, and habirgeoun,
And on his hanche ane roustie fell fachioun,
And in his hand he had ane roustie sword,
Wrything his face with mony angrie word.

164 gyte] gyis C; gate T; guise A
166 within] CT; into A
167 flasche] C; fasshe T; flush A
174 wonder] C; wonders T; good and A
176 wer] C; was TA
178 gyte] T; gyis C; guise A   gay] TA; *om* C
180 bair] CA; he beare T
182 weir] CA; bere T

190 Schaikand his sword, befoir Cupide he come,
With reid visage and grislie glowrand ene,
And at his mouth ane bullar stude of fome,
Lyke to ane bair quhetting his tuskis kene;
Richt tuilȝeour lyke, but temperance in tene,
195 Ane horne he blew with mony bosteous brag,
Quhilk all this warld with weir hes maid to wag.

Than fair Phebus, lanterne and lamp of licht,
Of man and beist, baith frute and flourisching,
Tender nureis, and banischer of nicht;
200 And of the warld causing, be his mouing
And influence, lyfe in all eirdlie thing,
Without comfort of quhome, of force to nocht
Must all ga die that in this warld is wrocht.

As king royall he raid vpon his chair,
205 The quhilk Phaeton gydit sum tyme v[n]richt;
The brichtnes of his face quhen it was bair
Nane micht behald for peirsing of his sicht;
This goldin cart with fyrie bemis bricht
Four ȝokkit steidis full different of hew
210 But bait or tyring throw the spheiris drew.

The first was soyr, with mane als reid as rois,
Callit Eoye, into the orient;
The secund steid to name hecht Ethios,
Quhitlie and paill, and sum deill ascendent;
215 The thrid Peros, richt hait and richt feruent;

190 sword] CA; brande T
191 glowrand] CA; glowyng T
192 bullar] CA; blubber T
194 tuilȝeour] C; tulsure T; Souldiour A
195 he] CA; *om* T
203 Must . . . is] C; Must go dye that al this worlde hath T; But all
    must die that in the world is A
204 his] CA; a T
205 gydit sum tyme] CA; somtyme gyded T   vnricht] vpricht
    CA; vnright T
211 soyr] CA; sorde T   215 richt (2)] CA; eke T

The feird was blak, callit Philologie,
Quhilk rollis Phebus doun into the sey.

Venus was thair present, that goddes [gay],
Hir sonnis querrell for to defend, and mak
Hir awin complaint, cled in ane nyce array,   220
The ane half grene, the vther half sabill blak,
[With] hair as gold kemmit and sched abak;
Bot in hir face semit greit variance,
Quhyles perfyte treuth and quhyles inconstance.

Vnder smyling scho was dissimulait,   225
Prouocatiue with blenkis amorous,
And suddanely changit and alterait,
Angrie as ony serpent vennemous,
Richt pungitiue with wordis odious;
Thus variant scho was, quha list tak keip: 230
With ane eye lauch, and with the vther weip,

In taikning that all fleschelie paramour,
Quhilk Venus hes in reull and gouernance,
Is sum tyme sweit, sum tyme bitter and sour,
Richt vnstabill and full of variance,   235
Mingit with cairfull ioy and fals plesance,
Now hait, now cauld, now blyith, now full of wo,
Now grene as leif, now widderit and ago.

With buik in hand than come Mercurius,
Richt eloquent and full of rethorie,   240
With polite termis and delicious,
With pen and ink to report all reddie,
Setting sangis and singand merilie;

216 callit] CT; and called A   Philologie] CT; Philogie A
218 gay] TA; *om* C   219 for] CA; *om* T
220 Hir] CA; His T
222 With] A; Quhyte C; White T
231 lauch, and with] CT; laughing and A
238 widderit] widdderit C; wyddred T; withered A

His hude was reid, heklit atouir his croun,
245   Lyke to ane poeit of the auld fassoun.

Boxis he bair with fyne electuairis,
And sugerit syropis for digestioun,
Spycis belangand to the pothecairis,
With mony hailsum sweit confectioun;
250   Doctour in phisick, cled in ane skarlot goun,
And furrit weill, as sic ane aucht to be;
Honest and gude, and not ane word culd lie.

Nixt efter him come Lady Cynthia,
The last of all and swiftest in hir spheir;
255   Of colour blak, buskit with hornis twa,
And in the nicht scho listis best appeir;
Haw as the leid, of colour nathing cleir,
For all hir licht scho borrowis at hir brother
Titan, for of hir self scho hes nane vther.

260   Hir gy[t]e was gray and full of spottis blak,
And on hir breist ane churle paintit full euin
Beirand ane bunche of thornis on his bak,
Quhilk for his thift micht clim na nar the heuin.
Thus quhen thay gadderit war, thir goddes seuin,
265   Mercurius thay cheisit with ane assent
To be foirspeikar in the parliament.

Quha had bene thair and liken for to heir
His facound toung and termis exquisite,
Of rethorick the prettick he micht leir,
270   In breif sermone ane pregnant sentence wryte.
Befoir Cupide veiling his cap alyte,
Speiris the caus of that vocatioun,
And he anone schew his intentioun.

245 to] CA; tyl T   250 ane] CT; *om* A   256 appeir] C; tapere
T; to appear A   258 hir (1)] CA; the T   260 gyte] T; gyse CA
262 bunche] CA; busshe T   264 thir] C; þe T; these A
267 liken] C; lykyng T; listned A   272 vocatioun] CA; vacatioun T

'Lo', quod Cupide, 'quha will blaspheme the name
Of his awin god, outher in word [or] deid,   275
To all goddis he dois baith lak and schame,
And suld haue bitter panis to his meid.
I say this by ʒone wretchit Cresseid,
The quhilk throw me was sum tyme flour of lufe,
Me and my mother starklie can reprufe,   280

'Saying of hir greit infelicitie
I was the caus, and my mother Venus,
Ane blind goddes hir cald, [and] micht not se,
With sclander and defame iniurious.
Thus hir leuing vnclene and lecherous   285
Scho wald ret[orte i]n me and my mother,
To quhome I schew my grace abone all vther.

'And sen ʒe ar all seuin deificait,
Participant of deuyne sapience,
This greit iniure done to our hie estait   290
Me think with pane we suld mak recompence;
Was neuer to goddes done sic violence:
Asweill for ʒow as for my self I say,
Thairfoir ga help to reuenge, I ʒow pray!'

Mercurius to Cupide gaue answeir   295
And said, 'Schir King, my counsall is that ʒe
Refer ʒow to the hiest planeit heir
And tak to him the lawest of degre,
The pane of Cresseid for to modifie:
As God Saturne, with him tak Cynthia.'   300
'I am content', quod he, 'to tak thay twa.'

275 or] TA; in C   276 lak] CA; losse T
278 ʒone wretchit] CA; yonder wretche T
280 starklie] CA; she stately T
283 Ane . . . and] Ane blind Goddes hir cald that C; She called a
    blynde goddes and TA
286 retorte in] T; returne on CA   287 abone] C; aboue TA
290 iniure] TA; Iniurie C   292 goddes] CT; goddesse A
297 Refer] CT; Vtter A

Than thus proceidit Saturne and the Mone
Quhen thay the mater rypelie had degest:
For the dispyte to Cupide scho had done
305   And to Venus, oppin and manifest,
In all hir lyfe with pane to be opprest,
And torment sair with seiknes incurabill,
And to all louers be abhominabill.

This duleful sentence Saturne tuik on hand,
310   And passit doun quhair cairfull Cresseid lay,
And on hir heid he laid ane frostie wand;
Than lawfullie on this wyse can he say,
'Thy greit fairnes and all thy bewtie gay,
Thy wantoun blude, and eik thy goldin hair,
315   Heir I exclude fra the for euermair.

'I change thy mirth into melancholy,
Quhilk is the mother of all pensiuenes;
Thy moisture and thy heit in cald and dry;
Thyne insolence, thy play and wantones,
320   To greit diseis; thy pomp and thy riches
In mortall neid; and greit penuritie
Thow suffer sall, and as ane beggar die.'

O cruell Saturne, fraward and angrie,
Hard is thy dome and to malitious!
325   On fair Cresseid quhy hes thow na mercie,
Quhilk was sa sweit, gentill and amorous?
Withdraw thy sentence and be gracious—
As thow was neuer; sa schawis th[rough] thy deid,
Ane wraikfull sentence geuin on fair Cresseid.

304 Cupide] CA; Cupide that T
318 in] CA; in to T
319 and] CA; *and* thy T
320 riches] C; richesse T; richnesse A
321 In] CA; In to T
325 On] CA; Of T
328 was] C; were T; wast A   through] T; thow CA
329 fair] CA; *om* T

Than Cynthia, quhen Saturne past away,   330
Out of hir sait discendit doun belyue,
And red ane bill on Cresseid quhair scho lay,
Contening this sentence diffinityue:
'Fra heit of bodie [here] I the depryue,
And to thy seiknes sall be na recure   335
Bot in dolour thy dayis to indure.

'Thy cristall ene mingit with blude I mak,
Thy voice sa cleir vnplesand hoir and hace,
Thy lustie lyre ouirspred with spottis blak,
And lumpis haw appeirand in thy face: 340
Quhair thow cummis, ilk man sall fle the place.
This sall thow go begging fra hous to hous
With cop and clapper lyke ane lazarous.'

This doolie dreame, this vglye visioun
Brocht to ane end, Cresseid fra it awoik,   345
And all that court and conuocatioun
Vanischit away: than rais scho vp and tuik
Ane poleist glas, and hir schaddow culd luik;
And quhen scho saw hir face sa deformait,
Gif scho in hart was wa aneuch, God wait!   350

Weiping full sair, 'Lo, quhat it is', quod sche,
'With fraward langage for to mufe and steir
Our craibit goddis; and sa is sene on me!
My blaspheming now haue I bocht full deir;
All eirdlie ioy and mirth I set areir.   355

334 heit] CA; heale T   here I the] T; I the now C; I do thee
      here A
335 sall be na recure] CT; there shall be no cure A
337 mingit] minglit C; menged T; mingled A
338 vnplesand] C; vnplesaunt TA   hoir] CA; heer T
341 fle] C; flye T; leaue A   342 This] C; Thus TA
345 to] CA; tyl T
349 face] CA; visage T
350 was] CA; were T   aneuch] C; I ne wyte T; enough A
352 for] CA; *om* T
353 goddis] C; goddes T; goddesse A
6

Allace, this day; allace, this wofull tyde
Quhen I began with my goddis for to chyde!'

Be this was said, ane chyld come fra the hall
To warne Cresseid the supper was reddy;
360   First knokkit at the dure, and syne culd call,
'Madame, ʒour father biddis ʒow cum in hy:
He hes merwell sa lang on grouf ʒe ly,
And sayis ʒour [beedes] bene to lang sum deill;
The goddis wait all ʒour intent full weill.'

365   Quod scho, 'Fair chyld, ga to my father deir
And pray him cum to speik with me anone.'
And sa he did, and said, 'Douchter, quhat cheir?'
'Allace!' quod scho, 'Father, my mirth is gone!'
'How sa?' quod he, and scho can all expone,
370   As I haue tauld, the vengeance and the wraik
For hir trespas Cupide on hir culd tak.

He luikit on hir vglye lipper face,
The quhylk befor was quhite as lillie flour;
Wringand his handis, oftymes said allace
375   That he had leuit to se that wofull hour;
For he knew weill that thair was na succour
To hir seiknes, and that dowblit his pane;
Thus was thair cair aneuch betuix thame twane.

Quhen thay togidder murnit had full lang,
380   Quod Cresseid, 'Father, I wald not be kend;
Thairfoir in secreit wyse ʒe let me gang
To ʒone hospitall at the tounis end,
And thidder sum meit for cheritie me send

357 goddis for] C; goddes T; goddesse A
360 syne] C; efte T; then A
363 beedes] T; prayers CA
372 lipper] CA; lepers T
374 oftymes] T; oftymes he C; he oft-times A
381 wyse] CT; wayes A
382 To] TA; Wnto C

To leif vpon, for all mirth in this eird
Is fra me gane; sic is my wickit weird!'   385

Than in ane mantill and ane bawer hat,
With cop and clapper, wonder priuely,
He opnit ane secreit ȝet and out thair at
Conuoyit hir, that na man suld espy,
Wnto ane village half ane myle thairby;   390
Delyuerit hir in at the spittaill hous,
And daylie sent hir part of his almous.

Sum knew hir weill, and sum had na knawledge
Of hir becaus scho was sa deformait,
With bylis blak ouirspred in hir visage,   395
And hir fair colour faidit and alterait.
Ȝit thay presumit, for hir hie regrait
And still murning, scho was of nobill kin;
With better will thairfoir they tuik hir in.

The day passit and Phebus went to rest,   400
The cloudis blak ou[erheled] all the sky.
God wait gif Cresseid was ane sorrowfull gest,
Seing that vncouth fair and harbery!
But meit or drink scho dressit hir to ly
In ane dark corner of the hous allone,   405
And on this wyse, weiping, scho maid hir mone.

384 eird] CA; erthe T
385 weird] CA; werthe T
386 Than] CA; Whan T
390 Wnto] C; There to TA
392 sent] CA; sende T
399 thairfoir] CA; there T
401 ouerheled] T; ouirquhelmit CA
402 was] CA; were T

THE COMPLAINT OF CRESSEID

'O sop of sorrow, sonkin into cair,
O catiue Creisseid, now and euer mair
Gane is thy ioy and all thy mirth in eird;
410 Of all blyithnes now art thou blaiknit bair;
Thair is na salue may saif [or sound] thy sair!
Fell is thy fortoun, wickit is thy weird,
Thy blys is baneist, and thy baill on breird!
Vnder the eirth, God gif I grauin wer,
415 Quhair nane of Grece nor ȝit of Troy micht heird!

'Quhair is thy chalmer wantounlie besene,
With burely bed and bankouris browderit bene;
Spycis and wyne to thy collatioun,
The cowpis all of gold and siluer schene,
420 Th[y] sweit meitis seruit in plaittis clene
With saipheron sals of ane gude sessoun;
Thy gay garmentis with mony gudely goun,
Thy plesand lawn pinnit with goldin prene?
All is areir, thy greit royall renoun!

425 'Quhair is thy garding with thir greissis gay
And fresche flowris, quhilk the quene Floray
Had paintit plesandly in euerie pane,
Quhair thou was wont full merilye in May
To walk and tak the dew be it was day,

title] CA; Here foloweth the complaynt of Creseyde. T
408 now] nowe T; for now CA
410 blaiknit] CA; blake *and* T
411 saif or sound] save or sound A; saif the of C; helpe T
412 weird] CA; werthe T 413 on breird] CA; vnberd T
414 eirth] CA; great T gif] C; if TA 415 nane] CA; men T
417 bankouris browderit] C; bankers brouded T; bonkers browdred A
419 The] CT; Thy A 420 Thy] TA; The C
421 saipheron sals] C; sauery sauce T; Saffron and sause A
sessoun] CA; facioun T
423 plesand] C; plesaunt T; pleasant A prene] C; pene T;
pin A 425 thir] C; thy TA
427 pane] CT; plain A 428 was] C; were T; wast A

And heir the merle and mawis mony ane, 430
With ladyis fair in carrolling to gane
And se the royall rinkis in thair ray,
In garmentis gay garnischit on euerie grane?

'Thy greit triumphand fame and hie honour,
Quhair thou was callit of eirdlye wichtis flour, 435
All is decayit, thy weird is welterit so;
Thy hie estait is turnit in darknes dour;
This lipper ludge tak for thy burelie bour,
And for thy bed tak now ane bunche of stro,
For waillit wyne and meitis thou had tho 440
Tak mowlit breid, peirrie and ceder sour;
Bot cop and clapper now is all ago.

'My cleir voice and courtlie carrolling,
Quhair I was wont with ladyis for to sing,
Is rawk as ruik, full hiddeous, hoir and hace; 445
My plesand port, all vtheris precelling,
Of lustines I was hald maist conding—
Now is deformit the figour of my face;
To luik on it na leid now lyking hes.
Sowpit in syte, I say with sair siching, 450
Ludgeit amang the lipper leid, "Allace!"

'O ladyis fair of Troy and Grece, attend
My miserie, quhilk nane may comprehend,
My friuoll fortoun, my infelicitie,
My greit mischeif, quhilk na man can amend. 455

432 ray] T; array CA   433-7 *om* T
438 burelie] CA; goodly T   441 peirrie] CA; pirate T
442 clapper] TA; Clappper C   443 and] CA; and my T
444 *om* T for] C; fair A
445 rawk as] C; ranke as T; rank and A hoir] C; heer T;
      hoar A   446-7 *om* T
448 Now is deformit] CA; Deformed is T
449 leid now lyking hes] CA; pleople hath lykyng T
450 Sowpit] CA; Solped T
451 Ludgeit] CA; Lyeng T leid] CA; folke T
453 *om* T   454 friuoll] CA; freyle T

Be war in tyme, approchis neir the end,
And in ʒour mynd ane mirrour mak of me:
As I am now, peraduenture that ʒe
For all ʒour micht may cum to that same end,
460   Or ellis war, gif ony war may be.

'Nocht is ʒour fairnes bot ane faiding flour,
Nocht is ʒour famous laud and hie honour
Bot wind inflat in vther mennis eiris,
ʒour roising reid to rotting sall retour;
465   Exempill mak of me in ʒour memour
Quhilk of sic thingis wofull witnes beiris.
All welth in eird, away as wind it weiris;
Be war thairfoir, approchis neir [ʒour] hour;
Fortoun is fikkill quhen scho beginnis and steiris.'

470   Thus chydand with hir drerie destenye,
Weiping scho woik the nicht fra end to end;
Bot all in vane; hir dule, hir cairfull cry,
Micht not remeid, nor ʒit hir murning mend.
Ane lipper lady rais and till hir wend,
475   And said, 'Quhy spurnis thow aganis the wall
To sla thy self and mend nathing at all?'

'Sen thy weiping bot dowbillis thy wo,
I counsall the mak vertew of ane neid;
[G]o leir to clap thy clapper to and fro,
480   And lei[f] efter the law of lipper leid.'

456 *printed after 460* T   in tyme] CA; therefore T
     the] CA; your T
459 that] CA; the T
467 away as wind] CA; as wynde away T
468 ʒour] your TA; the C
469 *om* T
473 remeid] CA; remedy T
474 till] CA; to T
477 thy weiping bot dowbillis] thy weiping dowbillis bot C; that
     thy wepyng but doubleth T; thy weeping doth double but A
479 Go] TA; To C
480 leif] leir CA; lerne T   lipper] CA; lepers T

Thair was na buit, bot furth with thame scho ȝeid
Fra place to place, quhill cauld and hounger sair
Compellit hir to be ane rank beggair.

That samin tyme, of Troy the garnisoun,
Quhilk had to chiftane worthie Troylus,   485
Throw ieopardie of weir had strikken doun
Knichtis of Grece in number meruello[u]s;
With greit tryumphe and laude victorious
Agane to Troy richt royallie thay raid
The way quhair Cresseid with the lipper baid.   490

Seing that companie, all with ane steuin
Thay gaif ane cry, and schuik coppis gude speid,
'Worthie lordis, for Goddis lufe of heuin,
To vs lipper part of ȝour almous deid!'
Than to thair cry nobill Troylus tuik heid,   495
Hauing pietie, neir by the place can pas
Quhair Cresseid sat, not witting quhat scho was.

Than vpon him scho kest vp baith hir ene,
And with ane blenk it come into his thocht
That he sumtime hir face befoir had sene,   500
Bot scho was in sic plye he knew hir nocht;
Ȝit than hir luik into his mynd it brocht
The sweit visage and amorous blenking
Of fair Cresseid, sumtyme his awin darling.

481 furth with thame] C; forthwith [?] thā T; forth-with then A
485 to] C; the T; a A
487 meruellous] meruellons C; marueylous T; marvellous A
489 richt] richt richt C; right TA
490 baid] C; stode T; bode A
491 that companie] that companie þai come C; that company come T;
    the troup they came A   ane] C; o T; a A
493 Worthie] Said worthie CA; Worthy T
495 thair] CA; her T
499 into] CA; in tyl T
501 plye] C; plyte TA
502 it] CA; he T

505   Na wonder was, suppois in mynd that he
        Tuik hir figure sa sone, and lo, now quhy:
        The idole of ane thing in cace may be
        Sa deip imprentit in the fantasy
        That it deludis the wittis outwardly,
510   And sa appeiris in forme and lyke estait
        Within the mynd as it was figurait.

        Ane spark of lufe than till his hart culd spring
        And kendlit all his bodie in ane fyre;
        With hait fewir, ane sweit and trimbling
515   Him tuik, quhill he was reddie to expyre;
        To beir his scheild his breist began to tyre;
        Within ane quhyle he changit mony hew;
        And neuertheles not ane ane vther knew.

        For knichtlie pietie and memoriall
520   Of fair Cresseid, ane gyrdill can he tak,
        Ane purs of gold, and mony gay iowall,
        And in the skirt of Cresseid doun can swak;
        Than raid away and not ane word [he] spak,
        Pensiwe in hart, quhill he come to the toun,
525   And for greit cair oft syis almaist fell doun.

        The lipper folk to Cresseid than can draw
        To se the equall distributioun
        Of the almous, bot quhen the gold thay saw,
        Ilk ane to vther prewelie can roun,
530   And said, 'Ʒone lord hes mair affectioun,
        How euer it be, vnto Ʒone Lazarous
        Than to vs all; we knaw be his almous.'

508 imprentit] C; enprynted T; imprinted A
513 all] CA; *om* T
514 ane] CA; in T
517 mony] CA; many a T
521 *printed twice* (*bottom of* C1ᵃ, *top of* C1ᵇ) C   mony] CA;
     many a T
522 swak] CA; shake T
523 he] TA; *om* C

'Quhat lord is ȝone,' quod scho, 'haue ȝe na feill,
Hes done to vs so greit humanitie?'
'Ȝes,' quod a lipper man, 'I knaw him weill;   535
Schir Troylus it is, gentill and fre.'
Quhen Cresseid vnderstude that it was he,
Stiffer than steill thair stert ane bitter stound
Throwout hir hart, and fell doun to the ground.

Quhen scho ouircome, with siching sair and sad,   540
With mony cairfull cry and cald ochane:
'Now is my breist with stormie stoundis stad,
Wrappit in wo, ane wretch full will of wane!'
Than [fel in swoun full] oft or [euer] scho [fane],
And euer in hir swouning cryit scho thus,   545
'O fals Cresseid and trew knicht Troylus!

'Thy lufe, thy lawtie, and thy gentilnes
I countit small in my prosperitie,
Sa [efflated] I was in wantones,
And clam vpon the fickill quheill sa hie.   550
All faith and lufe I promissit to the
Was in the self fickill and friuolous:
O fals Cresseid and trew knicht Troilus!

'For lufe of me thow keipt continence,
Honest and chaist in conuersatioun;   555

534 Hes done] C; That dothe T; Hath done A
536 it is] C; it is a knyght T; he is A
541 mony] C; many a TA   ochane] CA; atone T
543 ane wretch full will of wane] C; wretch fulwyl of one T; a
    wretchful will of wane A
544 fel in swoun] TA; swounit scho C   full oft or euer scho
    fane] oft or scho culd refrane C; ful ofte or she wolde fone T;
    full oft ere she would fane A
547 lawtie, and] CA; laude and al T
548 countit] CA; compted T
549 efflated] A; eleuait C; effated T
551 promissit to] C; promytted to T; promist unto A
552 the] C; thy T; it A   friuolous] CA; furious T
554 continence] gude continence C; countenaunce T; countenance A

Of all wemen protectour and defence
Thou was, and helpit thair opinioun;
My mynd in fleschelie foull affectioun
Was inclynit to lustis lecherous:
560   Fy, fals Cresseid; O trew knicht Troylus!

'Louers be war and tak gude heid about
Quhome that ȝe lufe, for quhome ȝe suffer paine.
I lat ȝow wit, thair is richt few thairout
Quhome ȝe may traist to haue trew lufe agane;
565   Preif quhen ȝe will, ȝour labour is in vaine.
Thairfoir I reid ȝe tak thame as ȝe find,
For thay ar sad as widdercok in wind.

'Becaus I knaw the greit vnstabilnes,
Brukkill as glas, into my self, I say—
570   Traisting in vther als greit vnfaithfulnes,
Als vnconstant, and als vntrew of fay—
Thocht sum be trew, I wait richt few ar thay;
Quha findis treuth, lat him his lady ruse;
Nane but my self as now I will accuse.'

575   Quhen this was said, with paper scho sat doun,
And on this maneir maid hir testament:
'Heir I beteiche my corps and carioun
With wormis and with taidis to be rent;
My cop and clapper, and myne ornament,
580   And all my gold the lipper folk sall haue,
Quhen I am deid, to burie me in graue.

558 in] CA; on T
562 for quhome] CA; for whan T; q*uhair*for L
563 thairout] CA; thrughout T; about L
564 Quhome] CTA; *þat* L
569 Brukkill] CA; Brittel T   into] C; vnto TA
570 vnfaithfulnes] CA; brutelnesse T
571 vnconstant] CA; inconstaunt T
576 on] CA; in T
577 beteiche] C; bequeth TA
579 and (1)] CA; my T
580 the] CA; these T

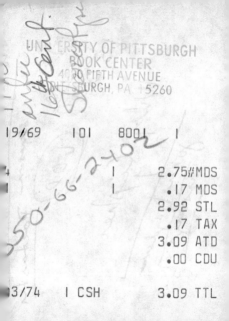

UNIVERSITY OF PITTSBURGH
BOOK CENTER
4000 FIFTH AVENUE
PITTSBURGH, PA 15260

19/69   101   8001   1

+   1   2.75#MDS
1   1   .17 MDS
                                 2.92 STL
                                  .17 TAX
                                 3.09 ATD
                                  .00 CDU

13/74   1 CSH   3.09 TTL

750) Johnson Poetasker

150.00
_____
600

Wiley Cipher

John Dryden
brave's 85

'This royall ring, set with this rubie reid,
Quhilk Troylus in drowrie to me send,
To him agane I leif it quhen I am deid,
To mak my cairfull deid wnto him kend.   585
Thus I conclude schortlie and mak ane end:
My spreit I leif to Diane, quhair scho dwellis,
To walk with hir in waist woddis and wellis.

'O Diomeid, thou hes baith broche and belt
Quhilk Troylus gaue me in takning   590
Of his trew lufe', and with that word scho swelt.
And sone ane lipper man tuik of the ring,
Syne buryit hir withouttin tarying;
To Troylus furthwith the ring he bair,
And of Cresseid the deith he can declair.   595

Quhen he had hard hir greit infirmitie,
Hir legacie and lamentatioun,
And how scho endit in sic pouertie,
He swelt for wo and fell doun in ane swoun;
For greit sorrow his hart to brist was boun;   600
Siching full sadlie, said, 'I can no moir;
Scho was vntrew and wo is me thairfoir.'

Sum said he maid ane tomb of merbell gray,
And wrait hir name and superscriptioun,
And laid it on hir graue quhair that scho lay,   605
In goldin letteris, conteining this ressoun:
'Lo, fair ladyis, Cresseid of Troy [the] toun,
Sumtyme countit the flour of womanheid,
Vnder this stane, lait lipper, lyis deid.'

583 drowrie] C; dowry TA   584 it] CT; *om* A
590 takning] C; tokenyng TA   593 Syne] C; Than TA
600 greit] C; *om* TA   was] CT; was ready A
603 said] CA; sayth T
605 quhair that] C; where as T; where A
607 fair ladyis] CT; clear Ladies fair A   Troy the] TA;
    Troyis C
608 countit] CA; compted T   609 lait] CT; laith A

610 Now, worthie wemen, in this ballet schort,
Maid for ʒour worschip and instructioun,
Of cheritie, I monische and exhort,
Ming not ʒour lufe with fals deceptioun:
Beir in ʒour mynd this sor[e] conclusioun
615 Of fair Cresseid, as I haue said befoir.
Sen scho is deid I speik of hir no moir.

FINIS

610 ballet] C; balade TA
614 sore] T; schort CA
FINIS] CA; Thus endeth the pyteful and dolorous testament of
fayre Creseyde: and here foloweth the legende of good women. T

NOTES

1–2. **doolie,** 'dismal', is a favourite adj. of Henryson's, but is not recorded before him. The etymology of it is doubtful (see *OED, doly, dowie*), and it is not certain what form Henryson himself used. T and R read here *doly* (but T reads *dooly* in 344); the spellings elsewhere in Henryson are always *dolly, dully,* or *dulye* (*Orpheus,* 134, 310, 600; *Thre Deid Pollis,* 50).

Henryson is combining two of the most conventional ways of beginning a poem: a *sententia* and an appropriate seasonal opening. For the peculiar weather, see Introduction, pp. 50–52. But he is also echoing the beginning of *Troilus*:

> help me for t'endite
> Thise woful vers . . .
> For wel sit it, the sothe for to seyne,
> A woful wight to han a drery feere,
> And to a sorwful tale, a sory chere.
> (I, 6–7, 12–14)

Henryson's lines were in turn imitated by Douglas:

> So weill according dewly bene annext
> *Th*ou drery preambill, with a bludy text
> (*Aen.,* VII, Prol. 165–6)

by Lindsay:

> But sad sentence sulde haue ane sad indyte
> (*Monarche,* Prol. 210)

and by Thomas Lodge:

> Such is the dolie season of the yeare
> (*A Margarite of America,* p. 15, in *Complete Works,*
> Hunterian Club, Vol. III [Glasgow, 1883]).

equiualent, 'correspondent'. Cf. Rolland, *Court of Venus,* ed. W. Gregor, STS I 3 (Edinburgh, 1884), I, 703–4: 'it is Equiualent / To all ressoun, and als correspondent . . .'

4. **tragedie.** In 63 below Henryson may be thinking of the definition in the *Monk's Tale*:

> Tragedie is to seyn a certeyn storie, . . .
> Of hym that stood in greet prosperitee,
> And is yfallen out of heigh degree
> Into myserie, and endeth wrecchedly.
> (VII, 1973, 1975–7; see also 2582 and 2627)

Cf. *Troilus*, V, 1786: 'Go, litel bok, go, litel myn tragedye'. Henryson's use of the term *tragedie* is discussed in Harth, 'Convention and Creation', pp. 44–8.

4–6. feruent has been taken by previous editors as 'severe' or 'bitter', but there seems to be no warrant for this meaning in any language. It is occasionally used as an adj. modifying *cold* or *frost* (see *OED*, *fervent*, 1c), but in its normal sense of 'burning'—a cold intense enough to give the impression of heat. It is barely possible that it here means 'stormy', since the word was sometimes used, in the sense 'boiling', of the raging sea or of tempests, as in 'The wedir was so fervent of wynd & eke of thundir' (*Tale of Beryn*, ed. F. J. Furnivall and W. G. Stone, EETS ES 105 [1909], 1583). But it is much more likely that *feruent* here means simply 'hot', as it does in 215 below.

Henryson is following traditional meteorology with learning and accuracy. The weather was traditionally hot for at least part of the time that the sun was in Aries: see Ptolemy, *Tetrabiblos*, II. 11 ('. . . part hot and pestilential. Its northern parts are hot and destructive') and Barth. Angl., VIII, x ('In the.ii.gree of Aries / or in the.ix.shall be great heete'), while Aries itself was 'the colerik hoote signe' (*Squire's Tale*, V, 51, and so Barth. Angl., VIII, x). And the hotness of spring was a poetic commonplace: see Tuve, *Seasons and Months*, p. 61. Like Douglas, who wrote that early in May 'corby gaspyt for *th*e fervent heit' (*Aen.*, XII, Prol. 174), Henryson was not concerned with the facts of a Scottish spring.

Hail was thought, according to a tradition which goes back to Aristotle's influential *Meteorologica* (347b–348b), to be caused by the mutual reaction of hot and cold. Extreme hot weather followed by a north wind logically brings on a hailstorm: 'For the moyste partis voiden and fleen heate of the ayre, and comen togethers in to the inner partyes of the clowde . . . And also the Northen wyn[d]e is colde and drye / and freseth and constraynethe the dewe . . . and tourneth it in to the substaunce of the haylle / as Beda sayth' (Barth. Angl., XI, x). See further S. K. Heninger, Jr., *A Handbook of Renaissance Meteorology* (Durham, North Carolina, 1960), pp. 55–6. There may also have been a popular connection between the north and hail: cf. the modern Scots saying 'When the wind is in the North / Hail comes forth' (Andrew Cheviot, *Proverbs, Proverbial Expressions, and Popular Rhymes of Scotland* [Paisley, 1896], p. 396).

5. Skeat, followed by later editors, argues that **Lent** is 'spring', that **in middis of the Lent**=OE *middewærd lencten*='April', and so that the time indicated is 'the *first week in April*, when the sun was still in Aries'. But *lent* in MSc means simply 'Lent', and, for that matter, there is no good evidence that *middewærd lencten*='April' (see Wright-Wülker, *Anglo-Saxon and Old English Vocabularies* [London, 1884], Vol. I, col. 176, for the gloss Skeat argues from). Henryson is simply saying that the time is the first month of spring: the sun enters Aries on the vernal equinox. *Lent* is mentioned because of its connotations of deprivation and death—if also of rebirth.

6. **gart,** though only in R, appears to be the true reading, since *can* awkwardly forces *descend* to bear the rare meaning 'cause to descend' (not attested in this construction: see *OED, descend,* 10). (Dickins glosses *can* as 'caused to', but there is no warrant for this.) Cf. *Orpheus,* 498–9: 'a rany clud . . . [down] fra the firmament / Scho gart discend'. *can* may have arisen from a misreading of *gart* as *gan* (=*can*), or from the scribal tendency to make each line a separate unit of sense.

7. C shows a mixture of constructions: *I micht defend* ('ward off') *the cauld* and *I micht me defend fra the cauld.* The unmetrical *me* in T may be an emendation, but it is possible (especially in view of the scribal tendency to lengthen aphetic forms) that the original reading was *I micht me fend.*

8. **oratur.** Probably a room for private worship (here, and in 120, for worship of Venus), though Lindsay uses the word for a private study (*Dreme,* 1031; *Beaton,* 2; *Monarche,* 6331). The cold drives the narrator from his unheated oratory to the fire in his chamber. Cf. Chaucer: 'In worshipe of Venus, goddesse of love, / Doon make an auter and an oratorie' (*Knight's Tale,* I, 1904–5); for other oratories of Venus see Lydgate, *Temple of Glas,* 696, and Schick's note to that line.

10. **sylit.** Probably not 'ceiled' and hence 'covered', 'overlaid', as Skeat, G. G. Smith, and Wood say (see *OED, ceil, ceiled, sile,* v.⁴), but the MSc form of 'seeled', here as elsewhere used in the sense of 'covered', 'concealed' (see *OED, sile,* v.³). The two verbs may, however, have become confused: see *OED, oversile,* and the imitation of these lines in *The Maitland Folio Manuscript,* ed. W. A. Craigie, STS II 7, 20 (Edinburgh, 1919–27), I, 205, lines 1–2. It is not clear what *scyled,* in T, is intended to be: in K it is glossed as 'scyled þat is hidden or shut vpp'.

cure, 'cover', with vocalisation of *v* before syllabic *r.*

11–14. Kinaston, and later A. S. Cook (*MLN,* **22** [1907], 62), point out that Venus can never have an elongation of more than 48°, and so can never be in opposition to the sun. But there is no need to assume, with Kinaston, 'Authoris error, qui . . . aliquantulum dormitare & in Astronomicis cæcutire videatur', or to follow Elliott's desperate suggestion that **in oppositioun** does not mean 'in opposition' (it must, since Venus is apparently rising in the east while the sun is setting, at a time near the equinox). Henryson, who demonstrates his disdain for the 'superstitioun of astrology' at the end of *Orpheus* (589), is using his considerable knowledge of it in the same ironic but not meaningless way as in the beginning of 'The Fox and the Wolf' (*Fables,* 628–55). Opposition, like the quartile aspect, is extremely malignant: Venus in opposition to the sun suggests an impossibly great malevolence. The unnatural astronomy is continued in 15–16, where it is said that Venus casts enough light to see by.

15–18. As Stearns points out (*Henryson,* p. 62) these lines are derived from Chaucer's *Book of the Duchess,* 336–43:

throgh the glas the sonne shon
Upon my bed with bryghte bemes,
With many glade gilde stremes;
And eke the welken was so fair,—
Blew, bryght, clere was the ayr,
And ful attempre for sothe hyt was;
For nother to cold nor hoot yt nas,
Ne in al the welken was no clowde.

Both passages contain the same beams shining through the glass, the same cloudless weather, and the same rhyme-words (*fair : air*).

17–19. 'whan the northen wind bloweth, the aire is the more dry & subtil. . . . Also for the Northe wynde is colde and drye, it pourgyth and clensyth reyne, and dryuyth awaye clowdes and mistes / and bryngeth in clerenes and faire weder' (Barth. Angl., IV, iii; XI, ii).

20. **Pole Artick,** 'the north celestial pole', 'the polestar'. 'The north wind, cold and snowy, blows straight from the north pole [*ab axe*] and makes an arid cold and dry clouds; it is also called "aparctias" ' (Isidore of Seville, *De natura rerum*, XXXVII, 1). '. . . the Northerne wynde . . . arysyth vnder the sterre that hyghte Polus Articus' (Barth. Angl., XI, iii). Henryson uses this traditional detail to emphasise the inhuman and distant origin of the baneful forces.

quhisling is probably right: cf. '*th*e wynd*is* lowde quhissilling' (Douglas, *Aen.*, I, ii, 6). *whiskyng*, in T, may be a paleographical error (*k* and *l* are very similar in some hands), perhaps suggested by the common sixteenth-century *whisking wind* (v. *OED, whisking*, ppl. a., 1b).

schill, 'shrill'. **loud and schill** is a stock phrase: see *OED, shill*, a. and adv.

24. A 'green heart' is a favourite Chaucerian expression: *Clerk's Tale*, IV, 1173; *Merchant's Tale*, IV, 1465; *Anelida*, 180.

27. 'But at that time I was prevented because of the great cold.'

29. **lufe be hait.** 'Hot love' is a commonplace in Chaucer, as elsewhere: e.g. 'the hote fir of love', *Troilus*, I, 490. Cf. Douglas,

Lufe is a kyndly passioun, engendryt of heyt
Kyndlyt in *th*e hart, ourspredyng al *th*e cors, . . .
And into agyt fail3eis, and is out quent . . .
    (*Aen.*, IV, Prol. 114–15, 120)

30. **3outheid,** 'youths'. The earliest citation of *youthhead* with this collective meaning in the *OED* is 1562.

32. **doif,** 'dull', 'spiritless'. *dolf* or *douf* are more normal spellings. Apparently there is ellipsis of *is* after *curage*.

curage is here used in the special sense of 'sexual desire'. See *MED, corage*, 2b, and Dunbar, *Tua Mariit Wemen*, 67 and *passim*.

34. **phisike**, 'natural or medical science'. Stearns suggests that these lines are derived from a misunderstanding of Chaucer's 'there is phisicien but oon / That may me hele' (*Book of the Duchess*, 39–40; Stearns, *A Modernization of Robert Henryson's Testament of Cresseid*, Indiana Univ. Humanities Series No. 13 [Bloomington, Indiana, 1945], p. 16). But Henryson would seem rather to be ironically perverting the common doctrine that the ailments of love can be cured only by the loved one (see Robinson's note to Chaucer's lines).

35. **I am expert**, 'I am experienced'. A latinism, repeated in *Orpheus*, 411.

36. **mend** is probably a preterite form (with absorption of the inflectional syllable): see *EDD*, *mend*, and Henryson's pret. or past part. forms *send* (74, 583) and *torment* (307). *made*, in T, is probably an emendation which arose from the apparent clash of tenses. One would expect here *bet* (pret. of *beet*): the earliest other example in the *OED* for the phrase *to mend a fire* is 1720.

   beikit, 'basked'. Henryson uses this verb in *Fables*, 757 and 1407, to suggest a dangerous complacency and immersion in sensual pleasures.

36–8. G. G. Smith compares Douglas's 'winter' prologue (Book VII, esp. pp. 89–93). Sitting by the fire and drinking is a traditional winter sport (cf. *Franklin's Tale*, V, 1252–3); Henryson is here modulating the season into the *winter nicht* of 39.

40. **quair**. Ordinarily used of a fairly short poem, such as might be contained in a single quire. All of the events referred to in the next two stanzas are in the fifth book of *Troilus*.

41–2. **worthie . . . worthie**. As G. G. Smith suggests, the repetition of *worthie* need not be taken as a slip: *lusty*, in T (42), is probably a wrong emendation. Henryson is careful to follow Chaucer, in whose poem Troilus is repeatedly called *worthy* and *worthiest* (so also in 485 below), but, unlike Criseyde, is never referred to as *lusty* (cf. *lustie Creisseid* in 69 below). Henryson, like Chaucer, opposes the beauty of Cresseid to the moral worth of Troilus. For the repetition of *worthie* in consecutive lines, see *Fables*, 1888–9.

   Chaucer, like other poets, was frequently called *worthy*: see Spurgeon, *Five Hundred Years of Chaucer Criticism*, I, 14, 22, 45, 53; and line 58 below.

44. Cf. 'Criseyde, brighte of hewe' (*Troilus*, V, 1573), 'Calkas doughter, with hire brighte hewe' (IV, 663), 'Hire [Criseyde's] hewe, whilom bright, that tho was pale' (IV, 740), and also 'every lady bright of hewe' (V, 1772). **hew** is perhaps emphasised here (by being rhymed with itself) because of the black and terrible colour of Cresseid's face later.

45. 'To breyde out of one's wit' is a common Chaucerian idiom: Troilus, after he has been deserted, says 'wel neigh out of my wit I breyde' (V, 1262). The *his* which appears in T is probably spurious: for **out of wit** (without the pronominal adjective) see *OED, wit,* 4.

46. **visage paill** is a Chaucerian expression (*Manciple's Prologue,* IX, 30; *Romaunt,* 420). The tearful Troilus of Book V has 'so ded an hewe' (559), and writes to Criseyde that he has lost 'myn hele and ek myn hewe' (1403).

47. Probably 'because of which despair, his tears recommenced', not 'because of which, despair renewed his tears'.

47–56. Henryson may have had particularly in mind *Troilus,* V, 1207–9:

> Bitwixen hope and drede his herte lay, (*Test.,* 47–8)
> Yet somwhat trustyng on hire hestes olde. (*Test.,* 50–1)
> But whan he saugh she nolde hire terme holde . . . (*Test.,* 54–5)

48. *Esperus* C; *esperous* T; *esperance* A. A famous crux. The reading in A is perhaps an emendation: the same emendation was made by Kinaston, who first wrote *Esperus* and then altered it to *Esperance,* adding a note in the margin 'esperance *þat* is hope', and also, independently, by Skeat, who wrote 'The reading *Esperus* in [C] is comic enough. Even Thynne has misread *esperans,* and has turned it into *esperous.*' But Bruce Dickins, in a letter to the *TLS* (11 December 1924, p. 850) argues for retaining *Esperus* 'in the sense of the Morning Star, which brings light to woeful hearts . . . And it is particularly appropriate that "Esperus," who is also Venus, should comfort the faithful lover.' (The essential part of Dickins's letter is quoted in Wood.) Charles Elliott, in 'Two Notes on Henryson's *Testament of Cresseid*', *JEGP,* 54 (1955), 241–54, repeats Dickins's arguments and adds more evidence for Esperus as a 'solace-bringer'.

It is true enough that both the evening star, bringing rest or lovers' meetings, and the morning star, bringing the dawn, can be used as symbols for joy. But there is no evidence that *Esperus* can be used flatly as an antonym of *wanhope,* whereas *esperance* is obviously appropriate. In *Garmont of Gud Ladeis,* 29, Henryson uses *esperance* as the opposite of *dispair,* and Chaucer puts Troilus 'Bitwixen hope and derk disesperaunce' (II, 1307). Since the two words could easily have been confused by an early scribe, there seems to be no reason to avoid the obvious emendation.

49. The alternation between joy and pain is a constant theme in *Troilus,* from I, 4 onwards. Troilus, waiting for Criseyde to return to Troy, says that she 'cause is of my torment and my joie' (V, 427).

50. **behest** is not common in MSc, but Criseyde's promise to return on the tenth day is called a 'behest' in *Troilus* (V, 1191, 1675).

comforting. Cf. 'Ne felte I swich a comfort, dar I seye; / She comth to-nyght, my lif that dorste I leye!' (*Troilus,* V, 1168–9).

52. **maist of eirdly thing.** An ambiguous expression which perhaps carries a reference to the end of *Troilus*. The usual expression is 'above' or 'over' all earthly things (see *DOST, erdly*), and 'earthly thing' was a disparaging theological term (e.g., *Fables*, 130, 151).

60. **quha will luik,** 'whoever will look may see'. See *DOST, luke,* v. 5c.

61. It is reasonably certain that this **vther quair** never existed. The mocking tone of the next stanza suggests this, and references to imaginary authorities, such as Chaucer's 'Lollius' and 'Trophee', are not uncommon in medieval literature.
   To brek my sleip. He may wish to stay awake because this is part of the service of Venus. Cf. 'The broken slepes' in the temple of Venus in the *Knight's Tale* (I, 1920), and 'Venus list not . . . take kepe / to suche men as wolle not do theyre payn / to please, serue, and brek mony a slepe' (*Secular Lyrics of the XIVth and XVth Centuries*, ed. R. H. Robbins, 2nd ed. [Oxford, 1955], p. 169, lines 8–10).

62. **fatall destenie.** An echo of *fatal destyne, Troilus*, V, 1. **fatall,** 'fated'. Henryson is suggesting that his poem about the final fortunes of Cresseid is a companion piece to Book V of *Troilus*, which tells of Troilus's end.

66. **authoreist,** 'possessed of authority'. The question of the truth in poetry is a preoccupation of Henryson's: cf. *Fables*, 1–18, 1099–1100, 1380–90, 1890–1. Chaucer uses **new** with the same connotation: 'Or ellis he moot telle his tale untrewe, / Or feyne thyng, or fynde wordes newe' (*Gen. Prol.*, I, 735–6).
   There is little to choose between *fenʒeit* (C) and *forged* (T).

67–8. The syntax of the stanza is loose, but it seems best to follow the punctuation in C, where there is a comma after **poeit** but not after **inuentioun,** so that **Maid** is parallel with **fenʒeit.**

70. T apparently emends because he takes **deid** ('death') to be 'died'.

71–2. Cf. Chaucer's 'syn I knowe youre delit, / I shal fulfille youre worldly appetit' (*Wife of Bath's Tale*, III, 1217–18), and Henryson's 'fulfilland evir my sensualitie / In deidly syn' (*Ressoning betuix Deth and Man*, 31–2).

73. It is possible that the original reading is preserved in A, and that the versions in C and T are editorial attempts to avoid the ellipsis of the pronominal subject.

74. **lybell of repudie.** *libellum repudii*, 'bill of divorce', occurs some six times in the Vulgate. Henryson may have in mind both Moses' statement that a woman who is divorced by her second husband cannot be taken back by her first husband, 'because she is defiled, and is

become abominable before the Lord' (Dt. 24:1-4), and also the passages where Christ denies the possibility of divorce and proclaims the sanctity of marriage (Mt. 19:3-9; Mk. 10:2-12).

Either *lybell of repudie* (C) or *lybel repudy* (T) is possible. The former may have had some slight currency: the anonymous English translator of Higden's *Polychronicon* uses 'libelle of repudy, of repulsion' to translate *repudium* (*Polychronicon*, ed. J. R. Lumby, Rolls Ser., Vol. VI [London, 1876], 381).

77. into the court, commoun. Probably **court** is the royal court, and **commoun,** 'promiscuous', is an adj. modifying **scho.** This interpretation is supported by the phrase in *The Spektakle of Luf*, 'went common amang þe grekis' (see Introduction, pp. 17-18). And the author of *The Laste Epistle of Creseyd to Troyalus* (printed in *The Works of William Fowler*, ed. H. W. Meikle, Vol. I, STS II 6 [Edinburgh, 1914], pp. 379-87) refers to the royal court, though not to Cresseid's prostitution: 'Of force the courte I left, & to / My fathers house did passe' (255-6). T, who reads *in the courte as commune*, presumably understood the line in this way, and inserted *as* in order to clarify it. For **commoun,** cf. Gower:

> every womman mihte take
> What man hire liste, and noght forsake
> To ben als comun as sche wolde.
>   (*Confessio Amantis*, V, 1427-9)

Previous editors have compared the terms *courtesan* and *to walk the streets*, but *courtesan* in the sense of 'loose woman' is not recorded before 1549 (*OED*), and the other phrase seems to go back only to the eighteenth century (see *OED, street*, 3c, 3f). An interesting but unclear parallel is provided by Bower, who quotes from *Babio*, 'Indisciplinata mulier / Cornuta capite, ut hœdus', which he translates as 'The unlatit woman the licht man will lait, / Gangis coitand in the curt, hornit lik a gait' (perhaps 'The unrestrained woman will seek the wanton man; she goes . . . [*coitand* is obscure] in the [royal] court, horned like a goat') (Fordun, *Scotichronicon*, ed. W. Goodall [Edinburgh, 1759], II, 376). A. J. Aitken has suggested to me that Henryson may have been thinking of the court as traditionally a place of wanton women. And Henryson is probably being intentionally vague, though the Chaucerian *And sum men sayis* (cf. *Troilus*, V, 804) makes it clear that he is damning Cresseid.

78. A per se, 'paragon' (see note in G. G. Smith; Whiting, *A per se*; Tilley, A275). Henryson is probably referring to Chaucer's 'Right as oure firste lettre is now an A, / In beaute first so stood she [Criseyde], makeles' (*Troilus*, I, 171-2).

flour. Both Troilus and Diomede call Criseyde a 'flower' in Book V (1317, 792). For Henryson's development of this image see lines 128, 137-9, 279, 435, 461, and 608. G. G. Smith points out that *flour* and *A per se* are associated in the poem ascribed (on no evidence) to Dunbar which begins: 'London, thou art of townes A *per se* . . . the flour of Cities all.'

79. **fortunait,** 'destined by fortune'. This latinate past part. elsewhere has the meaning 'favoured by fortune', while the weak past part. means neutrally 'fated'. There may be an ironic reference here to Pandarus's inquiry whether Criseyde was 'fortunat' (*Troilus*, II, 280). An exclamation mark has usually been put after *fortunait*, but this seems a more awkward punctuation.

81. An ironic reference to Cresseid's leprosy, which was caused by 'fleschelie lust', since *maculatus* was frequently used of lepers, as in Lev. 13:44, 'Quicumque ergo maculatus fuerit lepra'.

84. There is little to choose between **thow** (CA) and *the* (T). In the first case, **fall** means 'get', 'obtain' (*DOST, fall*, 7b); in the second, 'befall'.

87. **excuse,** 'exempt from blame'. Reminiscent of the Chaucerian narrator: e.g. 'And if I myghte excuse hire any wise, / For she so sory was for hire untrouthe, / Iwis, I wolde excuse hire yet for routhe' (*Troilus*, V, 1097–9).

88. **womanheid,** like **feminitie** in 80, may go back to Chaucer's frequent use of *wommanhede* and *wommanliche* in connection with Criseyde. Cf. 608 below.
   Criseyde is called wise and fair in the portrait of her in Book V (820, 808).

89–91. Henryson's narrator, like Chaucer's, blames Cresseid's troubles on a personified Fortune, and is impassioned by sympathy for the wronged Cresseid—so much so that here he breaks out into an exclamatory infinitive (see T. F. Mustanoja, *A Middle English Syntax*, Part I [Helsinki, 1960], p. 539): 'It is not at all because of your guilt—you have been injured by slander.'

92. **in** CA; *on* T. Thynne preserves the earlier usage. See 125 below (*on* CA; *in* T), and *OED, wise*, sb.[1] II, 2.

94. **or refute** T; *on fute* CA. **refute,** 'refuge' or 'protector', not recorded after 1535, is so much harder than *fute* that it must be preferred, even at the cost of one of Henryson's most famous lines. Cf. 335 below, where *recure* is erroneously changed to *cure* in A.

95. **Disagysit** CA; *Dissheuelde* T. The correct reading is uncertain. *Disagysit* is the usual MSc form, but the metre here requires *disgysit*. It is possible, however, that *far* should be omitted, as in T, and that the line should read *Disagysit passit out*. But *Dissheuelde* may point to an original *disshevely, dissheveled*, or another four-syllable derivative of OF *deschevelé* (for forms see *MED, dischevelē*). No forms of it are listed in *DOST*, but *Dyschowyll* occurs in *Wallace*, XI, 1014 (ed. J. Moir, STS I 6, 7, 17 [Edinburgh, 1885–9]; the 1570 ed. reads *Slomerit*, suggesting the late sixteenth-century printers may not have known the word). Either 'disguised' or 'dishevelled', 'uncoiffed', makes good

sense, since Cresseid is both secretive and distraught; *far* can be defended, even in view of the next line, as an indication of Cresseid's feelings. I have let C stand, but without conviction.

96. G. G. Smith suggests that '*Mansioun* may convey the special meaning of an ecclesiastical residence (for Calchas, the priest)', but this is doubtful. See *OED, mansion,* 3c. Henryson has promoted Calchas from the tent given to him by Chaucer (*Troilus,* V, 148–9, 845), and has generally urbanised the Greek camp.

97. **Beildit** is taken by G. G. Smith, Wood, and Dickins to mean 'decorated'. But it probably means simply 'constructed' (*OE byldan*). For parallel forms see *MED, bīlden,* and *DOST, beild.* There was sometimes confusion between this verb and *belde* (*OE beldan*), 'strengthen, shelter, and (hence) cover over', but there is no reason to suppose confusion here.
   was must be understood after **quhair.**

104. This Boethian sentiment is appropriate to a priest, and perhaps also to the conclusion of the poem.

106. 'according as the law was then'. Both the southern **tho** and the latinate **Cupido** may have been borrowed from Chaucer.

108. As Skeat points out, Calchas is a priest of Apollo in Chaucer, as elsewhere. Henryson turns him into a foil for Cresseid by making him a true servant of love, in character as well as in office.

109. The agreement of T and A gives **was neist** strong support. *was thame neist* (C) is in any case not very sensible: Venus and Cupid do not reside in their temple. The version of T and A is rougher metrically, but is satisfactory if **honourit** is given three syllables.
   chalmer, 'dwelling' (*MED, chaumbre,* 2). It is not clear whether **quhilk** in 110 refers to this or to the temple.
   neist and **breist,** like **preist,** have close *ē* (see *OED, next, breast*).

115. **deuoit** presumably goes with **in thair maneir,** though Elliott takes it with **sacrifice.** Cf. Chaucer's 'devout and humble in hir corage' (*Second Nun's Tale,* VIII, 131).

117. **kirk** and its southern forms were commonly used for heathen temples. See *OED, church,* 2.

119. **expuls,** 'expulsion', is a latinism elsewhere recorded only in Golding (*OED*).
   king. In *Troilus* Diomede boasts that if his father had lived, 'ich hadde ben, er this, / Of Calydoyne and Arge a kyng, Criseyde! / And so hope I that I shal yet, iwis' (V, 933–5).

120. **orature.** Probably part of Calchas's house and not, as Kinaston suggests, a small chapel in the church (p. 512; G. G. Smith, I, cxlix). See 8 above, and note.

123. A common motif in Chaucer: e.g. 'And on hir bare knees adoun they falle' (*Knight's Tale*, I, 1758).

124. Henryson may have in mind both the passage where Troilus, in his frenzy after Criseyde's departure, goes to his chamber and curses the gods (*Troilus*, V, 202ff.) and the later passage where he, unlike Cresseid, prays humbly to 'blisful lord Cupide' (V, 582ff.).

130. In *Troilus*, Criseyde says that her 'joies . . . now transmewed ben in cruel wo' (IV, 828, 830).

133. **abiect** is a noun, 'outcast' (not elsewhere recorded in MSc; first recorded in English in 1534).

134. Ellipsis of *there* before **is.**

135. Venus was occasionally described or portrayed as blind, though perhaps only in Germany. See E. Panofsky, *Studies in Iconology*, 2nd ed. (New York, 1962), pp. 113–14. But probably Cresseid is simply confusing Venus with Cupid, who, of course, is often represented as blind. See Stearns, *A Modernization . . .*, p. 38. It is clear that she is making a mistake, for which Cupid angrily upbraids her in 282–3, since neither Cupid nor Venus are shown as blind later in the poem. Her mistake is revealing, for she has confused blind lust with love. Panofsky demonstrates that 'in the fourteenth century the blindness of Cupid had so precise a significance that his image could be changed from a personification of Divine Love to a personification of illicit Sensualitie, and vice versa, by simply adding, or removing, the bandage' (p. 121). Cf. Chaucer, *Legend of Good Women*, G, 169–70, and Sidney, 'hath not shee throwne reason upon our desires, and, as it were given eyes unto *Cupid*?' (*Works*, ed. A. Feuillerat, I [Cambridge, 1939], 8).

The rhyme **goddes : face** is of a conventional MSc type: cf. *traiss* ('Thrace') : *goddess*, *Orpheus*, 46–7. In C, *goddis* is always 'gods' or 'god's', and *goddes* is usually 'goddess' (but 'gods' in 264 and [perhaps] 292). The similarity of the spellings often causes confusion, as in 292, 353, and 357, where A reads *goddesse*.

137–9. As J. A. W. Bennett points out (*The Parlement of Foules* [Oxford, 1957], p. 87n), this is a reminiscence of the *Roman de la Rose* and the well of Narcissus: 'Cupido, li fiz Venus, / Sema ici d'Amors la graine' (ed. E. Langlois, SATF, Vol. II [Paris, 1920], lines 1588–9). The line may come from the French or from the ME *Romaunt*: 'Venus sone, daun Cupido, / Hath sowen there of love the seed' (1616–17). The implications of the metaphor are explained by the context: 'For whoso loketh in that mirrour, / Ther may nothyng ben his socour / That he ne shall there sen somthyng / That shal hym lede into lovyng' (*Romaunt*, 1605–8). These lines are also reminiscent of the weather at the beginning of the poem, where freezing hail comes in springtime, and of the narrator, who wishes that Venus 'My faidit hart of lufe . . . wald mak grene' (24).

140. **forlane** is explained by Skeat and, tentatively, the *OED* as the past part. of *forlie*, 'sleep with', 'seduce'. But the parallel passages show clearly that it is connected in meaning with *forlay*, 'lay aside', 'abandon'. See the note in G. G. Smith; *MED, forleien*; and *DOST, forlane*. It is possible, however, that the correct reading is preserved in A, which has *forlorn*, rhyming with *shorn*. Douglas, in a stanza which begins, 'In fragil flesch зour [Venus and Cupid's] fykkil seyd is saw' (*Aen.*, IV, Prol. 8), apparently in imitation of Henryson, uses *beschorn* as a rhyme, and cf. *Orpheus*, 292.

144. For Cupid's majesty, see Bennett, *Parlement of Foules*, pp. 83–4. He is also called 'king' by later Scots poets: see *DOST, Cupide*.

Either **ringand** (C) or *tynkyng* (T) is possible, while *tingand* might account for both readings. (The 1598 and 1602 editions, and hence K, do in fact read *tinging*, but this must be a coincidence.) *t* and *r* are easily confused in black letter.

145. The universal power of love is a commonplace: Henryson may be remembering Chaucer's 'In hevene and helle, in erthe and salte see / Is felt thi [Venus's] myght' (*Troilus*, III, 8–9). And there may here be religious implications: love can lead either to heaven or to hell.

148. **generabill** is a latinism which is repeated in line 171, but elsewhere is not recorded before Puttenham. Here it probably has a passive meaning, 'capable of being generated', though an active meaning, 'capable of generating', is possible (with reference to the four qualities which join to generate the world). *Generabilis* is used in a passive sense in medieval Latin (see *Revised Medieval Latin Word-List*, ed. R. E. Latham [London, 1965]), though it occurs only in an active sense in classical Latin. (The passive sense given in lexicons is erroneous: see Manilius, *Astronomicon Liber Primus*, ed. Housman, 2nd ed. [Cambridge, 1937], Addenda, p. 103.)

148–9. Pecock shows that the (ostensible) theology of the *Testament* is just what a fifteenth-century writer would have expected pagans to hold. He remarks that the pagans concluded that planets and stars were uncreated and eternal: 'And ferthermore, for as myche as these men aspieden weel bi greet witt, that the seid parties of heuen reuliden ful myche the worchingis of bodies here binethe in the louзer world, and thei couthen not come ferther forto wite what was doon in eny bodi here binethe which deede was not reulid bi hem aboue, therfore thei helden and trowiden that the bodili heuen and hise seid parties reuliden al that was reuleable here bynethe among men and among othere bodies and thingis . . . therfore ech such man was stirid and moved forto chese to him summe of these planetis or sterris forto be to him his souereyn helper and lord of hise nedis, and therbi ech such man made to him sum planet or sterre forto be to him his God' (*The Repressor of Over Much Blaming of the Clergy*, ed. C. Babington, Rolls Ser. [London, 1860], Vol. I, 242–3).

influence is used in the technical sense: see Glossary.

150. **coursis variabill**: the course of fortune (*Troilus*, V, 1745), as opposed to 'the perdurable courses' of the stars (Boethius, IV, Met. 6).

151–263. Most of the details in the portraits of the seven planets are thoroughly traditional: Henryson was probably drawing on his memory rather than on any single source. A number of parallels are collected in Stearns, *Henryson*, pp. 73–96; a more trustworthy account of the traditions behind Henryson's portraits is given in Seznec, *Survival of the Pagan Gods*. The first three portraits, in particular, are connected with the Albricus tradition, and are stylistically similar to the short chapters of the *Libellus de imaginibus deorum* (see Seznec, pp. 170–9). (Like Albricus and many others, Henryson describes the seven planets in the order of the magnitude of their orbits.) Lindsay gives in his *Dreme* (386–488) a description of the seven planets which is in part drawn from the *Testament*.

151–68. Saturn is the most baleful of the planets, 'an euyll willed planete, colde, and drye / a nyght planete and heuy. And therfore by fables he is painted as an old man, his cercle is moost ferre fro the erthe / and neuerthelesse it is moost noyefull to the erthe. . . . he hathe . . . two dedelye qualitees, coldnesse and dryenesse' (Barth. Angl., VIII, xxiii). He causes pestilence in general, and, because he is cold and dry, leprosy in particular (see Introduction, pp. 32–3; note to 253–63; and Stearns, *Henryson*, p. 75). Cf. Chaucer's Saturn: 'I do vengeance and pleyn correccioun . . . myne be the maladyes colde . . . My lookyng is the fader of pestilence' (*Knight's Tale*, I, 2461, 2467, 2469). For the medieval metamorphoses of Saturn, see E. Panofsky, 'Father Time', in *Studies in Iconology*, pp. 69–93, and Klibansky, Saxl and Panofsky, *Saturn and Melancholy*, pp. 127–214. According to the *Libellus de imaginibus deorum* (pseudo-Albricus), Saturn 'was portrayed as an old man, grey, with a long beard, bent, sad and pale, with his head covered, in colour greyish' (in *Hygini, Augusti Liberti Fabularum Liber* . . . [Lyons, 1608], f. 170^b).

151–2. **sentence**, 'opinion', 'decision'. **Quhilk** probably refers to *Saturne* and not to *sentence*.

153. 'Saturn . . . became in later medieval art more and more the leader and representative of the poor and the oppressed, . . . he appears as . . . a ragged peasant, leaning on the tool of his trade. . . . He is the representative of the lowest rung of medieval society, to whom all intellectual activity is a closed book, and who spends his life in wresting a meagre subsistence from the soil. The latter days of life, when man becomes sterile and when his vital warmth diminishes so that he seeks only to crouch by the fire—these days are proper to Saturn' (Klibansky, Saxl and Panofsky, *Saturn and Melancholy*, pp. 203–4: cf. lines 29–36 above).

154. Cf. 'Hyt semyd by hys chere as he [Saturn] wold make a fray' (*The Assembly of Gods*, ed. O. L. Triggs, EETS ES 69 [London, 1896], line 284). G. G. Smith compares Dunbar's 'crabbit Saturn ald and haire' (*Golden Targe*, 114).

155–9. Saturn seems himself to have the symptoms of leprosy: a livid and discoloured complexion with a wrinkled face and sunken eyes. See lines 337, 339–40 and notes; also Aretaeus's description of leprosy: 'the colour is livid or black, the . . . skin . . . is greatly contracted so as to cover the eyes . . . The skin of the head is deeply furrowed, and the chinks are frequent, deep and rough . . .' (tr. Moffat, pp. 282–3). These symptoms appear because Saturn, like a leper, is cold and dry: 'by kynd colde causeth and maketh thynges to be discoloured yll . . . And so the vtter syde of the skynne made poore of heate maketh euyll coloured. As it appereth in lyppes and chekes. . . . Also kyndly drynesse maketh thynges rough. . . . And so the vtter partis ben vneuen with holownes sonke / & with hardnes arered . . .' (Barth. Angl., IV, ii–iii). His running nose and shivering come because he is, in Boethius's phrase, a *gelidus senex* (IV, Met. 1, 11). Cf. the old man in Henryson's *Ressoning betuix Aige and Yowth*, 'With cheikis lene and lyart lokis hoir; / His ene was how . . .' (11–12; Wood reads *clene* for *lene*).

This passage is imitated in *Philotus*: 'His eine half sunkin in his heid, / His Lyre far caulder than the leid, / His frostie flesch as he war deid . . .' (ed. A. J. Mill, in *Miscellany Volume*, STS III 4 [Edinburgh, 1933], lines 281–3).

155. **fronsit**, 'wrinkled'. See Apparatus. *fronsit* is almost certainly right: cf. *Fables*, 2819. The same scribal confusion occurs in Montgomerie's *Flyting*, 575, where the correct reading must be *fronsit*, though the existing texts have *froisnit, frozin*, and *frozen* (Alexander Montgomerie, *Poems*, Supplementary Volume, ed. G. Stevenson, STS I 59 [Edinburgh, 1910]). Scribes here probably attempted to give Saturn his traditional 'frosty face' (e.g. Lydgate, *Siege of Thebes*, 3). But a wrinkled face is equally traditional: 'Olde Saturne then aloft dyd lye, with rustey ryueled face . . . With frosen face aboute he loked and vyle deformed hewe' (from the preface to the 1560 version of *The Zodiake of Life*, Barnabe Googe's translation of Palingenius, ed. [in facsimile] Rosemond Tuve [New York, 1947]).

leid. 'led, withouten faille, / Ys, loo, the metal of Saturne' (Chaucer, *House of Fame*, 1448–9), and so Saturn's 'coloure is blacke, and leeddy' (Barth. Angl., VIII, xxiii). Henryson's Eurydice also has 'lyre . . . lyk unto the leid', when she is in Hades (*Orpheus*, 351). Cf. line 257.

156. The subject of **cheuerit** is apparently **teith**, though ellipsis of *he* is possible. Henryson is probably using loosely a stock phrase which normally takes a personal subject. Cf. 'my Gaist and I baith cheueris with the chin' (*Rauf Coilȝear*, 96, in *Scottish Alliterative Poems*, ed. F. J. Amours, STS I 27, 38 [Edinburgh, 1892–7]) and 'She neither chatterd with her teeth, / Nor shiverd with her chin' (*The Gay Goshawk* in Child, *English and Scottish Popular Ballads*, Vol. II [Boston, 1885–6], p. 367).

157. **how,** 'hollow', 'deeply'.

158. **meldrop**, 'mucus', from ON *mél-dropi*, the foam at a horse's mouth. Not elsewhere recorded before the nineteenth century: see

OED and *SND*. Saturn's nose runs because he is cold, and also because he is aged, as Kinaston points out: 'Juvenal, in describing old age, elegantly adds, among other characteristics, "noses running as in childhood" ' (*Sat*. X, 199; K, p. 516, G. G. Smith, I, cli).

at, in T (emended to *of* in K), is as likely to be right as **of** in CA.

160-1. Perhaps from the *Assembly of Gods*, 'A bawdryk of isykles about hys nek gay / He [Saturn] had' (285-6). Cf. Virgil's 'a rough beard stiff with ice' (*Aen*., IV, 251). Douglas imitates Henryson: 'gret ische schouchlis lang as ony speir' (*Aen*., VII, Prol. 62).

163. **Felterit**, 'tangled', 'matted'. Cf. 'Rycht syd and felterit hang his lyart haire' (*Clariodus*, ed. David Irving, Maitland Club [Edinburgh, 1830], I, 964).

ouirfret usually is used for embroidery or ornament, but Henryson's use is imitated by Douglas, 'With fros*tis* hair ourfret' (*Aen*., VII, Prol. 42, cf. also 162).

Henryson probably rhymed *hair* : *wair* : *bair*; since *boir* would be an unusual fifteenth-century MSc form (cf. 180 below). But *hoir* is used in rhyme in his *Ressoning betuix Aige and Yowth*, 11.

164. As Skeat and later editors (except Elliott) maintain, the correct reading is presumably **gyte**, 'cloak', 'gown', 'mantle', though Henryson may have used the earlier MSc form, *gyde*. T reads correctly *gyte* in 178 and 260 below, but here reads *gate*, probably a simple misprint (cf. his *fal* for *full* in this line). K copied *gate*, and then corrected this to *gite*. *gyte* would have been unfamiliar to Charteris: *DOST* records no use after the fifteenth century. But the word had some currency in England during the sixteenth century (see *OED*, *gite*[1]) and so is retained by T (in 178 and 260). The same confusion occurs with the Wife of Bath's 'gaye scarlet gytes' (III, 559), which turn into 'gyces' in one MS.

gytes are frequently *gay* (see *MED*, *gite*, n. [3]); Henryson probably uses the adj. for irony and to underline the contrast between Saturn and Jupiter (see 178 and note; for *gay* applied to Saturn see quotation in note to 160-1).

garmound here probably has the meaning 'suit (of clothes)'. See *DOST*, *garment*, 2, and cf. Henryson's *Garmont of Gud Ladeis*.

165. **out woir** (or *wair*, see note to 163) would seem to mean here 'carried out', 'caused to flutter out', though this meaning cannot be precisely paralleled. See *OED*, *wear*, v.[1] 22 and 23; *EDD*, *wear*, v.[2] 2; and also 467 below: 'away as wind it weiris'.

Saturn's tattered clothes are appropriate to his connection with abject poverty: see Panofsky, *Studies in Iconology*, p. 77.

166. Saturn's usual weapon is a sickle, but he is connected with archery in Caxton's *Recuyell of the Historyes of Troye*, where it is said that Saturn 'fyrste fonde the maner of shotyng and drawyng of the bowe' (ed. H. Oskar Sommer [London, 1894], I, 17: I owe this reference to Harth, 'Convention and Creation', p. 34). Hawes, perhaps following Caxton, also says that Saturn, 'as some poetes fayne . . .

founde shotynge / and drawenge of the bowe / Yet as of that / I am
nothynge certayne' (*The Pastime of Pleasure,* ed. W. E. Mead, EETS
OS 173 [London, 1928], 211–13; see p. 236 for the possible debt to
Caxton). The connection may have arisen because Saturn was thought
to have been a king of Crete, where archery was invented, according to
Isidore of Seville (*Etymologiae,* ed. W. M. Lindsay, 2 vols [Oxford,
1911], XVIII, viii; see also XIV, vi, 16).

Henryson's purpose in including 166–8 was presumably to show
Saturn as one who kills with cold, and to connect him with the earlier
hailstorm.

167. **flasche** would seem to be proved correct (see Apparatus) by the
1600 edition of Fairfax's *Tasso:* 'Her ratling quiuer at her shoulders
hong, / Therein a flash of arrowes feathered weele' (XI, st. 28). The
OED suggests that this passage, and the entries in Skinner's and
Phillips's dictionaries, are echoes of Henryson. The dictionary entries
are, indeed, copied from the glossary in Speght's 1602 edition: '*flash
of flames,* sheafe of Arrowes' (*sic*; in the text Speght reads *fasshe of
felone flains*). But Fairfax's use is probably independent, since the
English editions of the *Testament* before 1600 read *fasshe.* K reads *flash,*
perhaps emending, or perhaps following Speght's glossary. The
etymology of *flasche* is not clear, but it may be connected with *flask:*
see *DOST, flas; OED, flask*; and note in G. G. Smith.

168. 'aboue an hygh on his hede, / Cowchyd *with* hayle stonys, he
[Saturn] weryd a crowne of leede' (*Assembly of Gods,* 286–7).

169–82. Jupiter, the 'planet most benyng' (*Buke of the Ches,* in *Asloan
MS,* ed. Craigie, I, 81, line 6), 'attests concerning a sanguine makeup
and of ages designates youth toward its beginning and life and gladness,
truth and religion and patience and every fine precept; and of figures
a white man with ruddy face' (Robertus Anglicus, in *The Sphere of
Sacrobosco and Its Commentators,* ed. Lynn Thorndike [Chicago, 1949],
p. 210). He is the opposite of Saturn (172) in that his qualities are the
life-giving ones (171) of warmth and moisture.

171. **to** may be a mistake for *vnto.*

173. **burelie,** 'handsome' or 'strong'; not 'burly'. See line 417.
    browis and **brent** were often coupled: see *DOST, brent.* But it is
not always certain what the phrase is intended to mean: here 'smooth
brows' seems better (because of line 155) than 'arched eyebrows' or
'lofty brows'. See *MED, brant,* and *SND, brent.*

173–9. 'Iupiter is . . . In coloure syluery white / bright, and pleysynge
. . . he gyuethe whit[e] coloure and fayre, medlyd with rednesse.
And yeuyth fayre eyen and teethe / and fayre here, fayre berde and
rounde. . . . Vnder Iuppiter is conteyned honoure, rychesse, beast
clothynge' (Barth. Angl., VIII, xxiiii).

Stearns suggests (*Henryson,* pp. 79–80) that Henryson borrows the
details of Jupiter's appearance from the description of Idleness in

Chaucer's *Romaunt of the Rose*. But the resemblance probably shows only that Henryson is using conventional details.

174-5. Jupiter is not traditionally portrayed with a garland: Larry Benson points out that Henryson is here drawing upon 'the literary green man, the stock figure of the green-clad youth who so often appears in late medieval poetry' as a representative of youthfulness and vitality, and who is conventionally shown wearing a garland of flowers (*Art and Tradition in Sir Gawain and the Green Knight* [New Brunswick, N. J., 1965], pp. 63-5).

176. **as cristall wer his ene.** A traditional comparison. Cf. lines 337–8, and Whiting, *crystal* (3).

The agreement of T and A on *was* suggests that **wer** (C) may be an emendation. Cf. line 161.

177. The comparison of hair to gold wire is very common. A list of instances is collected in Lydgate, *Temple of Glas*, ed. J. Schick, EETS ES 60 (London, 1891), pp. 88–90, 136. See also 222 below.

178. The symbolism of green is ambiguous: see note to 220–1. But here it is opposed to Saturn's deadly grey and indicates vitality and life. Cf. 'The greyn [betakynnys] curage' (*Wallace*, IX, 116), and see *OED*, *green*, adj. 6. For the opposition between green and grey see Henryson's *Garmont of Gud Ladeis*, 39, and *DOST*, *gray*, a. 1c.

179. 'With golden hems or edgings gilded on every gore.' Cf. 'In purpour rob hemmit with gold ilk gair' (Gavin Douglas, *Palice of Honour*, in *Poetical Works*, ed. John Small, I [Edinburgh, 1874], p. 10, line 19).

180. The ellipsis of *he* in C and A is probably correct.

181. Jupiter 'was portrayed . . . sending thunderbolts to the lower regions from his right hand' (*Libellus de imaginibus deorum*, ff. 170[b]–171[a]). The thunderbolts were sometimes represented by a pointed shaft (as in Seznec, *Survival of the Pagan Gods*, p. 138).

182. The traditional enmity between Jupiter and Saturn goes back to the legend in which Jupiter vanquishes his father. Cf. Barth. Angl., 'Iupiter by his goodnes abatyth the malyce of Saturnus' (VIII, xxiiii; see further Stearns, *Henryson*, p. 78). But there is a strong hint in this line of the equation between Jupiter and Christ which was sometimes made, as in Dante's 'O highest Jove, who was on earth crucified for us' (*Purgatorio*, VI, 118–19). See Douglas's note to his *Aeneid*, I, v, 2 (also X, Prol. 156–7, with Coldwell's note), and Seznec, *Survival of the Pagan Gods*, pp. 99, 200.

183–94. Mars is a baleful planet: 'In colour he is bryght and shynynge and fyrye . . . he tokenethe wrathe / swyftenes / and wondes / and is redde and vntrue / and gylefulle' (Barth. Angl., VIII, xxv). See Chaucer's description of the temple of Mars, and Skeat's and Robinson's notes to it (*Knight's Tale*, I, 1967–2050). Poets frequently attach to him an *ire* : *fire* rhyme, since he rules over every occupation connected with either (e.g. Chaucer, *Anelida*, 50; Lydgate, *Troy Book*, IV, 2401).

185. **als feirs as ony fyre.** A common simile: see Whiting, *fire* (6).

186–8. Mars was traditionally heavily armed, and was portrayed 'like a man raging, sitting in a chariot, armed with a cuirass and other offensive and defensive arms, also wearing a helmet on his head, carrying a whip in his hand, and girded with a sword' (*Libellus de imaginibus deorum*, f. 171ª). See Seznec, *Survival of the Pagan Gods*, pp. 190–4; Stearns, *Henryson*, pp. 81–2.

187–8. **roustie.** G. G. Smith, followed by Wood, explains *roustie* as 'bronze', but there is no warrant for this (and iron is the metal of Mars). Hamer (*MLR*, **29** [1934], 344), followed by Elliott, suggests that it was 'the mediaeval custom not to wipe the sword clean of blood [but to leave it on] . . . until it rusted the blade, as a sign of its owner's prowess'. But it seems unnecessary to suppose this untidy custom: Henryson probably repeats *roustie* because of its ominous connotations, which may have arisen from the bloody colour of rust. William Nelson points out that Spenser's Rancor, Revenge, Danger, and Despair have rusty blades and knives ('Queen Elizabeth, Spenser's Mercilla, and a Rusty Sword', *Renaissance News*, **18** [1965], 113–17).

189. Cf. 'Her face scho wryit about for propir teyne' (*King Hart*, in Douglas, *Poetical Works*, I, 104, line 16).

190. There is little to choose between **sword** (CA) and *brande* (T).
   The orthographic confusion of C is shown by the parallel participles *Wrything* and *Schaikand*.

191. 'Mars . . . signifies . . . of human images a ruddy man with red hair and round face' (Robertus Anglicus, in *Sacrobosco*, p. 210).

192–3. **bullar,** 'bubble', is only Scots; the synonymous *blubber* (T) is not recorded in MSc (but see *DOST, blubbir*, v.). The simile is perhaps from Ovid (see Stearns, *Henryson*, pp. 82–3), or cf. Chaucer's 'As wilde bores gonne they to smyte, / That frothen whit as foom for ire wood' (*Knight's Tale*, I, 1658–9).

194. **tuilȝeour,** 'a brawler', 'a bully'. *tulsure* in T is meaningless; Speght unhelpfully glosses it (in his 1602 edition) as 'tilekil-like', which is in turn explained by Urry (in his 1721 edition) as 'Of a red tile-colour'. For Kinaston's correct emendation, see Introduction, p. 13. *Tuitlȝeour*, in G. G. Smith and Wood, is a misreporting of C.

195–6. Cf. *Fables*, 839–40: 'he hard ane busteous Bugill blaw, / Quhilk, as he thocht, maid all the warld to waig'. For **warld . . . to wag** see Whiting, *world* (1). **brag**, 'bray', 'trumpet-blast', is apparently used elsewhere only by Lindsay, who refers to Mars' 'bost & brag' (*Dreme*, 445), and by Douglas (see *DOST, brag*), who may also be imitating Henryson. But see *OED, brag*, v. 1.
   Mars is not usually shown with a horn; Stearns (*Henryson*, p. 83) suggests a connection between Mars and the traditional picture of March as a warrior blowing a horn. This is possible, but March is very rarely represented as a man with a horn in England, though

pictures of this sort are common enough in Italy (with the horn presumably representing the winds of March). See J. C. Webster, *The Labors of the Months in Antique and Mediaeval Art* (Evanston, Illinois, 1938), pp. 51, 58, 92.

197–203. The idea that the sun is the source of both light and life is a commonplace. Cf. Barth. Angl.: 'he is the wel of al light. . . . the son quikneth all thynge / and gyuethe all thynge lyfe, forme / and shape. . . . Also he hath vertu of nourysshinge . . . nothing bringeth forth fruit, nor groweth, but the son beme recheth therto. . . . Also he hath vertue of yeuynge lyfe . . .' (VIII, xxviii). See further Stearns, *Henryson*, pp. 84–5 and, for a discussion of whether the sun can be said to be the cause of generation, Michael Scot (?) in *Sacrobosco*, pp. 313–15.

197. Henryson is here playing on the phrase **lamp of licht,** which, like **lanterne,** was frequently used for 'paragon'. See *DOST, lamp,* 2c; *lantern(e,* 2b.

198–9. 'Tender nurse of man and beast, of both fruit and blossom'. For **flourisching,** see *MED, florishing* and *florishen.* Cf. Lydgate: 'And nexte Appollo, so cler, so schene & briȝt, / Þe daies eye & voider of þe nyȝt, / Cherischer of frut, of herbe, flour, & corne' (*Troy Book,* II, 5591–3).

200–1. 'And by his motion and his (astrological) influence causing life in every earthly thing in the world.'

202–3. The different readings of T and A may have been caused by the difficult syntax in C: 'all, by necessity, must go die (and turn) to naught'. (See *OED, die,* v.[1] 12.) Cresseid's death can be attributed to a lack of vital heat.

204. **chair,** 'chariot'.

205. **vnricht.** *vpricht* (CA) does not seem possible here, although Elliott argues for it. Cf. *Troilus,* V, 660–5: 'hym thoughte . . . that the sonne went his cours unright . . . And that his fader carte amys he [Phaeton] dryve.'

209–17. The first three of Henryson's four horses apparently have names derived ultimately from Ovid's 'volucres Pyrois et Eous et Aethon, / Solis equi, quartusque Phlegon' (*Met.* II, 153–4; for the early history of the horses of the sun see Paul Ehrenreich, *Die Sonne im Mythos* [Leipzig, 1915] and Hyginus, *Fabulae,* ed. H. I. Rose [Leiden, (1934)], pp. 127–8). But *Philologie* has long been a problem (see note to 216). Stearns, in 'Robert Henryson and the Fulgentian Horse', *MLN,* 54 (1939), 239–45 (partially repeated in *Henryson,* pp. 85–9, 134–5), points out that there is another set of names which derives from Fulgentius: Erythreus, Actaeon, Lampos, Philogeus. He argues that 'Henryson's exact source' is a ninth-century work once attributed to Bede, *De Mundi Coelestis Terrestrisque Constitutione* (*PL* 90, cols 881–910), where both the Fulgentian and Ovidian names are given, and that *Philologie* is derived from the Fulgentian *Philogeus* (*Philoges* in Pseudo-Bede).

But the situation is slightly more complicated than this. The four horses of the sun, whether under Ovidian or Fulgentian names, were often treated by medieval authors, who assigned to each horse a part of the day and often some physical characteristics. But the role and characteristics of each horse vary; the names occur in different forms in different authorities; and occasionally there is contamination between the Ovidian and the Fulgentian nomenclature (a series of lists is given in Stearns, *Henryson*, pp. 134–5). Henryson's list resembles that given in Pseudo-Bede, especially in that Pseudo-Bede lists Eous, Aethon, and Pyrois in that order, but there are, despite Stearns, no unique parallels, and some of the details of Henryson's list, such as the colours of his second and fourth horses, can be found only in other authorities. Henryson may be following an unknown source, or he may be working from memory, perhaps from memory of several different lists.

211. soyr, 'sorrel', 'reddish-brown'. *sorde,* in T, is meaningless: in many hands final *e* and *d* are easily confused. The horse of the early morning, whatever name was given to it, was usually described as red, because of the colour of the rising sun. Douglas imitates this line: 'Eous *the* steid, with ruby hamys red, . . . Of cullo*ur* soyr' (*Aen.*, XII, Prol. 25, 27).

212. Eoye must come from Ovid's *Eous*, though elsewhere Ovid's spelling seems to be retained. **orient** is presumably from a Latin source: e.g. 'Eous, id est, oriens' (Pseudo-Bede); 'sol oriens rubeat' (Boccaccio, *Genealogie Deorum Gentilium Libri,* ed. V. Romano, 2 vols [Bari, 1951], IV, iii).

213. Ethios. Generally spelled *Aethon* or *Ethon.* Aethon is not usually the second horse, but Pseudo-Bede places him second, probably because of the similarity to *Actaeon,* the second horse in Fulgentius; and some of the writers who elsewhere follow Fulgentius have substituted *Aethon* for *Actaeon.* (See Stearns, *Henryson*, pp. 134–5.)

214. The second horse is usually white, because the sun shines brightly in the morning. **sum deill ascendent,** 'somewhat rising up'. The earlier uses of *ascendent* recorded in English are all astronomical.

215. Peros. Ovid's *Pyrois* is not elsewhere spelled with an *e*.
   richt feruent. Either *richt* (CA) or *eke* (T) is possible, but *eke* is probably an attempt for elegant variation. *feruent,* 'fiery', 'ardent'. See 4 above and note. The third horse is often described as hot: Pseudo-Bede says that at that time the sun *fervet*; Boccaccio says that then *lux . . . videtur fervidior* (*Genealogie Deorum,* IV, iii).

216. Philologie. Although Skeat, followed by Dickins, emends to *Philegoney,* and G. G. Smith to *and callit Phlegonie,* it is probable that Henryson wrote a form which was ultimately derived from the Fulgentian *Philogeus,* not from the Ovidian *Phlegon* (see note to 209–17). But since *Philologie* is an awkward form, Elliott argues (in 'Two Notes on Henryson's *Testament of Cresseid*') that the correct reading is *and callit Philogey*. His main argument is that *Philology* was, thanks to Martianus Capella, a fairly common name, which a scribe could easily have substituted for the unfamiliar *Philogey*. But the reading of A, *and called Philogie*, supports his emendation. (The linguistic part of Elliott's argument is irrelevant: he does not realise that final open and close $\bar{e}$ had fallen together by the fifteenth century, and that Henryson habitually rhymes the resulting vowel with the suffix, from whatever source, corresponding to modern *-y*.)

It seems to me probable, however, that Henryson wrote *Philologie*, or a similar form with four syllables. It is difficult to explain how *and*, if original, could have disappeared: Elliott's suggestion, that it was omitted for metrical reasons, is unlikely, since *and callit Philologie* would still scan (*callit* is often monosyllabic). But it is easy to explain the insertion of *and* in A, a text full of 'corrections' and of words put in to pad out the metre. Similarly, *Philogie*, in A, is a predictable emendation. Speght, in the list of corrections in his 1598 edition, has 'Philologi, *read*, Phlegone', and Laing silently corrects to *Phlegonie*; an early editor would have been likely to have known the Fulgentian *Philogie* and so to have made that correction. A confusion in Henryson's mind between *Philogie* and *Philologie* seems entirely natural, when one considers the earlier confusion of these names. In Lydgate, for instance, 'Philology' is spelled *Phillogie*, *Philogye*, *Philloge*, etc. by five MSS and all the early prints in *Temple of Glas*, 130; *Philogie* by at least one MS in *Fall of Princes*, III, 66 (in Hammond, *English Verse*, 175); *Phylogenye* in *Epithalamium for Gloucester*, 179 (Hammond, 148); and is given other trisyllabic forms in *Siege of Thebes*, 833. A large number of MSS read incorrectly *philogie* in *Merchant's Tale*, IV, 1734 (see Manly and Rickert, *The Text of The Canterbury Tales* [Chicago, 1940], VI, 436). Henryson's contemporary, the author of the *Ovide moralisé en prose*, uses (for 'Phlegon') a composite form, *philegon* (p. 81).

For the black colour of Henryson's horse, cf. Boccaccio: 'Phegon [*sic*] goes from the colour of crocus to black [like the sunset] and is explained "loving the earth"' (*Genealogie Deorum*, IV, iii; *terram amans*, from the etymology of the Fulgentian *Philogeus*, shows further contamination between the two traditions).

218–38. Since Venus is, astrologically, benevolent, Henryson avoids any reference to the 'wel-willy planete' (*Troilus*, III, 1257), and instead describes a Venus who resembles Fortune. The not-uncommon identification of Fortune and Love is discussed in H. R. Patch, *The Goddess Fortuna in Mediaeval Literature* (Cambridge, Mass., 1927), pp. 90–8, as Stearns points out, and see also Edgar Wind, *Pagan Mysteries in the Renaissance* (London, 1958), p. 93, who shows that the connection between the two figures goes back to Pausanias.

220–1. **nyce**, 'extravagant', 'wanton' (*OED*, *nice*, 2). A Venus in two colours, to symbolise her two aspects, is at least as old as Apuleius (*Golden Ass*, X, 31). Here the green apparently stands for hope and joy, the black for despair and death. See lines 24, 138, 238, 401 and cf. Barclay:

8

> Mine habite blacke accordeth not with grene,
> Blacke betokeneth death as it is dayly sene,
> The grene is pleasour, freshe lust and iolite,
> These two in nature hath great diuersitie.
> (*Eclogues,* ed. B. White, EETS OS 175
> [London, 1928], Eclogue I, 107–10)

But it should be noted that the green is itself ambiguous, since green was commonly associated with frivolity and inconstancy. See *The Floure and the Leafe,* ed. Pearsall, pp. 36–7; and Harth, 'Convention and Creation', pp. 29–31, who points out that Lust, in *The Court of Love,* is 'in grene', with 'berd as blak as fethers of the crow' (1059–60). Green was sometimes associated with Venus: according to Lydgate her metal is 'coper, that wil ternyssh grene, / A chaungable colour, contrarye to sadnesse' (*Fall of Princes,* VII, 1239–40, quoted by Harth). See also *OED, Venus,* 7.

222. With, in A, is doubtless correct, though it may be an emendation. *Quhyte,* C, and *White,* T, may come from an unusual spelling of *With* (MSc spellings of *wytht* and *whith* are recorded). Kinaston, noticing the contradiction between white and gold, emended to *Bright.* The phrase *With hair as gold* occurs in *The Buik of Alexander,* ed. R. L. Graeme Ritchie, Vol. IV, STS II 25 (Edinburgh, 1929), p. 437, line 10995; see also Whiting, *gold* (8) and 177 above.

sched, 'parted'. In the *House of Fame* Venus appears with 'hir comb to kembe hyr hed' (136). The comb was a symbol of idleness and vanity, perhaps also of lechery. See D. W. Robertson, Jr., *A Preface to Chaucer* (Princeton, 1962), p. 198.

226. Prouocatiue, 'calling forth lust' (cf. Lindsay's imitation in his *Dreme,* 416). **blenkis amorous,** 'amorous glances'. Cf. line 503 and *Orpheus,* 81.

228–9. pungitiue, 'pricking', 'stinging' (first occurrence recorded in *OED*). These lines refer to the stock comparison between the serpent's tongue (thought to be his 'sting') and venomous speech. See *OED, serpent,* 1d, and Tilley, T407.

231. lauch and **weip** are probably absolute infinitives, which are sometimes used in MSc where we would expect a participle, as Mr K. Phillips has pointed out to me. See Mustanoja, *A Middle English Syntax,* I, 511. It has been suggested that they are preterites, but *lauch* cannot be a preterite form, and *weip,* as a strong preterite, would be very unusual in Henryson's time.

Stearns (*Henryson,* pp. 91–2) says that this line is derived from the *Book of the Duchess*: 'She [Fortune] ys fals; and ever laughynge / With oon eye, and that other wepynge' (633–4). But the image is not uncommon: Harth ('Convention and Creation', p. 15) remarks that Guido delle Colonne, who in connection with Criseyde attacks women's fickleness, says that women laugh with one eye and weep with the other, and that he is followed in this by other tellers of the Troilus story (e.g., Lydgate, *Troy Book,* III, 4290–2).

233.   O ladi Venus, modir of Cupide,
            That al þis wor[l]d hast in gouernau*n*ce . . .
                    (Lydgate, *Temple of Glas*, 321–2)

234–8. 'The dredful joye' of love is a commonplace, but Henryson
may have had in mind the description of love in the *Roman de la Rose*,
or its source in Alain de Lille (see Introduction, pp. 51–2 and fn.).
The rhetoric here resembles Chaucer's description of the effects of
'geery Venus': 'Now in the crope, now doun in the breres, / Now up,
now doun, as boket in a welle' (*Knight's Tale*, I, 1532–3).

238. Cf. 'ʒoutheid and his lustie levis grene' (*King Hart,* p. 85, line 6),
and also 24 and 221 above.

239–52. Mercury is, appropriately, a many-sided god, and Henryson
mentions most of his traditional attributes. He was 'god of fayre
spekynge and of wisdom' (Barth. Angl., VIII, xxvii), and figures in
poetry most often as 'souereyn & patrou*n* . . . Of rethorik and of
eloquence' (Lydgate, *Troy Book*, II, 2500–1). Line 243 refers to his
connection with music (as the inventor of musical instruments: see,
for instance, Isidore of Seville, *Etym.*, III, xxii, 8; III, xxi, 6), while
his function as god of thievery and lying is ironically alluded to in 252.
He is usually thought of as the god of merchants and of profit, but this
aspect is omitted here (unless it be hinted at by his obvious wealth),
and instead he is shown as a physician. The association between
Mercury and medicine is traditional, despite Stearns, and can probably
be traced back to Cicero's *De Natura Deorum*, where five Mercuries
are distinguished, of whom the fifth is said to have fled to Egypt after
killing Argus, and to have given laws and letters to the Egyptians, who
called him Theuth (III, xxii, 56). Lactantius repeats this, adding that
he was named Trismegistus (*PL* 6, col. 139), and Tertullian speaks of
'Mercury Trismegistus, master of all natural philosophers [*Physi-
corum*]' (*PL* 2, col. 567). This enumeration of different Mercuries is
intermittently and erratically perpetuated: so, for instance, Boccaccio:
'There were . . . many Mercuries, and although generally all are dis-
tinguished by the same ancient insignia, yet the same divine nature is
not attributed to all of them. For one is the god of medicine, another of
merchants, another, indeed, of thieves, and another of eloquence'
(*Genealogie Deorum*, XII, lxii; see also III, xx). But more usually these
gods were coalesced, so that the power over astrological medicine con-
nected with Hermes Trismegistus was attached to Mercury. Tris-
megistus was also one of the first 'Enditours, / Of old Cronique and ek
auctours' (Gower, *Confessio Amantis*, IV, 2411–2), which agrees with
lines 242–5. For his reputation in the Middle Ages, see F. A. Yates,
Giordano Bruno and the Hermetic Tradition (London, 1964).

242. **to report all reddie,** probably 'fully prepared to make a report'.
Mercury was sometimes represented as a scribe: see Seznec, *Survival
of the Pagan Gods*, pp. 159–60. Cf. *Fables*, 1356–8.

243. **Setting,** 'composing'. See *A Dictionary of Middle English
Musical Terms,* ed. G. B. Gerhard (Bloomington, Indiana, 1961),
s.v. *setten*.

244–5. heklit hoods are mentioned some five times in MSc: see *DOST, hek(k)illit.* But it is not certain precisely what sort of hoods they are, though the usual definition of *heklit,* 'having a border or fringe like a cock's hackle', is probably correct. Henryson describes the venerable poet Aesop as also wearing a red 'heklit' hood:

> His hude off Scarlet, bordourit weill with silk,
> On hekillit wyis, untill his girdill doun;
> His Bonat round, and off the auld fassoun . . .
> (*Fables,* 1351–3)

Editors since Kinaston (who adds the marginal gloss 'hecled *þat* is wrapped or folded') have adduced, to support 245, pictures of early poets in hoods, but this would seem to be irrelevant, since hoods in general were common enough: Henryson implies that poets wore hoods of a particular fashion. But I can find no clear evidence that poets were iconographically associated with any special style of hood. And it is suggestive that Douglas, when he borrowed 245, changed the headdress: 'And on his hed of lawrer tre a crown, / Lyke to sum poet of *the* ald fasson' (*Aen.,* XIII, Prol. 87–8).

Aesop's hood is 'untill his girdill doun', but Mercury's is 'atouir his croun', which suggests that Henryson was referring to one of the various methods of wearing a hood as a turban or hat with a fringe. See Joan Evans, *Dress in Mediaeval France* (Oxford, 1952), Plate 4 and *passim.* There is a good picture of Dante wearing this sort of headdress in Egerton MS 943 (reproduced in F. Saxl and H. Meier, *Catalogue of Astrological and Mythological Illuminated Manuscripts of the Latin Middle Ages,* Vol. III, 1 and 2: *Manuscripts in English Libraries,* ed. H. Bober [London, 1953], Part 2, Tafel XII, Abb. 30). Mercury's winged cap sometimes appears in medieval illustrations, through a misunderstanding, as such a crested or fringed headdress (see Seznec, *Survival of the Pagan Gods,* pp. 180–1; Saxl and Meier, Part 2, Tafel LXXXV, Abb. 218: the rooster-like appearance of Mercury in some of these pictures may also derive partly from the fact that a cock is one of his traditional attributes [see Tervarent, *Attributs et symboles,* col. 113]). It is tempting to suppose that Henryson is making a reference, perhaps a humorous one, to such an iconographic tradition.

246–51. These details are partly traditional. Skeat compares Chaucer's description of a physician, where the rhyme *apothecaries* : *letuaries* also appears, while Chaucer's 'In sangwyn and in pers he clad was al' corresponds to 'cled in ane skarlot goun' (*Gen. Prol.,* I, 425–6, 439). Elliott compares 'the "furrede hodes" and "cloke of Calabre" of Phisik in *Piers Plowman* (B Text . . . vi. 271–2)'. But the details are also historically accurate, even to the furs that were given to successful doctors. See John D. Comrie, *History of Scottish Medicine,* 2nd ed. (London, 1932), Vol. I, Ch. iv.

253–63. The moon is a cold and moist planet; the 'last of all', because closest to the earth; and 'swiftest in hir spheir', because she revolves about the earth the most rapidly. She is commonly thought of as being in herself neither benevolent nor malevolent, but taking on her quality by conjunction. 'Astronomers tell / that amonge all planetes the moone in rulynge hath moste power ouer disposition of mans bodye. For as Ptholomeus sayth . . . Vnder the moone is conteyned syken[e]sse / losse, fere and drede / and dommage. Therfore aboute the chaungynge of mans bodye, the vertue of the moone werketh principallye: and that fallethe through the sw[i]ftenesse of his meuynge . . . And Galene . . . sayth . . . that by coniunctyon of the bodye of the moone with sterres fortunat, cometh dredfull syknes to good ende, and with contrary planettes falleth the contrarye, that is to euyll ende' (Barth. Angl., VIII, xxix). Her partnership with Saturn is therefore generally ominous, and, in particular, Parr shows that Saturn and the moon were sometimes thought of as jointly causing leprosy ('Cresseid's Leprosy Again'). Kinaston had earlier pointed out, in a note which has been overlooked, that Paracelsus connected leprosy with Saturn and the moon (p. 525; G. G. Smith, I, clix). The passage to which Kinaston refers (in the *Archidoxis Magica*, now thought to be spurious) can be found in Paracelsus, *Sämtliche Werke*, I. Abteilung, Vol. 14, ed. Karl Sudhoff (Munich, 1933), p. 453.

Since Cresseid is both changeable herself and about to be changed by the gods, the moon is especially appropriate to her, being the 'most vnstable' of planets, with the 'mooste vncertayne and vnstedfast meuynge' (Barth. Angl., VIII, xxix, xxx). Cf. Lydgate:

> Now ful of liȝt, now hornyd pale is sche,
> Lady of chaunge and mutabilite,
> Þat selde in on halt hir any tyme;
> And so fare þei þat ben born in hir clyme,
> Þat ay delite in þingis þat ben newe,
> Whos hert is clad in many sondry hewe,
> So þei be diuers in her affecciouns.
>
> (*Troy Book*, II, 5613–19)

See also *Troy Book*, III, 4335–8, where Criseyde's iniquities prompt an attack on women in which their changeableness is compared to the moon's. Chaucer himself introduces the irony of having Criseyde say to Troilus, 'Now, for the love of Cinthia the sheene, / Mistrust me nought' (IV, 1608–9).

Henryson's description of the moon is echoed by Douglas (*Aen.*, III, Prol. 1–2) as well as by Lindsay (*Dreme*, 386–90).

255. The moon was frequently represented pictorially as a woman with a crescent moon attached to her head, so that she appeared to have horns (see F. Saxl, *Lectures* [London, 1957], I, 238–9 and II, Plate 161; also Saxl and Meier, Part 2, Tafel LXXIV, Abb. 187, 188). But since *busk*, 'to array, dress', often refers specifically to the dressing of a woman's hair or head (see *DOST, busker, busking*), Henryson is also thinking of a woman with a 'horned' headdress, a fashionable style in which a woman's hair (or false hair, or other material) was built up into two horns, and a kerchief or veil put over them. See *Accounts of the Lord High Treasurer of Scotland*, Vol. I (for 1473–1498), clxxxii–clxxxiii. Henryson may intend to be uncomplimentary, since this headdress was widely criticised. Bower says that 'to raise up horned veils is a sign of a bad and dangerous woman' (in Fordun, *Scotichronicon*, II, 373). See

further the note to 77 above; *Des Cornetes,* in *Satirical Songs and Poems on Costume,* ed. F. W. Fairholt, Percy Society (London, 1849), pp. 29–39; Lydgate, *Horns Away,* in Hammond, *English Verse,* pp. 110–3; and *Historical Poems of the XIVth and XVth Centuries,* ed. R. H. Robbins (New York, 1959), pp. 139, 323–4.

256. Either **appeir** (C) or *tapere* (T), 'to appear', is equally possible.

257. **Haw as the leid.** Cf. 155 and 340. The simile is proverbial (see Whiting, *lead,* [4]), as is the moon's lead colour: e.g. Hawes, 'dyane derlynynge / pale as ony lede' (*Pastime of Pleasure,* 1958).

    nathing cleir. Cf. Lydgate, 'derk Diane, ihorned, noþing clere' (*Temple of Glas,* 8).

258–9. The fact that the moon 'hath no light of her selfe, but boroweth & taketh of the plente of the sonne' (Barth. Angl., VIII, xxix) was repeated very frequently, since it was a fact useful for both allegory and astronomy, and also one which had not always been certain (see Augustine, *PL* 36, col. 132). Isidore of Seville, who discusses the question at length (*De natura rerum,* XVIII, XXI), quotes Lucan, 'Phoebe, when she was reflecting [*redderet,* lit. 'giving back'] her brother . . .' (I, 538), a possible source for 258.

    Since the moon has no light of its own, it 'conteyneth in it selfe a maner darkenesse and dimnesse / and that cometh of qualyte of his owne body, that is kyndly derke' (Barth. Angl., VIII, xxix). Henryson emphasises repeatedly (255, 257, 260) the moon's darkness and spots in order to make it, like Saturn, resemble the leprous Cresseid (see note to 155–9).

261–3. A reference to the common legend that the man in the moon is a thief carrying a stolen bundle of thorns. For the origins of the legend, see Oliver F. Emerson, 'Legends of Cain, Especially in Old and Middle English', *PMLA,* **21** (1906), 831–929; for bibliography, see Stith Thompson, *Motif-Index of Folk-Literature,* rev. ed. (Bloomington, Indiana, 1955–8), A. 751; and Edmund Reiss, 'Chaucer's Friar and the Man in the Moon', *JEGP,* **62** (1963), 481–5. The man in the moon is also called a 'churl' by Chaucer (*Troilus,* I, 1024) and in the ME 'Man in the Moon' poem (most recently printed in *The Harley Lyrics: The Middle English Lyrics of MS. Harley* 2253, ed. G. L. Brook, 2nd ed. [Manchester, 1956]).

262. Although Shakespeare represents 'the person of Moonshine' as carrying 'a bush of thorns' (*Midsummer-Night's Dream,* III, i), Henryson probably wrote not *busshe* (T), but **bunche** (C; spelled *bunsh* in A), using the word in its specificially Scottish sense of 'bundle'. Cf. line 439.

263. **na nar,** 'no nearer'. The moon's sphere marks the limit of the corruptible world.

266. Elsewhere in MSc, **foirspeikar** means 'One who speaks for another; an advocate' (*DOST, forspekare*). It may mean this here—

Mercury as the spokesman of the gods—but it would more naturally mean 'chairman', 'speaker'. *Prolocutor,* which *foirspekar* translates, was used in both senses (see *OED, prolocutor*).

Mercury is suitable for his position not only because of his skill in rhetoric, but also because of his nature: he is called *flexibilis* and *convertibilis,* and 'he torneth hym selfe soone to the planete / that he is ioyned with' (Boccaccio, *Genealogie Deorum,* II, vii; Barth. Angl., VIII, xxvii). Cf. also Isidore of Seville, who explains his name as coming from *medius currens,* 'because speech runs intervening between men' (*Etym.,* VIII, xi, 45).

267. liken is probably not a past part., as *DOST* suggests, but a phonetic spelling of *likand* (note the form *lykyng* in T). See note to 464 below, and Quintin Kennedy, *Two Eucharistic Tracts,* ed. C. H. Kuipers (Nijmegen, [1964]), p. 77. But *listned,* in A, is attractive: the corruption in C and T could be explained by the fact that *listin* appears in MSc only in early verse (see *DOST, listin*).

269–70. 'He might learn the practice of rhetoric, (how to) put a weighty opinion (*or* significant meaning) in a few words.'

273. intentioun is here equivalent to Latin *intentio,* 'charge', 'accusation'. See *OED, intention,* 13; *DOST, intent,* v.

278. Both C and T are metrically difficult here: it is possible, in view of *Fables,* 2853, that the original reading was *ʒone ʒonder wretche.*

283. See variants, and note to line 135. The agreement of T and A gives their reading strong support, but it is very difficult to see how their reading could have been corrupted into the version in C. I have ventured to suppose that Henryson wrote 'Ane blind goddes hir cald, and micht not se'. Cupid, slightly incoherent through rage, repeats in 282–3 Cresseid's words in 134–5, and adds that Cresseid herself is the one who cannot see. C's reading comes from a misunderstanding of the subject of *se*; in T and A the syntax of the first half of the line is simplified. But if this solution is correct, 284 is difficult: it is tempting to suppose that 284 and 285 are reversed.

285. vnclene. Cf. Lev. 13:8 '[the leper] shall be condemned of uncleanness'.

286. Either *returne* (C) or *retorte* (T) is possible; I have preferred *retorte* as being, in the sixteenth century, the harder reading (it is first recorded in the *OED* in 1557, but the word is not common until *c.* 1600). Again, either *on* (C) or **in** (T) is possible, but *in* is harder and follows the Latin idiom. Cupid is here using 'aureate terms'; cf. 288–9. **retorte in,** 'throw back on'; perhaps here both in the sense 'blame on' and 'throw back the charge against'.

287. quhome refers to Cresseid. Stearns (*Henryson,* p. 71) misinterprets it as referring to Venus and so draws a false parallel between the *Testament* and the *Assembly of Gods*.

288–9. **deificait** is first recorded *c.* 1475 (*MED*); **Participant** ('partaking') is first recorded in 1527 (*OED*).

290. As editors since Skeat have pointed out, the Scots form **iniure** (recorded only once in ME, in *Troilus*) is preserved in T and A; the English form *iniurie* (adopted into Scots in the later sixteenth century) is erroneously used in C.

291. 'I think we should make a return (for this injury) with a painful punishment.' Cf. *Fables*, 774.

293. **say**, 'speak'. See *OED, say,* v.¹ 3c, and cf. *Orpheus,* 127.

299. **modifie**, 'assess', 'determine'. A Scots legal term; see *OED, modify,* 5. **pane** is also used in the technical sense of 'punishment' (=*poena*).

302. **proceidit**, 'acted judiciously', is another legal term. See *OED, proceed,* 2d, and cf. Lydgate: 'Ye to be Iuge, and lyk as ye proceede / We shall obeye to youre ordynaunce' (*Minor Poems,* I, p. 198, lines 167–8).

311. **ane frostie wand.** Probably both a magic rod, depriving Cresseid of her vital warmth, and the white staff borne by the officer of a court of justice. Cf. *Fables,* 1269, 'the Crownar haif laid on him his wand', and, for magic wands, Kinaston's note (p. 494; G. G. Smith, I, cxxviii).

312. **lawfullie,** 'according to correct legal procedure'. Neither Skeat's explanation, 'in a low tone', nor Kinaston's emendation (by erasing the *l* he had written) to *awfully* has anything to recommend it.

314–40. For the symptoms of leprosy mentioned in Saturn's and Cynthia's speeches, see Introduction, pp. 25–6. In 314 Henryson is probably referring to the loss of hair which was often mentioned as a symptom of leprosy (e.g., Lanfranc, *Science of Cirurgie,* ed. R. von Fleischhacker, EETS OS 102 [London, 1894], p. 197; Aretaeus, tr. Moffat, p. 281), though the phrase would also fit the change in colour of hair which is sometimes cited as a symptom (Psuedo-Aristotle, *Problems,* X, 34; see also Lev. 13:3–37). In the phrase *wantoun blude,* Henryson is probably using *blude* in the sense of 'passion', 'temperament' (see *MED, blōd,* 7), but he may also be referring to the corruption, clotting, and granulation of the blood which is often given as a symptom of leprosy (see John of Gaddesden, *Rosa Anglica,* f. 57ª; Lanfranc, p. 196; Simpson, 'Leprosy . . . in Scotland', pp. 65–6).

316. **melancholy.** Accented on the second syllable. Henryson uses the term here as the opposite of *mirth,* but also with reference to its more technical meaning, the excess of black bile which is the cause of

leprosy (see Introduction, pp. 32–3), as well as of sadness (*is the mother of all pensiuenes*, 317). See Lindsay's imitation of these lines:

> I se thy spreit withoute mesoure
> So sore perturbit be malancolye,
> Causyng thy corps to vaxin cauld and drye.
> (*Dreme*, 157–9)

319. wantones here includes the meanings of both 'lasciviousness' (*play*) and 'arrogance' (*insolence*). Cf. line 549.

320. riches is 'richesse' (the spelling in T), not modern *riches*.

324. 'In dome and iugement he [Saturn] tokeneth sorowe / woo / and eleyngnesse' (Barth. Angl., VIII, xxiii).

325. T preserves the older idiom, 'to have mercy *of* someone', and may be correct.

326. amorous, 'loving', 'affectionate'; not necessarily in its modern sense. Cf. line 503 and *Fables*, 2848.

328. C reads *schawis thow*, which does not appear to make sense (although *schawis the* would be possible: see *OED*, *show*, 26c). **through,** the reading of T, is probably correct, with **schawis** in the sense 'is plain' (*OED*, *show*, 28d).

329. geuin is here monosyllabic, with loss of intervocalic *v*. Thynne presumably did not understand this, and so omitted **fair** to balance the metre.

332. bill is usually used, in legal contexts, for the formal charge of a plaintiff, but Chaucer uses *wrot the bille* for 'passed sentence' (*ABC*, 59). Or *bill* may be used here in its general sense of 'formal document'. Murison aptly compares this scene with Scott's *Heart of Midlothian*, Ch. 24.

333. sentence diffinityue, 'final sentence'. A common ME and MSc legal phrase.

334. heit (C) is clearly better than *heale* (T): the moon, being cold and moist, deprives Cresseid of warmth (though not of moisture—cf. 318). The inclusion of **here** in both T and A gives it strong support; the word-order in T is the hardest and the most likely to have been corrupted.

337. Criseyde's eyes are often called *clere* or *brighte* in *Troilus*, and are praised specifically in I, 304–5; III, 1352–5; V, 815–7. But Henryson also has in mind the *memento mori* tradition. Cf. his *Thre Deid Pollis*, 22–4:

> Thy crampand hair, & e[i]k thy cristall ene;
> full cairfully conclud sall dulefull deid;
> Thy example heir be us it may be sene.

The form *menged* in T suggests that Henryson wrote **mingit.**
mingle is rare before the sixteenth century.

338. voice sa cleir. Chaucer's Troilus remarks that he heard Criseyde
'with vois melodious, / Syngen so wel, so goodly, and so clere' (V,
577–8). It is stated in an ME sermon that 'be a ma*n* neu*er* so gret a
chau*n*ter, haue he neu*er* so cler voys, ʒit, & tis disese [leprosy] cu*m*
vp-on hym, it wil make hym a-non-rith for to lese it' (Grisdale, *Three
Middle English Sermons*, pp. 29–30, lines 258–60).

vnplesand, in C, is probably the original form. This is the first
instance under *unpleasing* in the *OED*, and the first instance under
unpleasant is 1535. Cf. the variants for line 423.

hoir CA; *heer* T; in K *heere* is crossed out and *hoarse* interlineated.
The same variants occur in line 445 (omitted in K). *OED* and *DOST*
suggest that *hoir*, 'hoary', is used here in an unusual sense. But it seems
better to assume the existence of a word *h—r* (with uncertain vowel),
meaning 'rough' or 'hoarse'. Cf. 'Houbeit ʒe think my harrand ["grating
utterance"] something har' (A. Montgomerie, *Poems*, ed. J. Cranstoun,
STS I 9–11 [Edinburgh, 1887], p. 131, line 61). See also *SND, haar,* 'a
burr or impediment in speech', and *OED, harr,* 'to snarl'.

339–40. The moon herself is *full of spottis blak* (260) and *haw* ('lead-
coloured', 257). A lead-coloured face is a symptom of leprosy: 'In
theym that haue the lepra . . . the face is leedisshe' (Barth. Angl., VII,
lxv); 'þe face [of lepers] . . . is su*m*what ledi' (Lanfranc, *Science of
Cirurgie*, p. 197).

342. This, 'thus'.

343. cop and clapper. The traditional accoutrements of a leper. The
cup was for receiving alms and the clapper for giving warning of a
leper's approach: cf. the biblical injunction that a leper 'shall cry out
that he is defiled and unclean' (Lev. 13:45). The clapper could be either
a separate rattle or the lid of a clap-dish. Henryson probably thought
of it as a separate rattle: see line 579 and note below; the Scots records
cited in Simpson, 'Leprosy . . . in Scotland', pp. 151–3; and the
picture in J. D. Comrie, *History of Scottish Medicine*, I, 195. But later
authors took it to be the lid of a clap-dish: cf. 'Wher me was giuen a
clappinge dishe / My wretched cromms to crave' in *The Laste Epistle
of Creseyd to Troyalus*, 263–4; and 'When Cresid clapt the dish, and
Lazer-like did goe' (George Turberville, *Tragical Tales, and Other
Poems* [reprinted from 1587 edition] [Edinburgh, 1837], p. 334).

348. hir schaddow culd luik, 'beheld her reflection'. Cf. *Fables,*
1664, 2392.

This scene is ironically reminiscent of the words which Chaucer's
Pandarus speaks to Criseyde, when he is trying to persuade her to
accept Troilus as a lover:

> 'The kynges fool is wont to crien loude,
> Whan that hym thinketh a womman berth hire hye,
> "So longe mote ye lyve, and alle proude,

Til crowes feet be growen under youre yë,
And sende yow than a myrour in to prye,
In which that ye may se youre face a morwe!" '
(II, 400–5)

Criseyde's mutability is used as a *carpe diem* argument by Pandarus, and as a proof of the vanity of sensual love by Henryson.

349. The variant *visage*, in T, is hard to account for: it is possible that **sa** was an early scribal addition, and that *visage* was then altered to **face** to preserve the metre. The same pair of variants occurs in Lydgate's *Fall of Princes*, II, 2737.

350. **wa** is here an adj., 'miserable'. *I ne wyte*, in T, may come from a spelling such as *inewcht* for *aneuch* (see *DOST*, *ineuch*).

353, 357. In both lines, C takes Cresseid to be referring to 'gods'; A understands 'goddess'; and the spelling in T is ambiguous (see note to 135 above). Although T and A agree on *to* in 357, in place of *for to* in C, this is probably coincident error. T elsewhere replaces *for to* with *to* (lines 219 and 352); A is probably here, as often, emending for metre— to accommodate the necessarily disyllabic *goddesse*.

358. **Be**, 'when'.

362–4. Cresseid has been **on grouf** ('prone', 'grovelling') because of her swoon; not, as Calchas thinks, in humble supplication. The dramatic irony is carried on more obviously in the next two lines.
    beedes (T), 'prayers'. *prayers*, in C, is a post-Reformation substitution. A similar Protestant expurgation of *bedis* is made in the 1553 print of Douglas's *Aeneid*: see Coldwell's edition, I, p. 102.

372–7. It has been suggested by Stearns (*Henryson*, p. 46), followed by Elliott, that there is a reference here to the fact that the duty of inspecting and reporting lepers sometimes fell upon the parish priest. It is true that for Scotland, as elsewhere, this was the duty of the ecclesiastical authorities: see Simpson, 'Leprosy . . . in Scotland', pp. 94–5. (This custom probably goes back to the biblical injunction that lepers shall be brought to the priest for diagnosis: Lev. 13:2, etc.) But it is not at all certain that Henryson is referring here to this custom.

373. **quhite as lillie flour.** Proverbial: see Whiting, *lily*; Tilley, L296; and *Orpheus*, 351.

374. The ellipsis of *he* in T is both harder and more characteristic of Henryson, while the different positions of *he* in C and A suggest it to be an addition.

376–7. Leprosy was generally thought to be incurable, except by divine intervention. Bernard de Gordon, for instance, claims only that physicians can impede the progress of the disease, and so prolong the life of a patient (*Lilium Medicinae*, p. 91). There is biblical authority

for this: e.g. 4 Kg. 5:7 ' "Am I God . . . to heal a man of his leprosy?" '
Cf. lines 307, 411.

382. The correct reading is uncertain, but the agreement of C and A
supports **To**. **hospitall** was normally accented on the first syllable, but
it is possible, as Skeat suggests, that it is accented here on the second
syllable. Skeat's evidence for this accentuation is not good, since the
aphetic forms of *hospital* go back to Italian or Levantine forms (see
OED, *spittle*, sb.¹), but cf. *Hospitelers* in *Romaunt of the Rose*, 6693.
It is possible, however, that the original reading was *Wnto ʒone spitall*,
and that *hospitall* was substituted as a more 'correct' form (cf. 391,
where A reads *Hospital*).

at the tounis end. Joseph Robertson, in his appendix to Simpson,
'Leprosy . . . in Scotland', points out that the lepers at Stirling were
described frequently as living *ad finem burgi*, and compares this line
(p. 164). In *Amis and Amiloun* a hut is built for the leper Amiloun at
'ʒe tounes ende' (line 1720). See also Introduction, p. 39, fn. 2.

383. When Amiloun becomes a leper, he says, 'Of no more ichil ʒe
praye, / Bot of a meles mete ich day, / For seynt charite' (lines 1606–8).

386. Cresseid's beaver hat has bothered commentators: J. A. W.
Bennett is probably right in his suggestion (quoted in Elliott) that
the hat is in fact worn by Calchas (lines 386–7 must then be taken as
modifying *He* in 388). Bennett further suggests that Henryson is
underlining Calchas's wish 'to leave unrecognized, with face obscured'.
Beaver hats were expensive and eminently respectable: cf. Chaucer's
Merchant (*Gen. Prol.*, I, 272). James IV paid ten shillings (about ten
days' wages for a common labourer) for one in 1489 (*Accounts of the
Lord High Treasurer of Scotland*, I, 146).

390. The agreement of T and A gives *There to* strong support, but in
view of *thair at* (388) and *thairby* (390), it may be a scribal repetition.
thairby is apparently used for 'from there', a meaning not recorded
in the *OED*.

397–8. 'Yet they assumed, because of her extreme distress and her
quiet [*or* constant] mourning, that she . . .'. **still** is ambiguous, but
'quiet' would seem to be the more aristocratic sort of mourning, and
also to fit the sense better in *Fables*, 1698: 'birdis blyith changit thair
noitis sweit / In ["into"] styll murning, neir slane with snaw and sleit.'

401. **ouerheled** (T) must be preferred to *ouirquhelmit* (CA) as the
harder reading. *Overhele*, 'to cover over', is not recorded in the *OED*
after 1513. Henryson uses it in *Fables*, 587.

407. Cresseid compares herself to a **sop**, a piece of bread soaked in
wine or another liquid, sometimes used to mean something of slight
value. But she is soaked in sorrow, not wine, and submerged in care.
For a similar use of *sop* as 'embodiment', cf. Rolland, *Court of Venus*,
II, 104, 'the sop of science . . . the flour of fairheid'. See also line 450
and note below.

408. C and A read *for now*: the omission of *for* in T may be incorrect (see note to 357 above). But the fact that Puttenham, who quotes 407–8 as an example of 'Ecphonisis. or the Outcry', assigning the lines to Chaucer, must be following a text which read only *now*, but nevertheless introduces an unauthorised *for*, suggests that *for* in C is also a scribal addition (*The Arte of English Poesie*, ed. G. D. Willcock and A. Walker [Cambridge, 1936], p. 212).

409. An echo of lines 384–5.

410. Either **blaiknit** (CA) or *blake &* (T) is possible. (1) *blaiknit* ('made pale') has the support of *Awntyrs off Arthure*, 203 (Thornton MS, in *Scottish Alliterative Poems*, ed. Amours), 'thi burlyche body es blakenede so bare'; and Dunbar, *Flyting*, 165, 'Thy cheik bane bair, and blaiknit is thy ble'. Cf. also *Fables*, 973. (2) *blake &* has the support of Chaucer's *Anelida*, 213, 'Myn herte, bare of blis and blak of hewe' (the usual interpretation of *blak* here as 'black' may be right, but see *MED*, *blak*, adj. 6, and for the confusion between OE *blāc* and *blæc*, and their reflexes, see *OED*, *black*). This line was probably in Henryson's mind, since he was following *Anelida*, but he need not have preserved Chaucer's syntax.

I have preferred the harder syntax and better authority of *blaiknit*. In either case, the imagery is connected with Cresseid's complexion, and perhaps also with *Troilus*, V, 1541–7, 'Fortune . . . Gan pulle awey the fetheres brighte of Troie / Fro day to day, til they ben bare of joie'. But *bare of blisse/joie* is not uncommon: see *MED*, *bār*, 10.

411. The diction carries with it an ironic reference to the conventional pains of love: e.g. *Troilus*, IV, 944, 'If to this sore ther may be fonden salve . . .'; *Anelida*, 242, '. . . my sores for to sounde'. The spelling *saif* (C) can stand either for *salve* or *save* (for *save* in the sense 'heal' see *OED*, *save*, v. 7). In favour of *save* is the fact that the verbs *salve* and *save* were sometimes coupled: see *OED*, *salve*, v.¹ 2b, quotations 1377 and *c.* 1470. But it is likely that a contemporary reader would have understood *saif* here as *salve*, because *salve*, unlike *save*, was often used in conjunction with *sore* (see *OED*, *salve*, v.¹ 1, 2). There was probably a widespread confusion between *save* and *salve*; see Lydgate's *Testament*, 443, where the MSS are almost equally divided between the two words (*Minor Poems*, I, 346).

Although **or sound** has only the very weak authority of A, it is probably correct: C and T show different attempts to avoid an unfamiliar word. The verb *sound*, 'heal', is not recorded after *c.* 1430 in the *OED*, but is used in *Anelida*, Henryson's model (quoted above). See also *Romaunt of the Rose*, 966, 'his soris sounde'; and Lydgate, *Troy Book*, IV, 2704–5, 'þer may no salue / Her sores sounde'.

413. **on breird**, 'sprouting'. See *Fables*, 10, 1796, 1904.

414–15. Both rhymes are true. Henryson probably wrote *ware* or *wair*, the spellings of T and A (cf. ON *váru*, pret. ind.; the MSc rhyme-form is perhaps restressed, or used as a conventional rhyme). **heird** = *heir it*; enclitic *it* is often reduced to *'d* in MSc. See *DOST*, *'d*.

416–33. The *ubi sunt* theme and the list of luxuries are both conventional. G. G. Smith compares the elaborate description of a fine lady's life given by the bawd in *Philotus*, 73–248. For lines 416–17, cf. the ME *Body and Soul*: 'Where ben . . . Thi chau*m*bres and þin hei3e halle, / Þat peynted weore*n* wi*th* feire floures' (ed. Linow, Vernon MS, lines 41–3), and, in a well-known sermon attributed to Augustine, 'ubi thalamus pictus, ubi lectus eburneus, ubi thorus regalis' (*Sermones ad fratres in eremo*, Serm. 48, *PL* 40, col. 1331: quoted by E. Gilson in *Les Idées et les lettres* [Paris, 1932], p. 16, and dated by him in the thirteenth century).

These stanzas are meant to suggest the immorality of Cresseid's earlier life. A good gloss on them is the passage in the *Parliament of Fowls* where Venus is shown with her porter Richesse and her two aids, Bacchus and Ceres (260–76).

417. 'With excellent bed and handsomely embroidered tapestry furniture-coverings.' **burely,** 'handsome, strong', was probably applied to beds, maidens, etc., because of a false connection with *bour,* 'bower'. See line 438. Cf. 'Where ben . . . Þi somers mid þi bourliche beddes, . . . Þi quyltes and þi couertoures' (*Body and Soul,* 25–6, 45).

418–21. Parr ('Cresseid's Leprosy Again', p. 491), followed by Elliott, suggests that Cresseid is lamenting that she will have to go on an invalid diet (medical writers advised that lepers should avoid food which produces melancholy). But this seems far-fetched, in view of the usual lepers' fare. See line 441 and note. In any case, luxurious food was a traditional item in *ubi sunt* lists. Cf. 'Where be nou alle þyne cokes snelle, / Þat scholde go greiþe þyne mete / Mid riche spiceries' (*Body and Soul,* 49–51) and 'Quhare is the meit and drynke delicious, / With quhilk we fed our cairfull cariounis' (Lindsay, *Dreme,* 295–6).

collatioun: a rere-supper or refreshment late at night. Such meals had a bad reputation: Robert of Brunne speaks of 'Rerë sopers yn pryuyte . . . [where] leccherye ys quene or kyng' (*Handlyng Synne,* ed. F. J. Furnivall, EETS OS 119, 123 [London, 1901–3], 7259, 7265); Lydgate says that Sardanapalus, 'a prynce off baudrie, / Fond rere soperis and fether beddis soffte' (*Fall of Princes,* II, 2259–60). Cf. Dunbar, *Of the Ladyis Solistaris at Court,* 14. Chaucer's Criseyde shares spices and wine with Diomede (V, 852).

420. sweit meitis. The first use of the term recorded after OE. They are probably dainties for the *collatioun* and not, as G. G. Smith suggests, pleasant meats. There is a recipe for sweet fried cakes with a saffron sauce in *Two Fifteenth-Century Cookery-Books,* ed. Thomas Austin, EETS OS 91 (London, 1888), p. 15.

Either *The* (C) or **Thy** (TA) may be right: A is suspect here because it reads (wrongly) *Thy* in 419 and 438.

421. Either **sessoun** (CA) or *facioun* (T) is possible: the confusion may have arisen because of such spellings as *sasoun* (with a tall *s*) and *fasoun. sessoun,* as a noun with the sense 'seasoning, flavour', is not elsewhere recorded before 1599, and is therefore harder.

425. thir, Henryson's normal pl. of *this,* does not seem appropriate here; *thy,* in T and A, may be right. But it is difficult to explain how *thy* could have been corrupted into *thir,* while on the other hand *thir* is elsewhere corrupted in T and A (see variants to 264).

426–7. Cf. *Fables,* 1680–3.

427. pane, in the sense of 'garden plot', is not recorded before 1819, and then not in the north (see *EDD*). It is likely that *pane* is used here simply in the sense of 'part' or 'division'. See Godefroy, *Dictionnaire de l'ancienne langue française, pan*; *OED, pane*; and Holland, *Buke of the Howlat,* 668, 670, 'a palace of pryce plesand allane . . . Pantit and apparalit proudly i*n* pane' (in *Asloan MS,* ed. Craigie, II, 115–16). But the text may be corrupt: see note to 433. As G. G. Smith notes, the word caused trouble for K, who wrote *gay* (in 425) and *pane,* but then altered them to *braue* and *paue;* and also for Speght, who put 'Pane, *read,* Way' in the list of corrections of his 1598 edition. K and perhaps Speght are trying to force the stanza into rhyme royal (Speght, following T, omits 433: see Introduction, pp. 10, 13). A, who preserves the correct rhyme scheme, emends to *plain.*

429. walk could mean either 'wake' or 'walk', but *Orpheus,* 93–5, proves that 'walk' is intended.

   tak the dew. Skeat's gloss, 'gather May-dew', is correct, though G. G. Smith explains the phrase as 'meaning little more than "go afield" '. It is an old custom, still carried on in Scotland and elsewhere, for girls to wash their faces with dew on May-day, thus acquiring beauty. See M. MacLeod Banks, *British Calendar Customs: Scotland,* Vol. II (London, 1939), pp. 222–4; and F. Marian McNeill, *The Silver Bough,* (Glasgow, 1957–), Vol. II, p. 65. As Skeat points out, the entries in Pepys' *Diary* (Mrs Pepys believed that May-dew was 'the only thing in the world to wash her face with') prove that any day in May was suitable for gathering dew (see entries for 28 May 1667, 10 May 1669, 11 May 1669). Henryson refers to this custom also in *Orpheus,* 95 (Asloan MS).

430. merle and mawis, 'blackbird and song-thrush'. Birds traditionally associated in Scottish, and later in English, poetry. See *OED, mavis, merle,* and cf. *Fables,* 871, 1338, 1710.

431. Henryson may have in mind the scene in *Troilus* where Criseyde walks in her garden with other women and listens to Antigone's song (II, 813ff.).

432. Either **ray** (T) or *array* (CA) is possible; *array* is perhaps a scribal 'correction' of the aphetic form.

433. on euerie grane. Skeat translates 'in every particular', but also suggests that *grane* might here have the meaning 'tint', an explanation which G. G. Smith prefers. *grane*, however, means in ME and MSc 'scarlet dye', or (usually in the phrase *in/of grain*) 'a fast dye'. There seems to be no authority for taking *euerie grane* to mean 'every colour'. So if *grane* is the correct reading here, it is necessary to take it as 'point, particular' (see *SND, grain,* n.¹). But it is tempting to suppose that *grane* and *pane* have been interchanged. *pane*, 'piece of cloth, portion of a garment', would make excellent sense here; *grane* would make acceptable sense in 427, since it is often used vaguely in poetry for 'seed', 'fruit', 'stalk', 'branch'. See *MED, grain*; *DOST, grain(e,* n.¹, n.²; 'girs gaye as þe gold and granes of grace' (Holland, *Howlat,* 28; cf. line 425 above) and 'fruct and flowring grane' (Dunbar, *All Erdly Joy Returnis in Pane,* 11).

439. 'As pilwes [& fether-beddis soft] been to chaumbris agreable, / So is hard strauh litteer for the stable', Lydgate, *Minor Poems,* II, p. 547. 'The farm of Shiels, in the neighbourhood of Ayr, has to give, if required, a certain quantity of straw for the lepers' beds . . .', Note LIV to Scott's *The Lord of the Isles.*

440. waillit wyne, 'chosen (choice) wine'. An alliterative phrase: cf. 'Walid wyne for to wete wantid þai none', *The "Gest Hystoriale" of the Destruction of Troy,* ed. G. A. Panton and D. Donaldson, EETS OS 39, 56 (London, 1869–74), line 386.

441. Fifteenth-century Scottish lepers may often have lived on rotten food. See *The Acts of the Parliaments of Scotland,* Vol. I, where it is said that 'gif ony wylde best be fundyn dede or wondyt [it shall be sent] . . . to þe hous of þe lepir men gif þar be ony sic ner by' (p. 328), and that any 'porci et salmones corrupti' brought to market shall be seized and sent to the lepers (p. 365).

pirate (T) may be correct; in any case it would seem to be a legitimate but unrecorded equivalent to **peirrie** (CA). For the Latin form, see Niermeyer, *Mediae Latinitatis Lexicon Minus* (Leiden, 1954—), *piratium* ('cider made of pears'), also *piretum* in *Promptorium Parvulorum* and *Catholicon Anglicum* (both quoted in *OED,* s.v. *perry*²). Cf. the variant readings *piriwhit* and *periwhit* in *Piers Plowman: The A Version,* V, 134. The correct gloss, '*pirate,* a drinke made of peares', is given in the glossary of Speght's 1602 edition.

444. Either **for** (C) or *fair* (A) is possible (cf. 431). The same set of readings occurs in Henryson's *Abbay Walk,* 2, where *fair* is probably correct.

445. rawk (C), 'hoarse, raucous', is not recorded before Henryson or after 1533 (*OED*). *ranke* (TA) is an emendation or a minim confusion: cf. *Fables,* 2789, *voce full rauk,* where the three earliest witnesses read *rauk* and the three latest read *rank* (which was sometimes used of loud noises: see *OED, rank,* a. 6b). John of Gaddesden remarks that in leprosy, 'vox raucescit' (*Rosa Anglica,* f. 57ª).

448. deformit the figour of my face. John of Gaddesden remarks that in leprosy the figure and the form (*figura et forma*, a stock medical phrase) of the face are corrupted (*Rosa Anglica*, f. 57ᵃ; see also Bernard de Gordon, *Lilium Medicinae*, p. 91).

450. Sowpit in syte, 'wearied *or* immersed in sorrow'. A traditional phrase: cf. 'Solpit in sorowe', Holland, *Howlat*, 42; *sowpit in site,* Kennedy, *The Passioun of Christ,* 1011 (*Poems,* ed. J. Schipper [Vienna, 1901]); 'sowpyt in syte', Douglas, *Aen.,* VIII, Prol. 5. The meaning of *sowpit* is not entirely clear: see *OED, sowp,* v.¹ and v.², and *sopit.* There may have been a confusion between the reflexes of OE *soppian,* 'to sop', and Latin *sopīre,* 'to put to sleep'. This line echoes 407.

454. friuoll (C) and *freyle* (T) have the same meaning: 'fickle, un-reliable' (see *DOST, frevoll; MED, frēle*). The former was common in MSc but not in English, and so is probably the correct reading. It is pronounced here as a monosyllable: cf. the spelling *fruell.* The same set of variants (in the comparative) occurs in Henryson's *Want of Wyse Men,* 45.

457. See Introduction, p. 46 and fn. 2.

461. It is remarked in an ME sermon that leprosy 'is defloratif of fairnes . . . be a man neuer so vair, it wil a-non-rith defade hym of al his bewte' (Grisdale, *Three Middle English Sermons,* pp. 29–30, lines 256–7, 264).

462–3. These lines may be derived from a mistranslation. Boethius, in his *Consolation* (III, Prose 6), quoted in Greek Euripides' *Andromache,* 319–20:

> ὦ δόξα δόξα, μυρίοισι δὴ βροτῶν
> οὐδὲν γεγῶσι βίοτον ὤγκωσας μέγαν.

'O reputation, reputation, you have raised to honour myriads of worth-less mortals.' In some MSS of Boethius this was incorrectly translated into Latin as 'O gloria, gloria, in milibus hominum nichil aliud facta nisi auribus inflatio magna.' (See Skeat's and Robinson's notes to Chaucer's translation, and also Joannes Murmellius's remarks on the various interpretations of this passage in his commentary on the *Consolation,* printed in *PL* 63, col.1010.) Chaucer translates this Latin into 'O glorie, glorie . . . thow n'art nothyng elles to thousandes of folk but a greet swellere of eres!', and his translation is imitated in Usk's *Testament of Love* (Bk II, Ch. viii, 66–9, in Skeat, *Chaucerian and Other Pieces*). But Henryson seems to be following the Latin, not Chaucer (**inflat,** 'puffed', was apparently suggested by *inflatio*). Cf. *Fables,* 474.

464. roising is listed in the *OED* as the only example of an adj. *rosing,* but probably it is simply a back-spelling of *rosen.* Cf. 425 above (*garding,* 'garden'), and note to 267. **rotting** may be either a similar

9

back-spelling of *rotten* or the concrete noun *rotting*, 'decomposed or putrid matter'.

reid may be correct here: a complexion 'red as rose' is common in romances (see *OED, red,* 1d), and cf. 211 above. But it is probable that Henryson wrote *rude* or *ruid,* 'complexion of those parts of the face which are naturally reddish', and that this somewhat archaic word was misunderstood, as it was by some of the Chaucerian scribes (see variants to *Miller's Tale,* I, 3317, and *Thopas,* VII, 727). For the common collocation of *rude* and *rose* or *rosen* see *OED, rud,* sb.¹, and cf. the passage, very reminiscent of the *Testament,* in Henryson's *Orpheus* (354–5): 'quhair is your rude as ross with cheikis quhyte, / your cristell ene with blenkis amorus'.

466. 'who furnishes a lamentable proof of such truths'.

467. Cf. Henryson's *Abbay Walk,* 10–12, and, for the proverbial simile, the first two quotations in *MED, blas.*

468. **ȝour** (TA; spelled *your*) and *the* (C) are of equal merit, but the agreement of T and A makes *ȝour* more likely to be original. See, however, the similar variants in 456.

469. **steiris.** *Steer* and *stir* were confused in MSc: *steiris* here can mean 'rule, govern' (*OED, steer,* 7; cf. 149 above) or, perhaps more probably, 'is active, bestirs herself' (*OED, stir,* 14b). The line may be an example of hendiadys: 'begins to . . .'

471. 'she lay awake the whole night through' (G. G. Smith).

473. **hir murning mend.** The construction is ambiguous: 'her mourning (might not) avail' (see *OED, mend,* v. 7b for *mend* used absolutely in MSc), or '(her lamentations might not) remove her sorrowing'. For the latter, cf. 'on the I call / To mend my murning' (*Orpheus,* 175–6), and 'god sendis . . . for murning remeid' (*Robene and Makyne,* 37–8).

474. Here and in *Fables,* 967, Henryson uses, in rhyme, a pret. form **wend** in place of the usual *went.* This form may be derived from the old pret. *wende:* see *OED, wend.* But see also the note to 36.

475. Proverbial: see Whiting, *wall* (10). Cf. Henryson's *Abbay Walk,* 30.

477. The text is uncertain here. C, though smooth metrically, does not make good sense: 'doubles only thy woe' (instead of doubling something else). *that,* in T; *doth,* in A; and the inversion of *bot dowbillis* in the ancestor of C and A were perhaps changes made to improve the metre.

478. A common proverb: see the note in G. G. Smith; Robinson's note to *Knight's Tale,* I, 3041–2; and Whiting, *virtue* (1) and *need* (3).

Henryson may be making an ironic reference to the advice Criseyde gives Troilus before she leaves Troy: 'Thus maketh vertu of necessite / By pacience' (*Troilus*, IV, 1586–7).

480. It seems certain that *leir* (modified to *lerne* in T) is a mistake for **leif**, presumably caused by the influence of *leir* in 479. Cf. 'To leif eftir thy lawis', *The Maitland Folio Manuscript*, ed. Craigie, I, 24, line 4. This mistake indicates that C, T, and A all go back to a faulty archetype.

481. **thame** (C) is clearly the right reading, especially since Cresseid is with the other lepers when she next appears. The later English texts read *than* or *then*, an erroneous expansion of *thā* in T, because they confuse *forth with* and *forthwith* (in T it is uncertain whether this is printed as one word or two). *then* in A is presumably an independent error, but one which arises from similar causes (A has the spelling *forth-with*). This coincidence suggests that there may have been a Scottish print of the *Testament* before 1532, in which *thā* appeared.

483. Although lepers were sometimes given a small allowance from the endowment of their spital, they traditionally supported themselves by begging, and were often given special permission to do so. See *The Acts of the Parliaments of Scotland*: 'Item at na lip*i*rous folk sit to thig nothir in kirk nor i*n* kirk ӡarde na i*n* nane vthir place wi*t*hin þe borowis bot at þare awin hospitale ande at þe porte of þe toune *and* vthir plac*is* outewith þe borowis' (Vol. II, p. 16: A.D. 1427).

486. **ieopardie of weir,** 'a daring enterprise of arms'. Cf. *Fables*, 1478.

490. **lipper,** 'leprous (persons)'. So in line 494. See *DOST*, *lipper*, 1c.

491. All the witnesses seem corrupt here: the version in A is the most tempting, but is probably an emendation, since *troop* is not recorded in the *OED* before 1545. My emendation rests on the conjecture that *come*, which appears in all witnesses (*came* in A), arose through an erroneous repetition of the first syllable of *companie*.
For the phrase **with ane steuin,** 'with one voice', see *OED*, *steven*, sb.¹ 1b.

493. The omission of *Said* in T produces a reading which is harder, and so slightly preferable. For a similar unheralded quotation see line 542.
Goddis lufe of heuin, 'love of God (*or* gods) of heaven'.

494. **part of,** 'give a share of' (*OED*, *part*, v. 11). **almous deid,** 'alms-giving' (*DOST*, *almous-dede*).

501. **plye** (C) is Scottish; *plyte* (TA) English.

505–11. For the historical background of this stanza see Stearns, *Henryson*, pp. 98–105. As Stearns points out, the general theory of psychology assumed here goes back to Aristotle, and Troilus's illusion may be ultimately derived from Aristotle's theory of illusions: 'the object of sense still remains perceptible even after the external object perceived has gone, and moreover . . . we are easily deceived about our perceptions while we have them, some in some circumstances and others in others; for instance the coward in his fear, the lover in his love, so that even by a very faint resemblance the coward thinks that he sees his enemy, and the lover the object of his love; and in proportion as he is more affected, so his imagination is stimulated by a more remote resemblance' (*De Somniis*, 460b; Stearns wrongly refers this passage to *De Somno*). Similar illusions and similar explanations were not uncommon: see note to line 508.

505–6. 'It was no wonder, even if he in his mind conceived her image so quickly', or, more loosely, 'if a picture of Cresseid immediately came into his mind'. Stearns's alternative explanation, 'bear in mind that he looked at her hastily', does not seem possible. There may be an allusion to the scene where Chaucer's Troilus muses on Criseyde until he thinks he sees her: 'Thus gan he make a mirour of his mynde, / In which he saugh al holly hire figure' (I, 365–6).

507. **idole,** 'image'. Presumably derived, as Stearns points out, from the late Latin *idolum*. According to the *OED*, the word was used in ME only with reference to religion, and 'The other uses are 16th c. adoptions of earlier Greek senses'.

508. **imprint** (em-, en-) is used commonly in ME and MSc for 'fix in the mind'. **fantasy,** like *imagination*, was sometimes used to denote that faculty (Aristotle's φαντασία) which records and preserves sense-impressions, or what we call *memory*. See Stearns, *Henryson*, p. 100; *MED*, *fantasie*, 1; and H. S. V. Jones, 'Imaginatif in Piers Plowman', *JEGP*, **13** (1914), 583–8. A similar account is given by Caxton of Dido, alone in her chamber: 'Desirynge the presence of Eneas by Imagyna-cyon impraynted wyth-in the fauntasme of her entendemente, Her semeth that she seeth hym there presente . . .' (*Eneydos*, ed. W. T. Culley and F. J. Furnivall, EETS ES 57 [London, 1890], p. 48). In the continuation of Lydgate's *Temple of Glas*, the lover says (78–81):

> ȝoure schap, ȝoure forme, & ȝoure fygure
> Amyd myn herte depeyntyd be:
> By god, thow I may ȝou nat se,
> The prent is there so depe I-graue . . .

509. **wittis outwardly.** The five senses, as opposed to the five 'inward wits'. See, e.g., Pecock, *Donet*, ed. E. V. Hitchcock, EETS OS 156 (London, 1921), pp. 9ff., and the references given in the *Assembly of Gods*, ed. Triggs, p. 91. Cf. Henryson's *Ressoning betuix Aige and Yowth*, 52, 63.

510. **lyke estait,** 'similar condition *or* bodily form'. See *MED*, *estat*, 1b. But probably with reference to Cresseid's changed *estait* (line 437).

511. as it was figurait, 'as it (the image) had been formed (in the *fantasy* or memory)'.

512–14. Cf. Chaucer's Troilus, who 'seyde he hadde a fevere . . . lest men of hym wende / That the hote fir of love hym brende' (I, 489–91). For **kendlit,** cf. 30 above.

517. Cf. 46 above and note, and also Chaucer's Troilus: 'The fyr of love . . . brende hym so in soundry wise ay newe, / That sexti tyme a day he loste his hewe' (I, 436–41).

mony (CA) is better than *many a* (T) here, as in 521 and 541: Henryson frequently uses *many* with a singular noun and no article (see *OED, many,* A.1a).

520–1. Probably a purse hanging from a jewelled girdle.

534. For the idiom *to do humanitie to,* 'to treat kindly', see *DOST, humanité.*

538–45. Henryson is using here, perhaps with intentional irony, language which was conventionally used to describe the grief of a woman deprived of her lover. See in Chaucer, for instance, *Troilus,* V, 708–42; *Anelida,* 169–75; *Book of the Duchess,* 103–23.

Stiffer than steill is a proverbial expression, but Henryson's use of it is unusual. See Whiting, *steel* (5).

540. ouircome, 'revived'. Cf. *Orpheus,* 400.

541. ochane. Gaelic *ochòin,* a cry of lamentation. For examples in English see *OED, ohone.* T emends to *atone,* 'together'. Wood suggests that **cald** might be 'called', but this seems impossible in the context. Her laments are cold because sad (cf. 'with ful colde sykynge3', *Gawain and the Green Knight,* 1982), and perhaps also because she, unlike Troilus, has been deprived of heat. *ochane* can be construed either as the first word of Cresseid's speech or as a noun parallel with *cry.* The punctuation of the early editions gives some slight support to the latter alternative (in C there is a full stop after *ochane* and in A a colon; T garbles the line).

543. Wrappit in wo may be a traditional phrase: cf. 'For mannes soule was wrapped in wo' in *Quia Amore Langueo* (*Religious Lyrics of the XIVth Century,* ed. Carleton Brown, 2nd ed. [Oxford, 1957], p. 234, line 6).

will of wane is a common phrase: 'bewildered, hopeless'. *will* is ON *villr,* 'astray', but *wane* may mean either 'hope' or 'dwelling-place'. See *OED, wane,* sb.²; *wone,* sb.² and sb.³; *will,* a.; also *Fables,* 300, and *Orpheus,* 245. G. G. Smith compares 'Wa Is me wretche in þis warld wilsome of wane' (Holland, *Howlat,* 43).

544. It is fairly certain that the original rhyme-word was **fane,** the normal MSc pret. of *fine,* 'to stop'. T, accustomed to equating MSc *ā* with southern *ō*, altered *fane* to the nonsensical *fone*, so preserving his rhyme; *refrane*, in C, presumably comes from a scribe who did not understand *fane* (a form not recorded in *DOST* after *c.* 1420). **fel in swoun** (TA) is to be preferred to *swounit scho* (C) because of the agreement of T and A. But *culd* (C) and *wolde* (TA) are both difficult, unless one supposes that Henryson incorrectly used *fane* as an infinitive form. I have conjectured that the auxiliary verb was introduced erroneously, and that the original reading was *or euer scho fane* (with monosyllabic *euer*). Note *ere* in A here, and *Or ever he ceissit* in *Fables*, 2587; and see *DOST, fine,* v.¹, for the expression *or (euer) he/she fane*.

549. The correct reading, **efflated** ('puffed out', Latin *efflāre*) is preserved in A, corrupted to the meaningless *effated* in T, and emended to *eleuait* in C. This word is not recorded in the *OED* until 1634, but note *inflat* in 463 above, also perhaps formed directly from the Latin (it is the first instance in the *OED* of this verb).

550. There are numerous references to the wheel of Fortune in *Troilus*, e.g. 'O ye loveris, that heigh upon the whiel / Ben set of Fortune' (IV, 323–4). Henryson also refers to it in *Fables*, 2418–19 and 2947.

552. **the self**, 'itself'. Cf. *Fables*, 2646.

554. *gude* in C is probably a scribal addition, as the agreement of T and A would suggest. The pret. and past part. of *keip* seem to be always disyllabic in Henryson. For **continence**, 'self-restraint', see Elyot: '*Shamfastnes* ioyned to *Appetite of generation* maketh *Continence*, whiche is a meane betwene *Chastitie* and *inordinate luste*' (*Gouernour*, ed. F. Watson [London, 1907], Bk I, Ch. 21). The spelling *countenaunce* in T and (with *-ance*) A suggests that they took it for the idiom 'to keep calm' (see *MED, contenaunce,* 2).

555. **chaist.** 'love . . . adorns a man, so to speak, with the virtue of chastity, because he who shines with the light of one love can hardly think of embracing another woman' (Andreas Capellanus, *The Art of Courtly Love,* tr. J. J. Parry [New York, 1941], p. 31: see also pp. 81 and 141).

557. **opinioun,** 'reputation'.

562. **for quhome** (CA), *for whan* (T), and *quhairfor* (L) are all possible: if *whan* is read, this line is not end-stopped ('for in times of difficulty there are few you can trust . . .').

563. **thairout,** 'in existence'. See *OED, thereout,* 2b.

566. Proverbial: see Whiting, *take* (1). 'Accept women as being what they are.'

567. A common image: see Chaucer, *Clerk's Tale,* IV, 995–6 and *Against Women Unconstant,* 12–13. For further examples see Whiting, *weathercock,* and *MED, fane,* n. (1), 3.

568–74. The syntax and punctuation of this stanza are difficult: the best solution is probably to take 570–1 (or 570–2?) as parenthetical, 'Expecting (to find) as great unfaithfulness in others (and to find them) as inconstant . . .' **Traisting,** 'expecting' (cf. *Fables*, 1424), has here a simple object: see *OED*, *traist*, v. 2c. For **vther** as a pl. pronoun see 287 above and *Orpheus*, 403, 404.

into ('in') in C is probably right: T and A presumably agree on *vnto* because they took the phrase *into my self I say* as a unit, and made the consequent emendation. Elliott apparently suggests that *into my self* be taken both with *vnstabilnes* ('the instability in myself') and *I say* ('I speak of myself'), but this seems impossible.

569. **Brukkill as glas.** A common expression: see Whiting, *glass* (1) and Aubrey Williams, 'The "Fall" of China and *The Rape of the Lock*', *PQ*, 41 (1962), 412–25. *Brittel* (T) is presumably an emendation to the southern form of the saying: see Tilley, G134 (*Brittel* is not recorded in *DOST*). *Brukkill* means 'morally frail', as well as 'brittle': see *Fables*, 2965, and *Orpheus*, 491.

570. The text is uncertain. (1) Henryson may have written **vnfaithfulnes** (CA), altered to *brutelnesse* by T (who would have been familiar with this Chaucerian word) under the influence of *Brittel* (T) in the line above. (2) Henryson may have written *brutelnesse* (T), under Chaucerian influence (cf. *Troilus*, V, 1832), and the Scottish printers, unfamiliar with this word (not recorded in *DOST*), may have altered it to *vnfaithfulnes*. (3) Henryson may have written *brukkilnes*, which was then altered to *vnfaithfulnes* in C for the sake of elegant variation and changed to the southern *brutelnesse* in T (cf. line 86, where C reads *brukkilnes* and T *brutelnesse*).

573. **ruse,** 'praise', is elsewhere balanced against *accuse*, 'blame': e.g. 'For if other men ruse hym, / We shall accuse hym', *Coliphizacio*, 33–4, in *The Wakefield Pageants*, ed. A. C. Cawley (Manchester, 1958).

577. **beteiche,** 'hand over, yield'. Frequently used for consigning a person to God or the devil: see *DOST*, *beteche*. Although both T and A read *bequeth*, this is probably a coincident error, produced by ignorance of the Scots *beteiche* (not recorded in English after the fifteenth century), or by the normal expectation of *bequeth* at the beginning of a testament.

578. **With wormis and with taidis.** *wormis* may be used vaguely for both the worms which are supposed to devour corpses (cf. 'wormis Keitching', *Fables*, 1932) and for reptiles or loathsome animals in general. Cf. 'Edderis, askis, and wormis meit for to be', in Henryson's *Ressoning betuix Deth and Man*, 38. Toads, like serpents, were commonly associated with corpses: see Tervarent, *Attributs et symboles*, cols. 135–6. In *Cursor Mundi* the third pain of hell is 'wormes þat sal neuer dei, / Fell dragons and tades bath' (Cotton 23226–7).

579. Either **and clapper** (CA) or *my clapper* (T) is possible: *and* may have been introduced by a scribe because of the common phrase *cop*

and clapper (see lines 343, 387, 442 above); alternatively, *my* may have been introduced by way of elegant variation, in order to avoid the series of *and*'s. The reading *my* shows that the cup and clapper were considered, by a scribe if not by Henryson, to be separate: see note to line 343.

582. In *Troilus*, III, 1368, Troilus and Criseyde 'entrechaungeden hire rynges'; a ruby (brooch) is mentioned three lines later; and Troilus is earlier said to own a ruby ring (II, 1087). But Henryson need not have made this connection, since ruby rings were common in ME and MSc literature (see *OED, ruby*), and since he says that Troilus *sent* it to Cresseid. The gift of a ring has a symbolic meaning: cf. Lindsay, *Squire Meldrum,* 1003–6:

> And he gaif hir ane lufe drowrie,
> Ane Ring set with ane riche Rubie,
> In takin that thair Lufe for euer
> Suld neuer frome thir twa disseuer.

The author of *The Laste Epistle of Creseyd to Troyalus* makes the meaning of this ring explicit:

> Except a ringe nought ells I haue
> W*h*ich thou me gave that night
> That ioyned was o*u*r hartes in one,
> And faythe to others plight;
> The w*h*ich I send in Paper lapte,
> Bewashed w*i*th my teares . . .
>
> (293–8)

583. **in drowrie,** 'as a love-token', or 'in affection'. Presumably both T and A emend to *dowry* because they are not familiar with *drowrie* (not recorded after *c.* 1500 in ME or after *c.* 1550 in MSc).

585. **deid,** 'death'.

587. **Diane.** Not Cynthia, but 'Dyane the goddesse chaste of woddis grene' (Dunbar, *Golden Targe,* 76), 'a goddesse pure / Ouer all desertys, forestes and chases' (*Assembly of Gods,* 57–8; the author of this poem also distinguishes between Diana and the goddess of the moon).
    spreit is commonly used for 'The soul of a person, as commended to God, or passing out of the body, in the moment of death' (*OED, spirit,* 2).

588. **wellis,** 'pools' or 'streams'; cf. *Fables,* 2618, and, for **waist woddis,** 2376 and 2441. Cf. 'Walis wyslie þe wayis be wodd*is* & wellis', Holland, *Howlat,* 305, and 'thay walkit be the syde of ane fair well', *Golagros and Gawane,* 40 (in *Scottish Alliterative Poems,* ed. Amours). One would expect (and Henryson may have written) *be,* not *in.*

589. **broche and belt.** In *Troilus* there is only a brooch, which Troilus gives to Criseyde and she in turn gives to Diomede (V, 1040, 1660–94). The belt was presumably introduced by Henryson because he took *broche* to mean 'buckle'. See *DOST, broch(e,* n. 2. The author of *The*

Laste Epistle of Creseyd to Troyalus apparently understood *broche* as 'buckle': 'Till that on Diomeds cote of armes / Thou spyed the little bruche' (239–40). (For the heraldic equation of brooches and buckles see Alexander Hay, *Estimate of the Scottish Nobility*, ed. C. Rogers [London, 1873], p. 14: 'The Erle of Rothos . . . gyveth the buckles called bruches in gold . . .' and the illustrations of the arms of this family in R. R. Stodart, *Scottish Arms*, Vol. I [Edinburgh, 1881], Plates C and 4.) Cresseid's belt probably has a symbolic meaning, as G. G. Smith suggests, but in view of lines 590–1 it is perhaps more likely to stand for the bond of true love than the girdle of chastity.

590. **takning.** Trisyllabic; cf. *tokenyng* TA.

600. The versions of this line in C and A are probably both derived from the metrically awkward version in T. I have followed the emendation in C, but it is possible that Henryson wrote the irregular but emphatic version of T.

This passage is reminiscent of Chaucer's *Troilus*: e.g. 'For sorwe of which myn herte shal tocleve', 'for sorwe . . . he bad his herte breste' (V, 613, 1567–8).

601. **I can no moir** may mean both 'I can do no more' and 'this is all I know'. See *DOST, can,* and cf. *Fables,* 144.

604, 606. 'And wrote on it her name and an inscription . . . in golden letters'. Or **superscriptioun** may mean 'title': it was used for the address on a letter (not recorded in this sense before 1518).

Cf. Lydgate: 'Telefus, out of marbil gray / Coriously a tombe made kerue . . . Wiþ lettris riche of gold . . . þat seide pleinly þus . . .' (*Troy Book,* II, 7520–30).

605. It is possible that both C and T are emending here for metrical reasons, and that Henryson wrote simply *quhair scho lay,* as in A.

607. The agreement of T and A gives strong support to **Troy the,** against *Troyis,* in C. *Troy the toun* is an unusual phrase, but Lydgate occasionally speaks of *Troye þe cite* (*Troy Book,* I, 1224; II, 1559, 3830, 3878: see also Mustanoja, *Middle English Syntax,* I, 237–40). Chaucer has usually *Troye toun; Troyes town* exists as a variant in *Troilus,* V, 768, and also as a variant in Lydgate's *Temple of Glas,* 95. But it is hard to account for the variant in the first half of the line in A, and so tempting to suppose that Henryson wrote *Lo, fair ladyis, clear Cresseid* [or *clear ladyis, fair Cresseid*] *of Troy toun.* Cf. Henryson's *Bludy Serk,* 47. *Troy the* might have arisen from a spelling *Troye,* since *y* and *þ* are often indistinguishable.

608. **flour of womanheid.** The phrase is used by Chaucer in *Womanly Noblesse,* 28. See note to line 88 above.

609. **lait.** The variant *laith* in A probably arose because *laith lipper* was a common phrase. See *DOST, lathe,* a. 1. **lipper** may be either a noun or an adjective: 'former leper', or 'formerly leprous'.

610. **ballet.** In MSc usually a short poem which is sung, but in ME often a short poem in rhyme royal. In this context it is a deprecatory term.

611. **for ȝour worschip,** 'in honour of you', 'to show you respect'. A Chaucerian irony.

614. Either **sore** (T) or *schort* (CA) is possible. I have preferred *sore*, since *schort* may have been repeated from 610 or, more likely, may have arisen under the influence of the stock phrase *short conclusion*: see 586 above; *Fables*, 2970; *Colkelbie Sow*, II, 166 (in *The Bannatyne Manuscript*, ed. W. Tod Ritchie, Vol. IV, STS II 26 [Edinburgh, 1930], p. 301); and *MED*, *conclusioun*, 5c.

APPENDIX

A

The fragment in the Ruthven MS
(lines 1–21).

] doly sassone onto ane cayrfull dit
Suld corespond & be eqewolent
Rycht so It wes quhen I begane to vryt
Thys tegrady with wedderis rycht ferwent
Quhen aries In myddis of þe lent   5
Schowris of haill gart fra þe northt decend
That scantly fra þe cald I mycht deffend

ʒit neuer þe les In tyll ane oriture
I stud quhar tytan hed his bamis brycht
with drawn dovne & sellit onder cure   10
And fayr wenus þe bewte of þe nycht
Wp rays & set onto þe west full rycht
Hyr goldin face In opycione
Of phebus derecture & descendin dovne

Out throw þe glas þe bamis byrst so fayr   15
That I mycht se on euery syd me by.
The northin wynd hed purifeyt þe ayre
And sched þe mysty cludys fray þe sky
The frost fresset with blastis bytterly
And poill artyk com wystland lovd & schyll   20
And causit me ra[mu]f agane my wyll

B

The fragment in the Book of the Dean of Lismore
(lines 561–7).

Luffar*is* be war and tak gwd heid about
quho*m* þ*at* ʒe luf q*uhai*rfor ʒe suffir pay*n*
I lat ʒou vit þ*air* is ryc*h*t few about
þ*at* ʒe may tr*ai*st to haif trew luf agay*n*
Preif quhe*n* ʒe vil ʒ*our* labo*u*r is in wane
þ*air*for I red ʒe tak þame as ʒe find
ffor þai ar sad as vidd*er*cok in wynd

BIBLIOGRAPHY

EDITIONS

Only the more important modern editions are listed here. Information about the earlier English editions of Chaucer which contain the *Testament* can be found in Hammond, *Chaucer*; a fairly complete though now out-of-date bibliography of Henryson is in William Geddie, *A Bibliography of Middle Scots Poets*, STS I 61 (Edinburgh, 1912); some of the more modern editions are listed in Stearns, *Henryson*, pp. 131–3.

CHALMERS — *Robene and Makyne, and The Testament of Cresseid*, ed. George Chalmers, Bannatyne Club (Edinburgh, 1824). The foundation for all later editions. Contains no notes or glossary, but has a succinct and generally accurate preface which outlines the bibliographical and biographical facts.

LAING — *The Poems and Fables of Robert Henryson*, ed. David Laing (Edinburgh, 1865). Valuable mostly for Laing's biographical and bibliographical researches.

SKEAT — *Chaucerian and Other Pieces*, ed. Walter W. Skeat (Oxford, 1897). Vol. VII of his edition of Chaucer. Contains a confused text of the *Testament*, but also the first useful set of annotations. Valuable mostly for its texts of other fifteenth-century poems.

G. G. SMITH — *The Poems of Robert Henryson*, ed. G. Gregory Smith, STS I 55, 58, 64 (Edinburgh, 1906–14). Still the best edition of Henryson. Contains the complete texts of C, T, and K, as well as important notes and a good glossary.

DICKINS — *The Testament of Cresseid*, ed. Bruce Dickins, rev. ed. (London, 1943). First published in 1925. Accurate and laconic.

MURRAY — *Selected Fables . . . The Testament of Cresseid and Robene and Makyne*, ed. H. M. R. Murray (London, 1930).

WOOD   *The Poems and Fables of Robert Henryson*, ed. H. Harvey Wood (Edinburgh, 1933). Rev. ed. (with no important changes), 1958. The only complete edition of Henryson now available.

MURISON   *Selections from the Poems of Robert Henryson*, ed. David Murison, Saltire Society (Edinburgh, 1952). Omits lines 169–301.

ELLIOTT   *Robert Henryson: Poems*, ed. Charles Elliott, Clarendon Medieval and Tudor Series (Oxford, 1963).

LIST OF WORKS CITED

This list contains works which are cited repeatedly or which are immediately important for the *Testament*. References to classical authors are to the Loeb texts and translations; references to the Bible are to the Vulgate (usually quoted in the Douay translation); references to Henryson's other works are to Wood's edition.

Accounts of the Lord High Treasurer of Scotland. Vol. I, 1473–98, ed. T. Dickson (Edinburgh, 1877).

The Acts of the Parliaments of Scotland. Vol. I, 1124–1423; Vol. II, 1424–1567; ed. T. Thomson and C. Innes ([Edinburgh], 1844, 1814).

ALAIN DE LILLE. *The Complaint of Nature*, tr. D. M. Moffat, Yale Studies in English, 36 (New York, 1908).

Amis and Amiloun, ed. MacEdward Leach, EETS OS 203 (London, 1937).

ANDREAS CAPELLANUS. *The Art of Courtly Love*, tr. J. J. Parry, Columbia Records of Civilization, 33 (New York, 1941).

Aretaeus, Consisting of Eight Books, on the Causes, Symptoms and Cure of Acute and Chronic Diseases, tr. John Moffat (London, [1785?]).

The Asloan Manuscript, ed. W. A. Craigie, STS II 14, 16 (Edinburgh, 1923–5).

The Assembly of Gods, ed. O. L. Triggs, EETS ES 69 (London, 1896).

The Bannatyne Miscellany, Bannatyne Club, Vol. II (Edinburgh, 1836).

BENNETT, H. S. *Chaucer and the Fifteenth Century*, Oxford History of English Literature (Oxford, 1947).

BENNETT, J. A. W. *The Parlement of Foules* (Oxford, 1957).

BERNARD DE GORDON. *Lilium Medicinae* (Lyons, 1559).

BLOOMFIELD, MORTON W. *The Seven Deadly Sins* ([East Lansing, Michigan], 1952).

BOCCACCIO, GIOVANNI. *Genealogie Deorum Gentilium Libri*, ed. V. Romano, Scrittori d'Italia, 2 vols (Bari, 1951).

BODEL, JEAN. 'Les Congés de Jean Bodel', ed. G. Raynaud, *Romania*, 9 (1880), 216–47.

[*Body and Soul*] 'Þe Desputisoun Bitwen Þe Bodi and Þe Soule', ed. W. Linow, *Erlanger Beiträge zur Englischen Philologie*, 1 (1889) (I. Heft), 1–209.

CHAUCER, GEOFFREY. *Works*, ed. F. N. Robinson, 2nd ed. (Cambridge, Mass., 1957).

Chaucerian and Other Pieces, ed. Walter W. Skeat (Oxford, 1897).

CLAY, ROTHA MARY. *The Mediaeval Hospitals of England* (London, 1909).

COGSWELL, FRED, tr. *The Testament of Cresseid* (Toronto, 1957).

COMRIE, JOHN D. *History of Scottish Medicine*, 2nd ed., 2 vols (London, 1932).

The Court of Love. In *Chaucerian and Other Pieces*, ed. Skeat.

CREIGHTON, CHARLES. *A History of Epidemics in Britain*, Vol. I (Cambridge, 1891).

'Cresseid in Scotland' (anon. rev.), *TLS*, 9 April 1964, p. 290.

CURRY, WALTER CLYDE. *Chaucer and the Mediaeval Sciences*, rev. ed. (New York, 1960).

Cursor Mundi, ed. Richard Morris, EETS OS 57, 59, 62, 66, 68, 99, 101 (London, 1874–93).

DICKSON, ROBERT, and JOHN PHILIP EDMOND. *Annals of Scottish Printing* (Cambridge, 1890).

DOUGLAS, GAVIN. *Virgil's Aeneid*, ed. David F. C. Coldwell, STS III 25, 27, 28, 30 (Edinburgh, 1957–64).

————. *Palice of Honour*. In *Poetical Works*, ed. John Small, Vol. I (Edinburgh, 1874).

DUNBAR, WILLIAM. *Poems*, ed. W. Mackay Mackenzie (London, 1932).

DUNCAN, DOUGLAS. 'Henryson's *Testament of Cresseid*', *Essays in Criticism*, 11 (1961), 128–35. Answered by Sydney J. Harth on pp. 471–80 of the same volume.

DURKAN, JOHN. 'Care of the Poor: Pre-Reformation Hospitals', in *Essays on the Scottish Reformation 1513–1625*, ed. David McRoberts, pp. 116–28.

ELLIOTT, CHARLES. 'Two Notes on Henryson's *Testament of Cresseid*', *JEGP*, 54 (1955), 241–54.

Essays on the Scottish Reformation 1513–1625, ed. David McRoberts (Glasgow, 1962).

FASTOUL, BAUDE. 'Che sont li Congié', in *Fabliaux et Contes des poètes françois*, ed. E. Barbazan, rev. M. Méon, Vol. I, 111–34 (Paris, 1808).

FEENY, PATRICK. *The Fight Against Leprosy* (London, 1964).

The Floure and the Leafe and The Assembly of Ladies, ed. D. A. Pearsall, Nelson's Medieval and Renaissance Library (London, 1962).

FORDUN, JOHN. *Scotichronicon*, ed. W. Goodall, 2 vols (Edinburgh, 1759).

FRACASTOR, GIROLAMO. *Syphilis or the French Disease*, ed. and tr. Heneage Wynne-Finch, with introduction by J. J. Abraham (London, 1935).

Sir Gawain and The Green Knight, ed. J. R. R. Tolkien and E. V. Gordon (Oxford, 1925).

GILBERTUS ANGLICUS. *Compendium Medicinae*, ed. Michael de Capella (Lyons, 1510).

GORDON, B. L. *Medieval and Renaissance Medicine* (London, 1960).

GOWER, JOHN. *The English Works*, ed. G. C. Macaulay, EETS ES 81, 82 (London, 1900–1).

GRIERSON, H. J. C. 'Robert Henryson', *The Modern Scot*, 4 (1933–4), 294–303. Also in *Aberdeen University Review*, 21 (1933–4), 203–12.

GRISDALE, D. M., ed. *Three Middle English Sermons from the Worcester Chapter Manuscript F. 10*, Leeds School of English Language Texts and Monographs, V (Kendal, 1939).

HAMMOND, ELEANOR PRESCOTT. *Chaucer: A Bibliographical Manual* (New York, 1908).

————, ed. *English Verse between Chaucer and Surrey* (Durham, North Carolina, 1927).

HARTH, SYDNEY J. 'Convention and Creation in the Poetry of Robert Henryson: A Study of *The Testament of Cresseid* and *Orpheus and Eurydice*' (dissertation, University of Chicago, 1960).

HASTINGS, JAMES, ed. *A Dictionary of the Bible*, 5 vols (New York, 1898–1904).

HAWES, STEPHEN. *The Pastime of Pleasure*, ed. W. E. Mead, EETS OS 173 (London, 1928).

HENDERSON, T. F. *Scottish Vernacular Literature*, 3rd ed. (Edinburgh, 1910).

HOLLAND, SIR RICHARD. *The Buke of the Howlat*, in *Asloan Manuscript*, ed. Craigie, II, 95–126.

ISIDORE OF SEVILLE. *Etymologiae*, ed. W. M. Lindsay, 2 vols (Oxford, 1911).

ISIDORE OF SEVILLE. *Traité de la nature* (*De natura rerum*), ed. Jacques Fontaine (Bordeaux, 1960).

JOHN OF GADDESDEN. *Rosa Anglica* (Pavia, 1492).

KENNEDY, QUINTIN. *Two Eucharistic Tracts*, ed. C. H. Kuipers (Nijmegen, [1964]).

King Hart (author unknown), in Douglas, *Poetical Works*, Vol. I.

KINSLEY, JAMES, ed. *Scottish Poetry: A Critical Survey* (London, 1955).

KLIBANSKY, R., E. PANOFSKY and F. SAXL. *Saturn and Melancholy* (London, 1964).

LANFRANC. *Science of Cirurgie*, ed. R. von Fleischhacker, Part I (all published), EETS OS 102 (London, 1894).

The Laste Epistle of Creseyd to Troyalus (author uncertain), in *The Works of William Fowler*, ed. H. W. Meikle, Vol. I, STS II 6, 379–87 (Edinburgh, 1914).

Libellus de imaginibus deorum (pseudo-Albricus), in *Hygini, Augusti Liberti Fabularum Liber . . .* (Lyons, 1608).

LINDSAY, SIR DAVID. *Works*, ed. Douglas Hamer, STS III 1, 2, 6, 8 (Edinburgh, 1931–6).

LYDGATE, JOHN. *Fall of Princes*, ed. H. Bergen, EETS ES 121–4 (London, 1924–7).

————. *The Minor Poems*, ed. H. N. MacCracken, EETS ES 107, OS 192 (London, 1911–34).

————. *Siege of Thebes*, ed. A. Erdmann and E. Ekwall, EETS ES 108, 125 (London, 1911–30).

————. *Temple of Glas,* ed. J. Schick, EETS ES 60 (London, 1891).

————. *Troy Book*, ed. H. Bergen, EETS ES 97, 103, 106, 126 (London, 1906–35).

MACARTHUR, LT.-GEN. SIR WILLIAM. 'Mediaeval "Leprosy" in the British Isles', *Leprosy Review*, **24** (1953), 8–19.

————. 'Some Notes on Old-Time Leprosy in England and Ireland', *Journal of the Royal Army Medical Corps*, **45** (1925), 410–22.

The Maitland Folio Manuscript, ed. W. A. Craigie, STS II 7, 20 (Edinburgh, 1919–27).

MORAN, TATYANA. 'The Meeting of the Lovers in the "Testament of Cresseid" ', *Notes and Queries*, New Series, **10** (1963), 11–12.

————. '*The Testament of Cresseid* and *The Book of Troylus*', *Litera*, **6** (1959), 18–24.

10

MUSTANOJA, TAUNO F. *A Middle English Syntax*, Part I: Parts of Speech. Mémoires de la Société Néophilologique de Helsinki, XXIII (Helsinki, 1960).

NEILSON, WILLIAM ALLAN. *The Origins and Sources of the Court of Love*, Studies and Notes in Philology and Literature, VI (Boston, 1899).

NEWMAN, GEORGE. 'On the History of the Decline and Final Extinction of Leprosy as an Endemic Disease in the British Islands', in *Prize Essays on Leprosy*, New Sydenham Society Publications, CLVII, 1–149 (London, 1895).

Ovide moralisé en prose, ed. C. de Boer (Amsterdam, 1954).

PANOFSKY, ERWIN. *Studies in Iconology*, 2nd ed. (New York, 1962). Contains essays on 'Father Time' (pp. 69–93) and on 'Blind Cupid' (pp. 95–128).

PARR, JOHNSTONE. 'Cresseid's Leprosy Again', *MLN*, 60 (1945), 487–91.

PERROW, E. C. 'The Last Will and Testament as a Form of Literature', *Transactions of the Wisconsin Academy of Sciences, Arts, and Letters*, 17, Part I (1913), 682–753.

Philotus, ed. A. J. Mill, in *Miscellany Volume*, STS III 4 (Edinburgh, 1933).

Piers Plowman: The A Version, ed. George Kane (London, 1960).

RÉAU, LOUIS. *Iconographie de l'art chrétien*. 3 vols in 6 (Paris, 1955–9).

RICE, WINTHROP HUNTINGTON. *The European Ancestry of Villon's Satirical Testaments*, Syracuse University Monographs, I (New York, 1941).

ROBERT OF BRUNNE. *Handlyng Synne*, ed. F. J. Furnivall, EETS OS 119, 123 (London, 1901–3).

ROGERS, SIR LEONARD and ERNEST MUIR. *Leprosy*, 2nd ed. (Bristol, 1940).

ROLLAND, JOHN. *The Court of Venus*, ed. W. Gregor, STS I 3 (Edinburgh, 1884).

ROLLINS, HYDER E. 'The Troilus-Cressida Story from Chaucer to Shakespeare', *PMLA*, 32 (1917), 383–429.

SACROBOSCO (JOHN HOLYWOOD). *The Sphere of Sacrobosco and Its Commentators*, ed. Lynn Thorndike (Chicago, 1949).

SAXL, FRITZ and HANS MEIER. *Catalogue of Astrological and Mythological Illuminated Manuscripts of the Latin Middle Ages*, Vol. III, 1 and 2: *Manuscripts in English Libraries*, ed. H. Bober (London, 1953).

Scottish Alliterative Poems, ed. F. J. Amours, STS I 27, 38 (Edinburgh, 1892–7).

SEZNEC, JEAN. *The Survival of the Pagan Gods*, tr. Barbara F. Sessions (New York, 1953).

SIMPSON, SIR JAMES Y. 'On Leprosy and Leper Hospitals in Scotland and England', in his *Archaeological Essays*, ed. John Stuart, Vol. II, 1–184 (Edinburgh, 1872).

SPEARING, A. C. 'Conciseness and *The Testament of Cresseid*', in his *Criticism and Medieval Poetry*, pp. 118–44 (London, 1964). Published also in *Speculum*, **37** (1962), 208–25.

SPEIRS, JOHN. *The Scots Literary Tradition*, rev. ed. (London, 1962).

SPURGEON, CAROLINE F. E. *Five Hundred Years of Chaucer Criticism and Allusion 1357–1900*, 2nd ed., 3 vols (Cambridge, 1925).

STEARNS, MARSHALL W. *Robert Henryson* (New York, 1949). Includes the substance of a number of earlier articles.

————, tr. *A Modernization of Robert Henryson's Testament of Cresseid*, Indiana University Publications, Humanities Series No. 13 (Bloomington, Indiana, 1945).

TERVARENT, GUY DE. *Attributs et symboles dans l'art profane 1450–1600*, Travaux d'humanisme et renaissance, XXIX. 2 vols (paginated consecutively) (Geneva, 1958–9).

THYNNE, FRANCIS. *Animadversions*, ed. G. Kingsley and F. J. Furnival, EETS OS 9 (London, 1865).

TILLYARD, E. M. W. *Poetry and its Background* (London, 1955). Originally published under the title *Five Poems 1470–1870* (London, 1948).

TUVE, ROSEMOND. *Seasons and Months: Studies in a Tradition of Middle English Poetry* (Paris, 1933).

[*Wallace*] *The Actis and Deidis of . . . Schir William Wallace*, ed. James Moir. STS I 6, 7, 17 (Edinburgh, 1885–9).

WITTIG, KURT. *The Scottish Tradition in Literature* (Edinburgh, 1958).

GLOSSARY

This glossary and index is intended to contain every form in the text; the line-references are intended to be complete except for entries where *etc.* is written. The definitions have almost always been adapted from those in *DOST, OED,* or *MED,* except for entries where a cross-reference to the notes appears (signalled by an *n* following a line-reference). Emendations are indicated by line-references in italics. ʒ (yogh) is alphabetised as *y.*

A per se, *n.* paragon, 78*n*

abak, *adv.* backwards, 222

abhominabill, *adj.* abominable, 308

abiect, *n.* outcast, one cast off, 133

abone, *prep.* above, 287

about, *adv.* on various sides, 36; *prep.* around, 180; concerning, 561

abraid, *pret.* started, burst; **out of wit abraid,** went out of his mind, 45

accuse, *v.* blame, 574

affectioun, *n.* fondness, 530; passion, desire, 558

agane, *adv.* again, 48, 584; back, 489; in return, 564

aganis, *prep.* against, 21, 475

age, *n.* age, old age, 29

ago, *past part.* gone away, 238, 442

air, *n.* air, 17

air, *adv.* early; **air and lait,** at all hours, incessantly, 82

all, *adj., n., adv.* all, every, everything, completely, 40, 64, 71, etc.; **at all,** in any way, 476

allace, *interj.* alas, 126, 139, 356, etc.

allone, *adv.* alone, 405

almaist, *adv.* almost, 525

almous, *n.* alms, 392, 528, 532; **almous deid,** alms-giving, 494

als, *see* **as**

alterait, *past part.* altered, 227, 396

alwayis, *adv.* always, 136

alyte, *adv.* a little, 271

amang, *prep.* among, 82, 98, 451

amend, *v.* set right, make better, 455

amiabill, *adj.* friendly, 169

amorous, *adj.* loving, affectionate, 226, 326, 528

and, *conj.* and, 2, 10, 11, etc.

ane, *indef. article* a, an, 1, 29, 31, etc., **a,** 535; **ane vther,** another, 61, 73, 518; *numeral* one, 518; **sic ane,** such a one, 251; **ilk ane,** each, 529; **mony ane,** many a one, 430; *adj.* one, 221, 231, 265, 491

aneuch, *adj., adv.* enough, 110, 350, 378

angerly, *adv.* angrily, 124

angrie, *adj.* angry, 189, 228, 323

anis, *adv.* once, 127

anone, *adv.* at once, 273, 366

answeir, *n.* answer, 295

appeir, appeiris, *v.* appear, 146, 256, 510; **appeirand,** *pres. part.* 340

apperance, *n.*; **be apperance,** seemingly, 143

appetyte, *n.* desire, 71

approchis, *v.* approaches, 456, 468

ar, *see* **be**

areir, *adv.* behind, 355, 424

Aries, 5*n*

armit, *pret. refl.* protected, 38

array, *n.* attire, dress, 220

art, *see* **be**

Artick, *adj.* arctic 20*n*

as, als, *adv., conj.* as, like, 30, 87, 90, etc.; as if, 175; such as, 300; **as than,** just then, 27; **as now,** just now, 574

ascendent, *adj.* ascending, rising towards the zenith, 214*n*

assaillit, *past part.* tried, made trial of, 35

assent, *n.*; **with ane assent,** unanimously, 265

asweill, *adv.* as well as, 293

at, *prep.* at, 112, 146, 192, etc.; from, 258

atouir, *prep.* down over, 162; above, over, 244

attend, *v.* note, mark with attention, 452

aucht, *pret.* ought, 251

auld, *adj., n.* old, 32, 106, 245

auster, *adj.* austere, stern, 154

authoreist, *past part.* possessed of authority, 66

away, *adv.* 330, 347, 467, 523

awin, *adj.* own, 220, 275, 504

awoik, *pret.* awoke, 345

ay, *adv.* always, 138

baid, *pret.* stayed, waited, 490

baill, *n.* misery, sorrow, 110, 413

bair, *n.* boar, 193

bair, *adj.* bare, uncovered, 123, 206; desolate, destitute (of), 410*n*

bair, *see* **beir**

bait, *n.* a halt for feeding horses, 210

baith, *adj.* both, 35, 54, 198, etc.

bak, *n.* back, 122, 262

ballet, *n.* song, poem, 610*n*

baneist, *past part.* banished, 413

banischer, *n.* banisher, 199

bankouris, *n. pl.* coverings for benches or seats, 417

bawer, *n. as adj.* beaver, 386

be, *inf.* 2, 81, 91, etc., **bene,** 363; **am,** *pres.* 1 *sg.* 35, 129, 133, etc.; **art,** *pres.* 2 *sg.* 105, 410; **is,** *pres.* 3 *sg.* 31, 33, 130, etc.; **ar,** *pres. pl.* 288, 567, 572, **is,** 563; **be,** *pres. subj.* 29, 66, 531, 572; **be,** *imp. sg.* 308, 327; **was,** *pret. sg.* 27, 53, 64, etc.; **war,** *pret. pl.* 109, 264, **wer,** 176, **was,** 161; **wer,** *pret. subj.* 414; **bene,** *past part.* 175, 267; **be war** (*see* **war**)

be, *prep.* by, 34, 41, 67; *conj.* when, as soon as, 358, 429. Cf. **by**

becaus, *conj.* because, 394, 568

bed, *n.* bed, 417, 439

beedes, *n. pl.* prayers, 363

befoir, befor, *prep., adv.* before, 114, 146, 190, etc.

beggar, beggair, *n.* beggar, 322, 483

begging, *pres. part.* begging, 342

beginnis, *pres.* begins, 469; **began,** *pret.* 3, 357, 516

behald, *v.* look at, 207

behest, *n.* promise, 50

behind, *prep.* behind, 122

beikit, *pret. refl.* warmed, basked, 36

beildit, *past part.* constructed, 97*n*

beir, *v.* bear, carry, 516; *imp.* 614; **beirand,** *pres. part.* 262; **bair, boir,** *pret.* 166, 180, 246, 594; **beiris . . . witnes** (*see* **witnes**)

beist, *n.* beast, 198

belangand, *pres. part.* pertaining, 248

bell, *n.* bell, 144

belt, *n.* belt, 162, 589

belyue, *adv.* quickly, at once, 331

bemis, *n. pl.* beams of light, 9, 15, 208

bene, *adv.* handsomely, 417

bene, *see* be

besene, *past part.* furnished, 416

best, *adj., adv.* best, 33, 104, 256

beteiche, *v.* hand over, yield, 577n

better, *adj.* better, 399

betuix, *prep.* between, 378

bewtie, *n.* beauty, 11, 313

biddis, *pres.* requests, 361

bill, *n.* a statement in writing, a formal document, 332n

bitter, *adj.* bitter, painful, severe, 234, 277, 538

bitterly, *adv.* bitterly, severely, 19

bla, *adj.* livid, livid or bluish from cold, 159

blaiknit, *past part.* made pale, 410n

blak, *adj.* black, 216, 221, 255, 260, 339, 395, 401

blaspheme, *v.* revile, treat with impiety, 274

blaspheming, *verbal n.* the uttering of blasphemy, 354

blastis, *n. pl.* blasts, strong gusts of wind, 19

blenk, *n.* glance, look, 499; **blenkis,** *pl.* 226

blenking, *verbal n.* glancing, 503

blew, *pret.* blew, sounded, 195

blind, *adj.* blind, 135, 283

blude, *n.* blood, 31, 314n, 337

blyith, *adj.* happy, glad, 237

blyithnes, *n.* happiness, gladness, 410

blys, *n.* happiness, 413

bocht, *past part.* bought, paid for, 354

bodie, *n.* body, 334, 513

borrowis, *pres.* borrows, 258

bosteous, *see* busteous

bot, *conj.* but, 27, 54, 116, etc.; *prep.* except, other than, 134, 442, 461, 463; *adv.* only, 477. *Cf.* but

boun, *past past. as adj.* ready, 600

bour, *n.* chamber, a lady's private apartment, 438

bow, *n.* bow, 166

boxis, *n. pl.* boxes, 246

brag, *n.* bray, trumpet-blast, 195n

brand, *n.* sword, 180

brast, *see* brist

breid, *n.* bread, 441

breif, *adj.* brief, 270

breird, *n.* the first shoots of grain; **on breird,** sprouting, sprouted, 413

breist, *n.* breast, 110, 261, 516, 542

brek, *v.* break, interrupt, stop, 61

brent, *adj.* smooth (?), 173n

bricht, *adj.* bright, fair, 9, 44, 173, 208

brichtnes, *n.* brightness, 206

brist, *v.* burst, break, 600; **brast,** *pret.* 15

broche, *n.* brooch, buckle, 589n

brocht, *pret., past part.* brought, 345, 502

brother, *n.* brother, 258

browderit, *past part.* embroidered, 417

browis, *n. pl.* brows, forehead, 173

brukkill, *adj.* brittle, morally frail, 569

brukkilnes, *n.* frailty, 86

buik, *n.* book, 58, 239

buit, *n.* help, remedy, 481

bullar, *n.* bubble, bubbling, 192

bunche, *n.* bunch, bundle, 262n, 439

burelie, burely, *adj.* strong, excellent, imposing, handsome, 173, 180, 417n, 438

burie, *v.* bury, 581; **buryit,** *pret.* 593

buskit, *past part.* arrayed, 255n

busteous, bosteous, *adj.* rough, rustic, rude, 153; strong, large, 166; harsh, violent, 195

but, *prep.* without, 94, 194, 210, 404; except, 574. *Cf.* bot

by, *prep.* beside, near (*post-positive*), 16; against, with reference to, 278; **neir by** (*see* **neir**). *Cf.* **be**

bylis, *n. pl.* boils, 395

cace, *n.* case, chance; **in cace,** by chance, 507

cair, *n.* sorrow, distress, 56, 130, 378, 407, 525; **cairis,** *pl.* 60

cairfull, *adj.* distressed, painful, sorrowful, 1, 236, 310, 472, 541, 585

Calchas, 97, 103, 106

cald, *see* **call**

cald, cauld, *n.* cold, 7, 27, 38, 318, 482; *adj.* 237; cold, gloomy, 541*n*

call, *v.* call, 360; **cald,** *pret.* named, 283; **callit,** *past part.* named, 212, 216, 435

can, *v.* did (*auxiliary to form past tense*), 28, 47, 55, etc.; can, 455; can do, know, 601; **culd,** *pret.* did (*also auxiliary to form past tense*), 252, 348, 360, etc.

cap, *n.* cap, 271

carioun, *n.* a dead body, 577

carrolling, *verbal n.* dancing or singing of carols, 431, 443

cart, *n.* chariot, 208

catiue, *adj.* wretched, miserable, 408

caus, *n.* cause, reason, 99, 272, 282

causit, *pret.* caused, 21, 136; **causing,** *pres. part.* 200

ceder, *n.* cider, 441

chair, *n.* chariot, 204

chaist, *adj.* chaste, pure, 555

chalmer, *n.* chamber, 28, 109, 416

change, *v.* change, transform, 80, 316; **changit,** *pret., past part.* 227, 517

chatterit, *pret.* chattered, shivered, 156

Chauceir, Chaucer, 41, 58, 64

cheikis, *n. pl.* cheeks, 159

cheir, *n.* countenance, bearing, 154; **quhat cheir?,** how are you?, 367

cheisit, *pret.* chose, 265

cheritie, *n.* charity, 383; **of cheritie,** for charity, 612

cheuerit, *pret.* shivered, 156*n*

chide, chyde, *v.* dispute, quarrel, 185, 357; **chydand,** *pres. part.* 470

chiftane, *n.* military commander, 485

chin, *n.* chin, 156

churle, *n.* churl, rustic, boor, 153, 261

chydand, chyde, *see* **chide**

chyld, *n.* boy, young servant, 358, 365

clam, *see* **clim**

clap, *v.* clap, 479

clapper, *n.* a leper's rattle, 343*n*, 387, 442, 479, 579

cled, *past part.* clothed, 220, 250

cleir, *adj.* clear, bright, 176, 257, 338, 443

clene, *adj.* clean, 420; *adv.* completely, 133

clim, *v.* climb, 263; **clam,** *pret.* 550

cloisit, *pret.* closed, 122

cloudis, *n. pl.* clouds, 18, 401

collatioun, *n.* collation, 418*n*

colour, *n.* colour, 255, 257, 396

come, *see* **cum**

comfort, *n.* comfort, 93; support, 202

comfort, *v.* comfort, encourage, 37

comforting, *verbal n.* comfort, encouragement, 50

commoun, *adj.* promiscuous, 77*n*

companie, *n.* company, band, 491; companionship, society, 75

compellit, *pret.* compelled, 483

complaint, *n.* formal statement of a grievance, 220; lamentation, plaintive poem, 407 (*title*)

comprehend, *v.* understand, 453

compylit, *past part.* written, described, 60

conclude, *v.* say in conclusion, 586

conclusioun, *n.* end, finish, 614
conding, *adj.* worthy, 447
confectioun, *n.* medicinal preparation, 249
consolatioun, *n.* consolation, comfort, 93
conteining, contening, *pres. part.* containing, having as a statement, 333, 606
content, *adj.* content, satisfied, 301
continence, *n.* continence, self-restraint, 554*n*
conuersatioun, *n.* conduct, behaviour, 555
conuocatioun, *n.* an assembly made by a summons, 346
conuoy, *v.* escort, protect, guide, 131; **conuoyit,** *pret.* 389
cop, *n.* a leper's cup or bowl, 343, 387, 442, 579; **coppis,** *pl.* 492; **cowpis,** *pl.* cups, bowls, 419
corner, *n.* corner, 405
corps, *n.* corpse, 577
correspond, *v.* correspond, be conformable, 2
counsall, *n.* counsel, advice, 296
counsall, *v.* counsel, advise, 478
countit, *past part.* reckoned, considered, 608; **countit small,** *pret.* reckoned as little, 548
coursis, *n. pl.* courses, procedures, movements, 150
court, *n.* court, entourage of a sovereign, 77*n*, 346
courtlie, *adv.* courtly, elegant, 443
cowpis, *see* **cop**
crabitlie, *adv.* ill-naturedly, 154
craibit, *adj.* ill-natured, 353
Cresseid, Cresseid, 42, 63, 69, etc.
cristall, *n., adj.* crystal, 176, 337
croun, *n.* crown, the top of the head, 244
cruell, *adj.* cruel, 323
cry, *n.* call, 492, 495; cry of grief, 472, 541
cryit, *pret.* cried, 125, 545
culd, *see* **can**

cum, *v.* come, 361, 366, 459; **cummis,** *pres.* 104, 341; **come,** *pret.* 20, 154, 183, etc.
cumming, *verbal n.* coming, arrival, 100
Cupide, 124, 134, 144, 146, 152, 190, 271, 274, 295, 304, 371; **Cupido,** 108
curage, *n.* disposition, spirit, sexual desire, 32*n*
cure, *n.* cover, 10*n*
custome, *n.* custom, 113
cut, *v.* cut, cut short, 39
Cynthia, 253, 300, 330

dark, *adj.* dark, 405
darknes, *n.* darkness, 437
darling, *n.* darling, 504
day, *n.* day, 54, 112, 356, 400; daylight, dawn, 429; **dayis,** *pl.* 336
daylie, *adv.* daily, 392
debait, *n.* contention, strife, 184
decayit, *past part.* decayed, ruined, 436
deceptioun, *n.* deception, 613
declair, *v.* state, announce, 595
defame, *n.* defamation, 284
defence, *n.* protector, 556
defend, *v.* make defence, 7*n*; support, maintain against opposition, 219
deformait, deformit, *past part.* deformed, 349, 394, 448
degest, *past part.* digested, considered, 303
degre, *n.* degree, rank, 298
deid, *n.* deed, act, 275, 328; **almous deid** (*see* **almous**)
deid, deith, *n.* death, 70, 585, 595
deid, *adj.* dead, 32, 581, 584, 609, 616
deificait, *past part.* deified, 288
deill, *n.* a part; **sum deill,** *adv.* somewhat, to some extent, 214, 363
deip, *adv.* deeply, 508
deir, *adj.* dear, beloved, 105, 365
deir, *adv.* dearly, at a high cost, 354

delicious, *adj.* delightful, 241

deludis, *pres.* deludes, deceives, 509

delyte, *n.*; **set his haill delyte . . . vpon,** set his whole desire upon, desired only, 73

delyuerit, *pret.* delivered, 391

deme, *v.* judge, give as a judgement, 85

deming, *n.* suspicion, 118

depryue (fra), *v.* deprive (of), 334

desolait, *adj.* solitary, abandoned, 76

destenie, desteny, destenye, *n.* destiny, fate, 62, 121, 470

destitute, *adj.* deprived, devoid, 92

desyre, *n.* desire, object of desire, 101

desyrit, *pret.* desired, 52

deuine, deuyne, *adj.* divine, 127, 289

deuoit, *adj.* devout, pious, 115

dew, *n.* dew, 429*n*

Diane, 587

did, *see* **dois**

die, *v.* die, 203, 322

different, *adj.* different, 172, 209

diffinityue, *adj.* final, determinative, 333*n*

digestioun, *n.* digestion, 247

Diomeid, 43, 71, 101, 119, 132, 589

direct, *adv.* directly, 14

disagysit, *past part.* disguised, 95*n*

discend, *v.* descend, 6; **discendit,** *pret.* 331; **discending,** *pres. part.* 14, 147

diseis, *n.* discomfort, distress, 320

dispyte, *n.* scorn, injury, 304

dissensioun, *n.* dissension, discord, 184

dissimulait, *past part. as adj.* dissembling, deceitful, 225

distres, *n.* distress, 57, 70, 89

distributioun, *n.* distribution, 527

doctour, *n.*; **doctour in phisick,** doctor of medicine, 250

doif, *adj.* dull, spiritless, 32

dois, *pres.* do, perform, render, cause, 276; **did,** *pret.* 143, 367; **done,** *past part.* 290, 292, 304, 534

dolour, *n.* sorrow, 336

dome, *n.* judgement, judicial sentence, 324

done, *see* **dois**

doolie, *adj.* doleful, dismal, 1*n*, 344

douchter, *n.* daughter, 103, 367

doun, *adv.* down, 10, 14, 76, etc.

dour, *adj.* stern, harsh, 437

dowbillis, *pres.* doubles, 477; **dowblit,** *pret.* 377

draw, *v.* move, 526; **drew,** *pret.* pulled, 210

dreame, *n.* dream, 142, 344

drerie, *adj.* doleful, sad, 470

dressit, *pret. refl.* turned, proceeded, 404

drew, *see* **draw**

drink, *n.* drink, 37, 404

drowpit, *pret.* drooped, were lowered, 157

drowrie, *n.* love-token, love, 583*n*

dry, *n.* dryness, 318

dule, *n.* sorrow, 472

duleful, *adj.* sorrowful, 309

dure, *n.* door, 122, 360

dwellis, *pres.* dwells, lives, 587; **dwelland,** *pres. part.* 98

dyte, *n.* a written work, manner or style of writing, 1

efflated, *past part.* puffed out, 549*n*

efter, *prep.* after, following, 183, 253; according to, 480; **efter that,** after the time that, 43; *conj.* according as, 106

eik, *adv.* also, 314

eird, eirth, *n.* earth, 414; **in (this) eird,** on (this) earth, 384, 409, 467

eirdlie, eirdly, eirdlye, *adj.*

earthly, terrestrial, mortal, 52, 201, 355, 435

eiris, *n. pl.* ears, 463

electuairis, *n. pl.* electuaries (medicines in which the ingredients are combined with honey or syrup to form a paste), 246

ellis, *adv.* else, otherwise, 460

eloquent, *adj.* eloquent, 240

end, *n.* end, conclusion, death, 69, 345, 456, etc.; extremity, 382; **fra end to end,** throughout, 471

endit, *pret.* ended, died, 63, 598

ene, *see* eye

Eoye, 212*n*

equall, *adj.* equal, impartial, 527

equiualent, *adj.* correspondent, 2*n*

esperance, *n.* hope, *48n*

espy, *v.* observe, perceive, 389

estait, *n.* rank, position, 290, 437; condition, bodily form, 510*n*

Ethios, 213*n*

euer, *adv.* at any time, 126; always, 545; **or euer,** before, *544. Cf.* **euermair, how euer, quhat euer**

euerie, *adj.* every, 16, 179, 427, 433

euermair, euer mair, *adv.*; **for euermair,** for all time, 315, 408

euin, *adv.* properly, precisely, 261

exclude, *v.* shut out, banish, remove, 315; **excludit,** *pret., past part.* 75, 133

excuse, *v.* exempt from blame, 87

exempill, *n.* example, *exemplum,* warning, 465

exhort, *v.* admonish, urge, 612

expert, *adj.* experienced, skilled, 35

expone, *v.* explain, make known, 369

expuls, *n.* expulsion, 119

expyre, *v.* come to an end, die, 515

exquisite, *adj.* choice, carefully chosen, 268

extasie, *n.* frenzy, stupor, trance, 141

eye, *n.* eye, 231; ene, *pl.* 157, 176, 191, etc.

face, *n.* face, 13, 137, 155, etc.

fachioun, *n.* falchion, a large sword with a curved blade, 187

facound, *adj.* eloquent, 268

faidit, *past part. as adj.* faded, withered, 24, 396; **faiding,** *pres. part. as adj.* 461

faillit, *pret.* failed, was defective, 34

fair, *n.* fare, entertainment, 403

fair, *adj.* beautiful, handsome, 11, 42, 63, etc.; bright, clear, 15; as courteous term of address, 365

fairnes, *n.* beauty, 88, 313, 461

faith, *n.* faith, fidelity, 551

fall, *v.* get, obtain, 84*n*; **fell, fel,** *pret.* fell, 123, 142, 525, etc.

fals, *adj.* faithless, treacherous, 134, 546, 553, etc.; spurious, 236

fame, *n.* fame, reputation, 434

famous, *adj.* celebrated, 462

fand, *see* find

fane, *pret.* stopped, *544n*

fantasy, *n.* imagination, memory, 508*n*

far, *adv.* far, 95, 113; widely, to a great extent, 172; **far furth** (*see* **furth**)

fassoun, *n.* manner, style, appearance, 245

fast, *adv.* firmly, securely, 122; quickly, persistently, 158

fatall, *adj.* fated, 62

father, *n.* father, 97, 172, 182, etc.

fay, *n.* faithfulness, fidelity, 571

fecht, *v.* fight, 185

fedderit, *past part.* feathered, 168

feill, *n.* knowledge, idea, 533
feird, *adj.* fourth, 216
feirs, *adj.* fierce, impetuous, 185
fell, *adj.* cruel, destructive, 187, 412
fell, fel, *see* **fall**
felloun, *adj.* cruel, destructive, 167
fellowschip, *n.* company, companions, 94
felterit, *past part.* tangled, matted, 163
feminitie, *n.* womanliness, 80
fenȝeit, *past part.* invented, imagined, 66
feruent, *adj.* extremely hot, burning, fiery, ardent, 4n, 215
few, *adj. as n.* few, 563, 572
fewir, *n.* fever, 514
fickill, fikkill, *adj.* fickle, changeable, false, 469, 550, 552
figour, figure, *n.* form, appearance, 448; image, representation, 506
figurait, *past part.* formed, shaped, 511
filth, *n.* filth, moral foulness, 80
find, findis, *v.* meet, encounter, discover, 566, 573; **fand,** *pret.* learned by reading, 43, 62
firmament, *n.* the vault of heaven, 170
first, *adj., adv.* first, 151, 211, 360
flanis, *n. pl.* arrows, 167
flasche, *n.* sheaf (of arrows), 167n
fle, *v.* flee, run away from, 341
fleschelie, *adj.* fleshly, carnal, 81, 232, 558
Floray, Flora, 426
flour, *n.* flower, 373, 461; perfection, embodiment, 128, 279, 608; choicest individual, best, 78n, 435; **flouris, flowris,** *pl.* 175, 426
flourisching, *n.* blossoms, bloom, 198n
flowing, *pres. part.* flowing, 31
foirspeikar, *n.* chairman, speaker, 266n

folk, *n.* people, 526, 580
fome, *n.* foam, 192
for, *prep.* on account of, because of, 27, 47, 263, etc.; for the sake of, on behalf of, for the benefit of, 247, 293 (2), 383, 493, 562, 611; for fear of, 118, 207; in place of, 438, 439, 440; in return for, as a punishment for, 371; notwithstanding, 459; during, for the space of, 315; **for to** (+ *inf.*), in order to, 111, 219, 299; **for to** (+ *inf.*), to, 267, 352, 357, 444; **for the best,** 104. *conj.* because, since, 22, 35, 58, etc.
for quhy, *conj.* for the reason that, because, 53
force, *n.*; **of force,** of necessity, 202
forlane, *past part.* abandoned, laid aside, 140n
forme, *n.* shape, 510
fortoun, *n.* fortune, chance, 412, 454; (*personified*) 89, 469
fortunait, *adj.* destined by fortune, 79n
foull, *adj.* vile, loathsome, 83, 558
four, *numeral* four, 209
fra, *prep.* from, 6, 7, 18, etc.; *conj.* from the time that, as soon as, 101. *Cf.* **fro**
fraward, *adj.* adverse, perverse, ill-humoured, 323, 352
fre, *n.* noble, generous, 536
freisit, *pret.* became icy cold, 19
fresche, *adj.* fresh, 426
friuoll, *adj.* fickle, unreliable, 454n
friuolous, *adj.* trifling, wanton, 552
fro, *adv.*; **to and fro,** back and forth, 479. *Cf.* **fra**
froist, *n.* frost, extreme cold, 19, ¶39; **froistis hoir,** hoarfrost, 163
fronsit, *past part. as adj.* wrinkled, 155
frostie, *adj.* frosty, icy, 311

frute, *n.* fruit, 198

fulfillit, *past part.* filled completely, satiated, 72

full, *adj.* full, 235, 237, 240, 260; *adv.* very, exceedingly, 97, 100, 105, etc.; exactly, 12

furrit, *past part.* clothed or adorned with furs, 251

furth, *adv.* forth, out, 481; **als far furth,** as far, 87

furthwith, *adv.* immediately, 594

fy, *interj.* fie, 560

fyne, *adj.* excellent, choice, 246

fyre, *n.* fire, 28, 33, 36, 185, 513

fyrie, *adj.* fiery, 208

ga, go, *inf., pres., imp.,* 82, 342, 365; (+*simple infinitive, pleonastic*) 203, 294, 479; **gane,** *inf.* (*used for rhyme*) 431; **gane, gone,** *past part.* gone, departed, 368, 385, 409. *Cf.* **gang, went, ȝeid**

gadderit, *past part.* gathered, assembled, 264

gaif, *see* gif

gair, *n.* gore (wedge-shaped piece of cloth forming part of a garment), 179

gane, *see* ga

ganecome, *n.* return, 55

gang, *inf.* go, 381. *Cf.* ga

garding, *n.* garden, 425

garland, *n.* garland, wreath, 174

garmound, *n.* garment, suit of clothes, 164*n*, 178; **garmentis,** *pl.* 422, 433

garnischit, *past part.* ornamented, decorated, 433

garnisoun, *n.* garrison, body of armed men, 484

gart, *pret.* caused (+*simple infinitive*), 6

gaue, *see* gif

gay, *adj.* handsome, beautiful, bright, 164, 174, *178*, *218*, 313, 422, 425, 433, 521; *adv.* handsomely, brightly, 97

generabill, *adj.* capable of being generated, 148*n*, 171

gentill, *adj.* noble, courteous, of a pleasant disposition, 326, 536

gentilnes, *n.* courtesy, nobility, kindliness, 547

gest, *n.* guest, 105, 402

gif, *v.;* **God gif,** *subj.* God grant, 414; **gaue,** *pret.* gave, 127, 152, 295, 590; pronounced, delivered, 151; **gaif,** *pret.* made, put forth, 492; **geuin,** *past part.* pronounced, delivered, 329

gif, *conj.* if, whether, 64, 65, 350, etc.

giglotlike, *adv.* like a wanton woman, 83

gilt, *n.* guilt, 90

gilt, *past part.* gilded, decorated with gold, 179

girdill, gyrdill, *n.* girdle, belt, 167, 520

giuing, *verbal n.;* **for giuing of,** for fear of giving, 118

glas, *n.* glass, 15, 569; mirror, 348

glitterand, *pres. part.* glittering, 177

glorious, *adj.* glorious, illustrious, 41

glowrand, *pres. part. as adj.* staring, 191

go, *see* ga

god, *n.* (pagan) god, 14, 170, 183, 275, 300; God (*in exclamations*), 350, 402, 414; **goddis,** *gen.* 493; **goddis,** *pl.* 276, 353, 357, 364; **goddes,** 264, 292

goddes, *n.* goddess, 135*n*, 218, 283

gold, *n.* gold, 222, 419, 521, 528, 580

goldin, *adj.* golden, 13, 177, 179, etc.

gone, *see* ga

gottin, *past part.* obtained, 101

gouernance, *n.;* **in ... gouernance,** under control, under (one's) sway, 233

goun, *n.* gown, 250, 422

grace, *n.* favour, divine grace, 138, 287

gracious, *adj.* benevolent, kind, 327

grane, *n.* point, particular, 433*n*

graue, *n.* grave, 581, 605

grauin, *past part.* buried, 414

gray, *adj.* grey, 260, 603; *n.* grey cloth, 164

Grece, Greece, 79, 415, 452, 487

Greikis, Greeks, 82, 98

greissis, *n. pl.* herbs, plants, grass, 425

greit, *adj.* great, extreme, 27, 50, 149, etc.; thick, 161

grene, *adj.* green, 221; full of vitality, youthful, flourishing, 24, 138, 238; *n.* green cloth, 178

grew, *pret.* grew, increased, 138

grislie, *adj.* grisly, terrible, 191

grouf, *n.*; **on grouf,** prone, face downwards, 362

ground, *n.* ground, 539

groundin, *past part.* as *adj.* ground sharp, 181

gude, *adj.* good, 252, 421, 561; **gude speid** (*see* **speid**)

gudelie, gudely, *adj.* goodly, 59, 422

gyde, *v.* guide, direct, 131; **gydit,** *pret.* 205

gyrdill, *see* **girdill**

gyte, *n.* cloak, gown, mantle, *164n, 178,* 260

habirgeoun, *n.* habergeon (a sleeveless coat or jacket of armour), 186

hace, *adj.* hoarse, 338, 445

had, *see* **haue**

haill, *n.* hail, 6

haill, *adj.* whole, 73

hailstanis, *n. pl.* hailstones, 168

hailsum, *adj.* wholesome, health-giving, 249

hair, *n.* hair, 160, 177, 222, 314

hait, *adj.* hot, 29, 215, 237, 514

hald, *past part.* regarded, esteemed, 447

half, *n.* half, 211 (2), 390

hall, *n.* hall (the large public room of a building), 358

hanche, *n.* haunch, 187

hand, *n.* hand, 166, 181, 188, 239; **tuik on hand,** took charge of, set oneself to carry out, 309; **handis,** *pl.* 374

hang, *pret.* hung, 160

harbery, *n.* shelter, lodging-place, 403

hard, *adj.* hard, 186; severe, cruel, 324

hard, *see* **heir**

harnes, *n.* armour, 186

hart, *n.* the heart (as the seat of life, feelings, or love), 24, 56, 350, 512, 524, 539, 600

hat, *n.* hat, 386

haue, *v.* have, possess (*and as auxiliary with past participles*), 35, 84, 277, etc.; **hes,** *pres.* 60, 89, 148, etc.; **had,** *pret.* 9, 17, 44, etc.; **hauing,** *pres. part.* 496

haw, *adj.* leaden, livid, bluish, 257, 340

he, *pron. 3 pers. masc. sg., nom.* 49, 50, 52, etc.; **him,** *dat., acc.* 48, 165, 183, etc.

hecht, *pret.* promised, vowed, 23

hecht, *past part.* called, named, 213

heid, *n.* head, 157, 174, 311

heid, *n.* heed, careful attention, 495, 561

heidit, *past part.* headed, tipped, 168

heir, *v.* hear, 145, 430; listen, 267; **heird,** hear it, 415*n*; **hard,** *pret.* heard, 143; heard of, 596

heir, here, *adv.* here, now, 297, 315, 334, 577

heit, *n.* heat, vital heat, 318, 334

heklit, *past part.* fringed, shaped like a cock's hackle, 244*n*

hell, *n.* hell, 145

help, *v.* help, 34, 294; **helpit,** *pret.* 557

here, *see* **heir**

hes, *see* **haue**

heuie, *adj.* dejected, despondent, 116

heuin, *n.* heaven, 145, 493; the firmament, 263

heuines, *n.* heaviness, dejection, 56

hew, *n.* colour, 209; facial colour, complexion, 44, 46, 517

hewmound, *n.* helmet, 186

hiddeous, *adj.* hideous, 445

hie, *adj.* high, exalted, 26, 290, 434, etc.; extreme, great, 397; **hiest,** *superl.* highest, 297; **hie,** *adv.* high, 550

him, *see* **he**

hir, *see* **scho**

hir, *possess. adj. 3 sg. fem.* her, 13, 15, 26, etc.

his, *possess. adj. 3 sg. masc.* his, 9, 47, 53, etc.

hoir, *adj.* hoary, white, 163; rough, hoarse, 338*n*, 445

honest, *adj.* honest, honourable, 252, 555

honour, *n.* honour, reputation, 434, 462

honourit, *past part.* honoured, worshipped, 109

horne, *n.* horn (a wind instrument), 195; **hornis,** *pl.* horns, 255*n*

hospitall, *n.* charitable house, leper-house, 382*n*

hounger, *n.* hunger, 482

hour, *n.* hour, appointed time, 54, 375, 468

hous, *n.* house, 342, 391, 405

how, *adv.* hollow, deeply, 157

how, *adv.* how, 45, 79, 598; **how sa?,** how is that?, 369; **how euer,** in whatever way, by whatever means, 531

hude, *n.* hood, 244

humanitie, *n.* kindness, 534*n*

humbill, *adj.* humble, 25

hy, *n.* haste, 123, 361

I, *pron. I pers. sg., nom.* 3, 7, 9, etc.; **me,** *dat., acc.* 16, 21, 36, etc.

ice, *n.* ice, 168; **ice schoklis,** *pl.* icicles, 160

idole, *n.* image, 507*n*

ieopardie, *n.* daring enterprise of arms, battle, prowess, 486

ilk, *adj.* each, 341; **ilk ane,** each one, 529

imprentit, *past part.* imprinted, fixed firmly in the mind, 508*n*

in, *prep.* in, on, within, into, to, 5, 13, 28, etc.; *adv.* in, 399

inclynit, *past part.* inclined, disposed, 559

inconstance, *n.* inconstancy, fickleness, 224

incurabill, *adj.* incurable, 307

indure, *v.* endure, 336

infelicitie, *n.* ill fortune, misery, 281, 454

infirmitie, *n.* illness, 596

inflat, *adj.* puffed, inflated, 463

influence, *n.* influence ('The supposed flowing or streaming from the stars or heavens of an etherial fluid acting upon the character and destiny of men, and affecting sublunary things generally' [*OED*]), 149, 201

iniure, *n.* injury, 290

iniurious, *adj.* offensive, abusive, 284

ink, *n.* ink, 242

inquyre, *v.* inquire, 99

insolence, *n.* pride, licentiousness, 319

instructioun, *n.* instruction, 611

intent, *n.* intention, purpose, mind, 364; mind, 116

intentioun, *n.* charge, accusation, 273*n*

intill, *prep.* into, 142

into, *prep.* in, into, 77, 117, 120, etc.

inuentioun, *n.* poetic invention, fabrication, 67

ioly, *adj.* fine, splendid, 59

iowall, *n.* costly article, precious ornament, 521

ioy, *n.* joy, happiness, 49, 130, 236, 355, 409

ire, *n.* anger, 183

is, *see* **be**

it, *pron.* it, 3, 30, 39, etc.

Iuppiter, Jupiter, 169

keip, *n.* care, regard; **tak keip,** pay attention, 230

keiper, *n.* custodian, warden, 107

keipt, *pret.* kept, 554

kemmit, *past part.* combed, 222

kend, *past part.* known, 585; recognised, 380

kendillis, *pres.* catches fire, is aroused, 30; **kendlit,** *pret.* set burning, 513

kene, *adj.* sharp, fierce, 193

kest, *pret.* cast, directed, 498

kin, *n.* family, 398

king, *n.* king, 119, 144, 204, 296

kirk, *n.* church, temple, 117

knaw, *v.* know, perceive, recognise, 532, 535, 568; **knew,** *pret.* 376, 393, 501, 518

knawledge, *n.* recognition, 393

kneis, *n. pl.* knees, 123

knicht, *n.* knight, 546, 553, 560; **knichtis,** *pl.* 487

knichtlie, *adj.* knightly, noble, 519

knokkit, *pret.* knocked, 360

labour, *n.* labour, 565

lady, ladie, *n.* lady, gentlewoman, 44, 72, 92, etc.; (*as title*) 253; **ladyis,** *pl.* 431, 444, 452, etc.

laid, *pret.* laid, put, 311, 605

lait, *adv.* late, 82; *adv. or adj.* formerly, former, 609

lak, *n.* shame, insult, 276

lamentatioun, *n.* lament, 68, 597

lamp, *n.* lamp, source (of light), 197*n*

lang, *adj.* long, 161, 363; *adv.* 362, 379

langage, *n.* manner of speaking, words, 86, 91, 352

lanterne, *n.* lantern, 197*n*

last, *adj.* last, 254; **at the last** (*as n.*), at last, 112

lat, *v.* let, 573; **lat ʒow wit,** make known to you, 563; **ʒe let,** *imp.* allow, 381

lattit, *past part.* hindered, prevented, 27

lauch, *v.* laugh, 231

laud, laude, *n.* fame, glory, 462, 488

law, *n.* law, 106, 480

lawest, *adj. superl.* lowest, humblest, 298

lawfullie, *adv.* according to correct legal procedure, 312

lawn, *n.* a fine linen, an article of dress made out of lawn, 423

lawtie, *n.* loyalty, fidelity, 547

lay, *see* **ly**

lazarous, *n.* leper, 343, 531

lecherous, *adj.* lecherous, 285, 559

left, *see* **leif**

legacie, *n.* will, testament, 597

leid, *n.* lead, 155, 257

leid, *n.* person, man, 449

leid, *n.* people, 451, 480

leif, *n.* leaf, 238

leif, *v.* leave, bequeath, 584, 587; **left,** *pret.* left, abandoned, 40; **left . . . fra,** *past part.* abandoned by, 140

leif, *v.* live, survive, subsist, 384, 480; **leuit,** *pret., past part.* 49, 375

leine, *adj.* lean, emaciated, 159

leir, *v.* learn, 269, 479

Lent, *n.* Lent, 5*n*

let, *see* **lat**

letteris, *n. pl.* letters, 606

leuing, *verbal n.* living, manner of life, 285

leuit, *see* **leif**

licht, *n.* light, 197, 258

lie, *v.* lie, speak falsely, 252

liken, *pres. part.* liking, choosing, 267*n*

lillie flour, *n.* the flower of the (white) lily, 373

lipper, *adj.* (*attributive*) leprous, 372, 451, 474, 480, 526, 535, 580, 592; (*as collective n.*) lepers, 490, 494; *n. or adj.* leper, leprous, 609; *n.* (*attributive*) leper-, 438

lippis, *n. pl.* lips, 159

list, listis, *v.* (+*simple infinitive*) chooses, likes, 230, 256

listis, *n. pl.* hems, edgings, 179

litill, *adj.* little, 152

lo, *interj.* Lo! Behold!, 274, 351, 506, 607

lokkis, *n. pl.* locks, hair, 162

lord, *n.* lord, nobleman, gentleman, 530, 533; **lordis,** *pl.* 493

loud, *adv.* loud, 20

louers, luifferis, *n. pl.* lovers, 140, 308, 561

ludge, *n.* a small dwelling (especially a temporary building to house lepers or plague-victims), 438

ludgeit, *past part.* dwelling, residing, 451

lufe, luif, *n.* love 24, 29, 128, 135, 137, 279, 512, 547, 551, 554, 564, 591, 613; **luifis,** *gen.* 22; **for Goddis lufe,** for the love of God, 493

lufe, *v.* love, 562

luifferis, *see* **louers**

luik, *n.* look, appearance, 154, 502

luik, *v.* look at, 348; observe, take notice, 60; **luik on,** look at, 449; **luikit on,** *pret.* looked at, 372

lumpis, *n. pl.* lumps, protuberances, 340

lust, *n.* lust, sexual desire, 81; **lustis,** *pl.* 559

lustie, *adj.* beautiful, lovely, 69, 339

lustines, *n.* delightfulness, loveliness, 447

ly, lyis, *v.* lie, 143, 362, 404, 609; **lay,** *pret.* 162, 310, 332, 605

lyart, *adj.* streaked with grey, grey, 162

lybell, *n.* formal declaration, 74*n*

lyfe, *n.* life, 201, 306

lyke, *adj.* similar to, 155;

similar, 510; *adv.* after the manner of, 343; **lyke to,** after the manner of, 193, 245; (*as suffix*) 194

lyking, *verbal n.* pleasure, desire, 449

lyre, *n.* face, complexion, 155, 339

maculait, *past part.* spotted, defiled, 81

madame, *n.* madam (*as form of address*), 361

magnificence, *n.* magnificence (*as title of honour*), 26

maid, *see* **mak**

mair, *adj. comp.* greater, 530; *adv. comp.* more, 72; **euer mair** (*see* **euer**); **no moir,** *n.* nothing more, 102, 601; *adv.* no longer, 616

maist, *adv. superl.* most, 52, 447

mak, *v.* make, produce, 24, 39, 51, etc.; **maid,** *pret., past part.* 68, 126, 129, etc.

malitious, *adj.* malicious, evil-disposed, 324

man, *n.* man, 29, 198, 341, etc.; **men,** *pl.* 77, 85, 145; **mennis,** *gen. pl.* 463

mane, *n.* mane, 211

maneir, *n.*; **in thair maneir,** in their behaviour, 115; **on his maneir,** in his behaviour, 153; **on this maneir,** in this way, 576

manifest, *adj.* clearly revealed, obvious, 305

mansioun, *n.* mansion, house, 96

mantill, *n.* cloak, 386

Mars, 183

mater, *n.* matter, subject, statements or allegations which come under the consideration of a court, 303

mawis, *n.* mavis, song-thrush, 430

May, May, 175, 428

may, *v.* can, may, 87, 411, 453,

11

etc.; **micht,** *pret.* 7, 16, 121, etc.

me, *see* **I**

meid, *n.* wages, reward; **to his meid,** in recompense, 277

meit, *n.* food, 383, 404; **meitis,** *pl.* 440; **sweit meitis,** dainties, 420*n*

melancholy, *n.* gloom, excess of black bile, 316*n*

meldrop, *n.* mucus from the nose, 158*n*

memoriall, *n.* remembrance, 519

memour, *n.* memory, 465

men, mennis, *see* **man**

mend, *v.* remedy, improve, 476; avail, remove, 473*n*; *pret.* added fuel to, 36*n*

merbell, *n.* marble, 603

mercie, *n.* mercy, 325

Mercurius, Mercury, 239, 265, 295

merilie, merilye, *adv.* pleasantly, happily, 243, 428

merle, *n.* blackbird, 430

meruellous, *adj.* marvellous, 487

merwell, *n.* marvel; **hes merwell,** is struck with astonishment, 362

micht, *n.* strength, power, 459

micht, *see* **may**

middill, *n.* middle, waist, 180

middis, *n.*; **in middis,** in the middle, 5

ming, *v.* mingle, 613; **mingit,** *past part.* 236, 337

mirrour, *n.* mirror (that which reflects something to be avoided, a warning), 457

mirth, *n.* happiness, joy, 316, 355, 368, 384, 409

mischance, *n.* ill-luck, disaster, 84

mischeif, *n.* misfortune, distress, 455

miserie, *n.* misery, 453

mistie, *adj.* misty, 18

modifie, *v.* assess, determine, 299

moir, *see* **mair**

moisture, *n.* moisture (as inherent in all plants and animals; one of the four elements), 318

mone, complaint, lamentation, 406

Mone, Moon, 302

monische, *v.* admonish, exhort, 612

mony, *adj.* many (*with sg. n.*), 189, 195, 249, etc.; **mony ane,** many a one, 430

mortall, *adj.* mortal, deadly, 321

mother, *n.* mother, 135, 280, 282, 286; cause, origin, 317

mouing, *verbal n.* motion, 200

mouth, *n.* mouth, 192

mowlit, *past part. as adj.* mouldy, 441

mufe, *v.* move, provoke, anger, 352

murning, *verbal n.* sorrowing, lamentation, 398, 473

murnit, *past part.* lamented, 379

must, *v.* must, it is necessary that, 203

my, *possess. adj. 1 sg.* (*before consonants*) 21, 24, 28, etc.; (*before vowels*) 454; **myne** (*before vowels*), 8, 579; **my self** (*see* **self**)

myle, *n.* mile, 96, 390

mynd, *n.* mind, 457, 502, 505, etc.; **beir in ȝour mynd,** remember, 614

na, *adj., adv.* no, not any, 263, 325, 335, etc.; **no moir** (*see* **mair**)

name, *n.* name, 274, 604; **to name,** by name, 213

nane, *pron.* no one, 134, 207, 415, etc.; **nane vther,** not any other, not any, 259

nar, *adv. comp.* nearer, 263

narratioun, *n.* narrative, account, 65

nathing, *n.* nothing, 476; *adv.* not at all, in no way, 90, 257

nature, *n.* nature, 34

neid, *n.* poverty, destitution, 321; necessity, 478

neidis, *pres.*; **me neidis** (*impersonal*), it is necessary for me, 57

neir, *adv.* near, almost, close at hand, 45, 113, 456, 468; **neir by,** *prep.* close to, 496

neist, *adj.* nearest to, 109; **nixt,** *adv.* in the next place, 183, 253

neuer, *adv.* never, at no time, 292, 328

neuertheles, *adv.* nevertheless, 8, 85, 518

new, *adj. as n.*; **of the new,** anew, 66

nicht, *n.* night, 11, 39, 199, 256, 471

nixt, *see* **neist**

no moir, *see* **mair**

nobill, *adj.* noble, 132, 398, 495

nocht, *adv.* not, 30, 57, 65, 501; *n.* nought, nothing, 202, 461, 462; **not,** *adv.* 103, 117, 252, etc.

nois, *n.* nose, 158

none, *n.* mid-day, 114

nor, *conj.* nor, 65, 415, 473

north, *n.* north, 6

northin, *adj.* northern, 17

not, *see* **nocht**

now, *adv.* now, 129, 131, 139, etc.

number, *n.* number, numbers, 487

nureis, *n.* nurse (that which nourishes or fosters), 171, 199

nyce, *adj.* extravagant, wanton, 220

O, *interj.* O, 78, 134, 323, etc.

obedience, *n.* obedience, 23

ochane, *interj. as n.* alas, 541*n*

odious, *adj.* hateful, offensive, 133, 229

of, *prep.* of, from, out of, made of, about, concerning, 5, 6, 11, etc.; in, 209, 255, 257, 289; to, 14, 118; for, 33, 612; as regards, 24, 447; over, 148; *adv.* off, 592

oft, *adv.* often, 544; **oft syis,** often, 525

oftymes, *adv.* many times, 374

on, *prep.* on, in, 16, 123, 125, etc.; against, 332

only, *adj.* single, sole, 53

ony, *adj.* any, 118, 185, 228; *as pron.* 460

opinioun, *n.* reputation, 557

opnit, *pret.* opened, 388

oppin, *adj.* open, plain, 305

oppositioun, *n.* opposition (the position of two planets when exactly opposite to each other, as seen from the earth), 13

oppres, *v.* press down, burden, 55; **opprest,** *past part.* 306

or, *conj.* or, 66, 85, 96, etc.; **or euer,** before, 544

oratur, orature, *n.* oratory, small chapel, 8*n*, 120

orient, *n.* east, 212

ornament, *n.* adornment, 579

ouerheled, *pret.* covered over, 401*n*

ouircome, *pret.* recovered, revived, 540

ouirfret, *past part.* ornamented over, overspread, 163*n*

ouirspred, *past part.* spread, covered over, 339, 395

our, *possess. adj. 1 pl.* our, 290, 353

out, *adv.* out, 125, 165, 388; **out of,** *prep.* out of, 45, 95, 158, 331; **throw out** (*see* **throwout**)

outher, *adv.* either, 275

outwaill, *n.* outcast, 129

outward, *adj.* external, 33

outwardly, *adv.* externally, 509

paill, *adj.* pale, whitish, 46, 214

paintit, *past part.* depicted, adorned, 261, 427

pane, paine, *n.* pain, suffering, punishment, grief, 49, 291, 299*n*, 306, 377, 562; **panis,** *pl.* 277

quair, *n.* quire, small book, 40*n*, 61

quene, *n.* queen, 22, 426

querrell, *n.* accusation, cause, 219

quha, *pron. interrog., rel.* who, whoever, 60, 64, 131, etc.; if anyone, 230, 267; **quhome,** *dat., acc.* 23, 31, 202, etc.; **quhome that,** whom, 562

quhair, *conj., adv.; interrog., rel.* where, wherever, 97, 121, 143, etc.; in which, when, 435, 444; **quhair that,** when, in a case in which, 34; where, 605

quhais, *possess. adj. rel.* whose, of which, 146

quhat, *pron., adj.; interrog., rel.* what, 70, 351, 367, etc.; **quhat euer,** whatever, 85

quheill, *n.* wheel (of Fortune), 550

quhen, *adv., conj.* when, whenever, as soon as, 3, 5, 9, etc.

quhetting, *pres. part.* sharpening, 193

quhilk, *pron. rel.* which, who, 33, 52, 62, etc.; *adj.* which, 47*n*; **the quhilk,** *pron.* which, who, 89, 205, 279; **the quhylk,** 373

quhill, *conj.* until, 48, 112, 482, etc. *Cf.* **quhyle**

quhisling, *pres. part.* whistling, 20

quhite, *adj.* white, fair, 373

quhitlie, *adj.* whitish, pale, 214

quhome, *see* **quha**

quhy, *adv.* why, 325, 475; (*elliptically*) the reason why, 506; **for quhy,** because, 53

quhyle ... quhyle; quhyles ... quhyles, *adv.* at one time ... at another time, now ... now, 49, 224; **ane quhyle,** *n.* a short time, 517

quhylk, *see* **quhilk**

quod, *pret.* said, 103, 274, 301, etc.

rage, *n.* furious passion, violent desire, 31

raid, *pret.* rode, 204, 489, 523

rais, *pret.* rose, 347, 474

rank, *adj.* absolute, downright, 483

rauischit, *past part.* carried away, entranced, 142

rawk, *adj.* hoarse, raucous, 445

ray, *n.* array, dress, 432

recompence, *n.* return, retribution, 291

recure, *n.* remedy, cure, 335

red, *see* **reid**

reddie, reddy, *adj.* ready, prepared, 242, 359; likely, liable, 515

refer, *v. refl.* entrust, commit, 297

refute, *n.* refuge, protector, 94*n*

regrait, *n.* lamentation, distress, 397

reheirs, *v.* repeat, relate, 57

reid, *adj.* red, 191, 211, 244, 464*n*, 582

reid, *v.* counsel, advise, 566; **red,** *pret.* read, 332

reioisit, *pret.* gladdened, 48

remeid, *n.* remedy, 33

remeid, *v.* remedy, provide a remedy, 473

remufe, *v.* go away, 21

renew, *v.* recommence, 47*n*

renoun, *n.* renown, fame, 424

rent, *past part.* torn, 578

report, *v.* relate, make a report, 68, 242

reprufe, *v.* blame, accuse, 280

repudie, *n.* divorce, rejection, 74*n*

responsaill, *n.* response, reply, 127

ressauit, *past part.* received, taken, 44

ressoun, *n.* statement, 606

rest, *n.* rest, 400

rethorick, rethorie, *n.* rhetoric, eloquence, 240, 269

retorte, *v.;* **retorte in,** throw back on, 286*n*

retour, *n.* return, 51

retour, *v.* return, change into 464

reuenge, *v.* take vengeance, 294

reuerence, *n.* veneration, respect, 25, 152

reull, *n.* rule; **in reull,** under control, under (one's) sway, 233

reull, *v.* govern, control, 149

riches, *n.* richesse, wealth, 320

richt, *adj.* right, 181

richt, *adv.* very, altogether, 4, 94, 169, etc.; just, 3; straight, 12

rin, *v.* run, flow, 158

ring, *n.* ring, 582, 592, 594

ringand, *pres. part.* ringing, 144

rinkis, *n. pl.* men, warriors, 432

rois, *n.* rose, 211

roising, *adj.* rosy, 464*n*

rollis, *pres.* rolls, drives, 217

rotting, *adj. or verbal n.* rotten; decomposed matter, 464*n*

roun, *v.* whisper, 529

roustie, *adj.* rusty, 187*n,* 188

royall, *adj.* royal, 204, 424, 432, 582

royallie, *adv.* royally, magnificently, 489

rubie, *n.* ruby, 582

ruik, *n.* rook, 445

ruse, *v.* praise, extol, 573

rypelie, *adv.* with mature consideration, 303

sa, *adv.* so, thus, as, 3, 15, 30, etc.; **so,** 436, 534; **how sa?,** how is that?, 369

sabill, *adj.* sable, black, 221

sacrifice, *n.* sacrifice, a sacrificial offering, 115; **maid ȝow sacrifice,** made a sacrifice to you, 126

sad, *adj.* steadfast, constant, 567; sorrowful, 540

sadlie, *adv.* sorrowfully, 601

said, *see* say

saif, *v.* salve, heal, 411*n*

saipheron, *n. as adj.* saffron, 421

sair, *n.* disease, suffering, 411; *adj.* grievous, painful, 450, 482,

540; **sore,** *614;* **sair,** *adv.* grievously, painfully, 307, 351; **soir,** 46, 100

sait, *n.* seat, throne, abode, 331

sall, *v.* shall, will, must, ought to, 87, 131, 322, etc.; **suld,** *pret.* 2, 51, 84, etc.

sals, *n.* sauce, 421

salue, *n.* remedy, 411

samin, *adj.* same, 58, 484; **same** (*pleonastic*), 125, 459

sangis, *n. pl.* songs, 243

sapience, *n.* wisdom, 289

sat, *pret.* sat, 497, 575

Saturne, 151, 172, 300, 302, 309, 323, 330

saw, *see* se

sawin, *past part.* sown, planted, 137

say, sayis, *v.* say, speak, 77, 85, 111, etc.; **saying,** *pres. part.,* 281; **said,** *pret., past part.* 100, 125, 141, etc.

scantlie, *adv.* scarcely, 7

schaddow, *n.* shadow, reflected image, 348

schaikand, *pres. part.* shaking, brandishing, 190; **schuik,** *pret.* 492

schame, *n.* shame; **dois . . . schame . . . to;** inflicts dishonour on, 276

schawis, *pres. impersonal,* is plain, appears, 328*n;* **schew,** *pret.* showed, made known, 273; granted, 287

sche, *see* scho

sched, *past part.* scattered, put to flight, 18; parted (of hair), 222

scheild, *n.* shield, 516

schene, *adj.* bright, shining, 419

schew, *see* schawis

schill, *adv.* resonantly, shrilly, 20

Schir, *n.* Sir (*as a title of honour*), 536; (*placed before a common noun, and forming with it a term of address*), 296

scho, *pron. 3 pers. fem. sg., nom.*

she, 24, 51, 53, etc.; **sche** (*in rhyme*), 351; **hir**, *dat., acc.* 74, 75, 90, etc.

schoklis, *see* **ice schoklis**

schort, *adj.* short, 39, 610

schortlie, *adv.* briefly, in a few words, 586

schouris, *n. pl.* showers, downfalls, 6

schuik, *see* **schaikand**

sclander, *n.* calumny, defamation, 284

scornefull, *adj.* scornful, contemptuous, 86

se, *v.* see, perceive, 16, 432; have the faculty of sight, 283; experience, 375; watch over, 527; **seing**, *pres. part.* 403, 491; **saw**, *pret.* 54, 99, 349, 528; **sene**, *past part.* 500; **is sene on me**, is evident by me, is to be seen in me, 353

se, *see* **A per se**

secreit, *adj.* secret, secluded, 120, 381, 388

secund, *adj.* second, 213

seid, *n.* seed, 137, 139

seiknes, *n.* sickness, malady, 307, 335, 377

self, *pron.* self; **my self**, 293, 569, 574; **thy self**, 476; **hir self**, 117, 259; **the self**, itself, 552

semit, *pret.* seemed, appeared, was seen, 223

sen, *conj.* seeing that, considering that, 132, 288, 477, 616

send, *v.* send, 383; *pret.* 74, 583; **sent**, *pret.* 392

sene, *see* **se**

sentence, *n.* judgement, decision, sentence, 309, 327, 329, 333; opinion, decision, 151; opinion, meaning, 270

sermone, *n.* discourse, speech, 270

serpent, *n.* serpent, snake, 228

seruit, *past part.* served, presented, 420

sessoun, *n.* a period of the year (mentioned with reference to the conditions of weather), 1; seasoning, flavour, 421

set, *v.* put, place, set, 355; setting, *pres. part.* composing, 243; **set**, *pret.* 12, 73; *past part.* ornamented, 582

seuin, *numeral* seven, 147, 264, 288

sey, *n.* sea, 217

sic, *adj.* such, 84, 89, 292, etc.; **sic ane**, such a one, 251

siching, *pres. part.* sighing, 100, 601; *verbal n.* 450, 540

sicht, *n.* eyesight, 207

siluer, *n., adj.* silver, 144, 419

sing, *v.* sing, 444; **singand**, *pres. part.* 243

skarlot, *adj.* scarlet, 250

skirt, *n.* skirt, lap, 522

sky, *n.* sky, 18, 401

sla, *v.* kill, 476; **slane**, *past part.* destroyed, 139

sleip, *n.* sleep, 61

small, *adj.* little, of small value, 548

smyling, *verbal n.* smiling, 225

so, *see* **sa**

soir, *see* **sair**

solempne, *adj.*; **ane solempne day**, a day of special religious observances, 112

sone, *n.* son, 108; **sonnis**, *gen. sg.* 219

sone, *adv.* soon, quickly, 592; **sa sone**, so quickly, 30, 506

sonkin, *past part.* sunken, hollow, 157; submerged, 407

sop, *n.* sop, 407*n*

sore, *see* **sair**

sorrow, *n.* sorrow, grief, 55, 407, 600

sorrowfull, *adj.* sorrowful, 402

sound, *n.* sound, noise, 146

sound, *v.* heal, 411*n*

sour, *adj.* sour, unpleasant, 234, 441

sowpit, *past part.* wearied, immersed, 450*n*

soyr, *adj.* sorrel, reddish-brown, 211

spak, *see* **speik**

spark, *n.* spark, 512

speid, *n.*; **gude speid,** speedily, quickly, 492

speik, *v.* speak, 366, 616; **spak,** *pret.* 523

speir, *n.* spear, 161, 181

speiris, *pres.* asks, inquires, 272

spheir, *n.* sphere (one of the concentric transparent globes revolving around the earth which bear the various heavenly bodies), 254; **spheiris,** *pl.* 147, 210

spilt, *past part.* injured, ruined, 91

spittaill hous, *n.* hospital, leper-house, 391

sport, *n.* amusement, diversion, 40

spottis, *n. pl.* spots, 260, 339

spreit, *n.* soul, 587*n*; **in spreit,** with regard to (one's) immaterial intelligent part (as opposed to the body), 142; **spreitis,** *pl.* vital functions, faculties, 37

spring, *v.* spring, fly, 512

spurnis, *pres.* strike, kick, 475

spycis, *n. pl.* spices, 248, 418

stad, *past part.* burdened, beset, 542

stane, *n.* stone, tombstone, 609

starklie, *adv.* strongly, harshly, 280

starnis, *n. pl.* stars, 170

steid, *n.* steed, large high-mettled horse, 213; **steidis,** *pl.* 209

steill, *n.* steel, 538

steir, *v.* rule, govern, 149

steir, *v.* disturb, provoke, 352; **steiris,** *pres.* is active, bestirs herself, 469*n*

stert, *pret.* sprang, rushed, 538

steuin, *n.* voice; **with ane steuin,** with one voice, in accord, 491

stiffer, *adj. comp.* stronger, harder, 538

still, *adj.* quiet, constant, 398*n*

still, *adv.* still, yet, 116

stormie, *adj.* stormy, tempestuous, 542

stound, *n.* pain, pang, attack, 538; **stoundis,** *pl.* 542

strife, *n.* dispute, contention, 184

strikken, *past part.* struck, 486

stro, *n.* straw, 439

stude, *pret.* stood, was, 9, 192

succour, *n.* help, aid, 376

suddanely, *adv.* suddenly, at once, 227

suffer, *v.* suffer, undergo, 322, 562

sugerit, *past part. as adj.* sweetened with sugar, 247

suld, *see* **sall**

sum, *pron.* some, 393, 572, 603; *adj.* 67, 77, 383; **sum deill** (*see* **deill**)

sumtyme, sum tyme, sum-time, *adv.* at one time, 23, 205, 279, etc.; **sum tyme . . . sum tyme,** at one time . . . at another time, 234

superscriptioun, *n.* inscription, 604

supper, *n.* supper, 359

supplie, *n.* assistance, support, 138

suppois, *imperative as conj.* although, even if, 505

swak, *v.* fling, dash, 522

sweit, *n.* a condition or fit of sweating, 514

sweit, *adj.* sweet, charming, 234, 249, 326, 503; **sweit meitis** (*see* **meit**)

swelt, *pret.* died, 591; fainted, swooned, 599

swiftest, *adj. superl.* swiftest, 254

sword, *n.* sword, 188, 190

swoun, *n.* faint, fainting-fit, 599; **in swoun,** into a faint, *544*

swouning, *verbal n.* fainting, 545

syde, *n.* direction, place, 544

syis, *see* **oft syis**

sylit, *past part.* covered, concealed, 10*n*

syne, *adv.* then, immediately afterwards, 360, 593

syropis, *n. pl.* medicated syrups, 247

syte, *n.* sorrow, grief, 450

taidis, *n. pl.* toads, 578

taikning, takning, *verbal n.*; **in ta(i)kning,** as a token, 232, 590

tak, *v.* take, receive, accept, 300, 301, 438, etc.; exact, 371; obtain, gather, 429; accept, put up with, 566; **tak to,** bring to, attach, 298; **takand,** *pres. part.* 83; **tuik,** *pret.* 37, 40, 61, etc.; apprehended, conceived, 506; seized, 515; **tuik . . . in,** admitted, 399; **tuik on hand** (*see* **hand**)

takning, *see* **taikning**

tarying, *verbal n.* delaying, 593

tauld, *past part.* told, related, 370

teiris, *n. pl.* tears, 47

teith, *n. pl.* teeth, 156

temperance, *n.* self-restraint, moderation, 194

tempill, *n.* temple, 107, 114

tender, *adj.* tender, kind, 199

tene, *n.* anger, 194

termis, *n. pl.* words, expressions, language, 59, 241, 268

testament, *n.* testament, will, 576

thair, *possess. adj. 3 pl.* their, 115, 147, 149, etc.

thair, *adv.* there, in that place, 43, 218, 267, etc.; **thair at,** at that place, 388

thairby, *adv.* from there, 390*n*

thairfoir, *adv.* for that, for that reason, therefore, 103, 294, 381, etc.

thairout, *adv.* outside, without, 38; in existence, 563

thame, *see* **thay**

than, *adv.* then, at that time, 37, 55, 76, etc.; **as than,** just then, 27; **than,** *conj.* than, 532, 538

that, *rel. pron.* who, which, 63, 64, 160, 203; *dem. pron.* that, this, 377; *dem. adj.* 44, 139, 218, etc.; *conj.* 16, 22, 51, etc.;

so that, 7, 389; (*pleonastic*) 34, 458, 562, 605; **efter that,** after the time that, 43

thay, *pron. 3 pers. pl., nom.* they, 264, 265, 303, etc.; **they,** 399; **thame,** *dat., acc.* 378, 481, 566

thay, *dem. adj.* those, 301

the, *def. art.* the, 4, 5, 6, etc.

the, *see* **thou**

therupon, *adv.* on that subject, with reference to that, 25

thidder, *adv.* thither, 383

thift, *n.* theft, 263

thin, *adj.* thin, lean, 159

thing, *n.* thing, object, 507; (*sg. in collective sense*) 52, 201; **all thing,** everything, all things, 148, 171; **thingis,** *pl.* 466

think, *v.*; **me think,** *impersonal,* it seems to me, 291; **thocht,** *pret.* thought, intended, 26

thir, *dem. adj.* these, 264, 425*n*

this, *dem. pron.* this, 141, 278, 358, 575; *dem. adj.* this, 4, 65, 69, etc.

this, *adv.* thus, 342

tho, *adv.* then, at that time, 106, 440

thocht, *n.* thought, mind, 499

thocht, *conj.* although, even if, 29, 572

thocht, *see* **think**

thoillit, *pret.* suffered, endured, 70

thornis, *n. pl.* thorn branches, thorn bushes, 262

thou, thow, *pron. 2 pers. sg., nom.* (*used to familiars and inferiors, or for rudeness, as in 134, 325, 328*) 79, 84, 103, etc.; **the,** *dat., acc.* 91, 315, 334, 551

thrid, *adj.* third, 215

throw, *prep.* through, 210; on account of, 90, 138; 279, by means of, 67, 486; by, 91; **through,** by, *328*

throwout, throw out, *prep.* through, right through, 15, 539

thus, *adv.* thus, in this way, 49, 230, 264, etc.

vnfair, *adv.* unhandsomely, roughly, 163

vnfaithfulnes, *n.* unfaithfulness, 570

vnplesand, *pres. part. as adj.* unpleasant, displeasing, 338*n*

vnricht, *adv.* not in the right way, improperly, 205

vnstabill, *adj.* changeable, variable, 235

vnstabilnes, *n.* instability, changeableness, 568

vnto, wnto, *prep,* unto, to, 96, 114, 145, etc.; towards, directed towards, 12

vntrew, *adj.* untrue, faithless, 571, 602

vnworthie, *adj.* worthless, despicable, 129

vocatioun, *n.* summoning, 272

voice, *n.* voice, 176, 338, 443

vp, *adv.* up, 76, 347, 498

vpon, *prep.* upon, on, 73, 112, 174, etc.; against, 124

vprais, *pret.* rose, 12

vs, *see* **we**

vsit, *pret.* was accustomed, 111

vther, *adj.* other, 40, 221, 463; **ane vther,** another, 61; **the vther,** *absolute,* the other one, 231; **nane vther,** not any other, not any, 259; **vther,** *pron. pl.* others, 287, 570; **vtheris,** 446; **ane vther,** another, 73; **not ane ane vther knew,** neither knew the other, 518; **ilk ane to vther,** each one to another, 529

wa, *adj.* grieved, miserable, 350. *Cf.* **wo**

wag, *v.* shake, 196

waillit, *past part. as adj.* chosen, choice, 440

waist, *adj.* waste, uninhabited, 588

wait, *see* **wit**

wald, *see* **will**

walk, *v.* walk, 429*n,* 588; **walkit,** *pret.* 76

wall, *n.* wall, 475

wand, *n.* rod, staff, 311*n*

wane, *n.;* **will of wane,** bewildered, hopeless, 543*n*

wanhope, *n.* hopelessness, despair, 47

wantones, *n.* lasciviousness, arrogance, 319, 549

wantoun, *adj.* unruly, lascivious, 314

wantounlie, *adv.* voluptuously, luxuriously, 416

war, *adj.* prepared, careful, alert; **be war,** *imp.* 456, 468, 561

war, *adj. comp.* worse, 460 (2)

war, *see* **be**

warld, *n.* world, 196, 200, 203

warne, *v.* warn, tell, 359

was, *see* **be**

way, *n.;* **the way,** in the direction, along the road, 490

we, *pron. 1 pers. pl., nom.,* we, 291, 532; **vs,** *dat., acc.* 182, 494, 532, 534

wedder, *n.* weather, 4, 150

weid, *n.* clothing, 165

weill, *adv.* well, 38, 251, 364, etc.

weip, *v.* weep, shed tears, 103, 231; lament with tears, 121; **weiping,** *pres. part.* 351, 406, 471; *verbal n.* 477; **weipit,** *pret.* 46

weir, *n.* war, 196, 486

weir, *v.* ward off, 182

weird, *n.* destiny, one's appointed lot, 385, 412, 436

weiris, *pres.* fades, wastes, goes, 467; **out woir,** *pret.* carried out, caused to flutter out, 165*n*

welcum, *interj.* welcome, 105

wellis, *n. pl.* springs, pools, streams, 588

welterit, *past part.* overturned, tossed about, 436

welth, *n.* well-being, prosperity, 467

wemen, *n. pl.* women, 556, 610

went, *pret.* went, 114, 400; **wend,** 474*n*

wer, *see* **be**

werie, *adj.* weary, discontented, 102

wes, *see* **be**

west, *n.* west, 12

wichtis, *n. pl.* creatures, human beings, 435

wickit, *adj.* evil, cruel, 91, 385, 412

widdercok, *n.* weathercock, 567

widderit, *past part. as adj.* withered, wasted, 165, *238*

will, *n.* wish, inclination, 21; **with better will,** with more goodwill, 399

will, *adj.* astray, 543*n*

will, *v.* will, wish to, want, 60, 274, 565, 574; **wald,** *pret.* 24, 102, 117, etc.

wind, *n.* wind, 17, 150, 165, 467, 567; air, 463

winter, *n. as adj.* winter, 39

wisdome, *n.* wisdom, 88

wit, *n.*; **out of wit,** out of one's mind, 45; **wittis,** *pl.* senses, 509*n*

wit, *inf.* know, 563; **wait,** *pres.* 64, 65, 350, etc.; **witting,** *pres. part.* 497

with, *prep.* with, by, 25, 46, 81, etc.

withdraw, *v.* take back, retract, 327; **withdrawin,** *past part.* taken away, caused to disappear, 10

within, *prep.* within, inside of, 8, 166, 511, 517

without, *prep.* without, with absence of, 202; **withouttin,** 593

witnes, *n.*; **witnes beiris,** furnishes evidence, 466

witting, wittis, *see* **wit**

wnto, *see* **vnto**

wo, *n.* grief, misery, 237, 477, 543, 599; *adv.* **wo is me,** I am grieved, 602

woddis, *n. pl.* woods, 588

wofull, *adj.* sorrowful, miserable, 56, 69, 121, etc.

woik, *pret.*; **woik the nicht,**

stayed awake during the night, 471

woir, *see* **weiris**

womanheid, *n.* womanliness, womankind, 88, 608

wonder, *n.*; **na wonder was,** it was not surprising, 505; *adv.* surprisingly, very, 161, 174, 387

wont, *past part.* accustomed, 428, 444

word, *n.* word, speech, 189, 252, 275, etc.; **wordis,** *pl.* 229

wormis, *n. pl.* worms, 578*n*

worschip, *n.*; **for ȝour worschip,** in honour of you, 611

worthie, *adj.* honourable, excellent, 41, 42, 58, 485, 493, 610

wox, *pret.* grew, became, 102

wraik, *n.* vengeance, 370

wraikfull, *adj.* vengeful, vindictive, 329

wrait, *see* **wryte**

wraith, *n.* wrath, 182

wrappit, *past part.* enveloped, entangled, 543

wretch, *n.* a miserable person, 543

wretchit, *adj.* miserable, 278

wretchitlie, *adv.* with great misery, 63

wringand, *pres. part.* wringing, 374

wrocht, *past part.* wrought, created, 203

wryte, *v.* write, 3, 270; **wrait,** *pret.* 64, 604; **writtin,** *past part.* 41

wrything, *pres. part.* twisting, distorting, 189

wyne, *n.* wine, 418, 440

wyre, *n.* wire, 177

wyse, *n.* manner, way; **in this wyse,** 92*n*; **on this (same) wyse,** in this way, 125, 312, 406; **in secreit wyse,** secretly, 381

wyte, *v.* blame, 134

ȝe, *pron.* 2 *pers. pl., nom. (used*

also as a respectful sg. form)
you, 127, 136, 288, etc.; **ȝow,**
dat., acc. 126, 293, 294, etc.

ȝeid, *pret.* went, 481

ȝes, *adv.* yes (*stronger than* ay),
535

ȝet, *n.* gate, door, 388

ȝit, *conj.* yet, still, but, 8, 29, 85,
etc.; **nor ȝit,** *adv.* and also
not, 415, 473

ȝokkit, *past part. as adj.* yoked,
209

ȝone, *dem. adj.* that, 278, 382,
530, 531; *pron.* 533

ȝour, *possess. adj. 2 pl.* your, 138,
361, 363, etc.

ȝoutheid, *n.* youths, 30

ȝow, *see* ȝe